Critical Psychology

The International Journal of Critical Psychology

Issue 5

Embodiment

ISSN 1471 4167
ISBN 0 85315 961 0

Cover design Art Services
Cover image © Tim Davison
Typeset by Derek Doyle and Associates, Liverpool, UK, printed by Bookcraft, UK

Critical Psychology is published three times per year by
Lawrence & Wishart
99a Wallis Road
London E9 5LN
United Kingdom

Editor
Valerie Walkerdine (University of Western Sydney)
Email: v.walkerdine@uws.edu.au

Editorial Assistant
Barbara Graham
Email: ijcp@uws.edu.au

Individual subscriptions £40
Institutional subscriptions £120

For advertising information contact contact
editorial@l-w-bks.demon.co.uk

In the essay 'Resistance in women's talk: thinking positively about breast cancer', by Professor Celia Kitzinger, that appeared in issue IV *Under the Covers*, a setting error was made. The way the data extracts have been set does not reflect the transcription conventions of conversation analysis and is therefore misleading for professionals in the sector.

We wish to apologise to Professor Kitzinger for this mistake and inform our readers that correct copies of the transcripts are available from Lawrence and Wishart. For further information please contact: vanna@l-w-bks.demon.co.uk

Contents

Book Reviews

Editorial

Valerie Walkerdine

This issue of the journal engages with two different but important foci: *the body and embodiment*, an issue brought to our attention through feminist and other work on bodies and materiality; in addition, the final selection of papers continues the theme of *counter stories* which was explored in issue 4.

The matter of bodies and their theoretical place within critical psychology is an important one, especially for traditions of critical work informed mostly by theories of discourse. In what sense does the body and embodiment matter in understanding both subjectivity and the place of psychology? The papers in this issue tackle the matter in a number of different ways. Nikki Sullivan, for example, explores inscriptions on the body in the form of scars, cuts, tattoos. In particular she is concerned with the reading of these as marks of self-mutilation, understood as signs of a psychological disorder which impels the subject to disfigure the body. Psychologically, the skin functions as a communicative border between the inside and the outside, so that what the body speaks is something on the surface, which is indicative of a depth. Of course, such an understanding is very common within discourses of psychopathology. However, this understanding ignores the marking of the body itself, understanding it always as a sign of something else. Sullivan uses the work of Lyotard to understand 'fleshly disfiguration' as duplicitous, that is, it may tell us something about what is beneath but the marks themselves have a narrative that demands to be read; and it is the taking seriously of that narrative that Sullivan asks of us. That narrative of course varies considerably, but needs to be understood within a social and cultural practice of which it is a part.

Nicole Vitellone considers the take-up of male sex drive discourse within an AIDS culture, by means of an analysis of the object of the condom and its place within safe heterosex campaigns. Examining in particular Wendy Hollway's (1984) argument about male sex drive discourse, Vitellone concludes that the discursive inscription of the condom in safe heterosex, especially the 'if it's not on, it's not on' campaign, means that the male sex drive discourse is not challenged by safe sexual practices which still understand the condom as a sign of male virility.

Lawrence Johnson discusses the mind-body problem, focusing on psychological and then psychoanalytic discourses which would want to understand the mind as part of the body, and conversely the body as part of the mind. In considering the way in which both types of discourse reduce the complexity of the boundary between mind and body and the understanding of the phenomenon in general, he argues for a critical polytextualism in which mind, body and the boundaries between them are inscribed within a variety of intersecting discourses. He argues cogently that what is at stake is not the opening out of the boundaries of one discipline in response to challenges from another, but the 'radical abandonment of all boundaries that have traditionally separated one discipline from another, one corpus from another, one body of ideas from another'. This argument is terribly important for critical psychological work on embodiment as well as the issue of disciplinary boundaries within our field of study on the other.

Christopher Peet discusses Michael Polanyi's understanding of scientific enquiry. According to Polanyi, scientific method can be described as a set of discursive and technical practices in which the person of the scientist is inscribed as having a central place and in which science becomes a passionately embodied act. In this context, the constitution of the knowing of the scientist and the production of her/his own subjectivity is seen not as peripheral to science but absolutely central to it.

Robert Steele explores embodiment in a different way, by thinking about debates about sexual abuse and in particular the issue of recovered memory. He analyses Daniel Schachter's recent positivist history of research on memory distortion in which Schachter supports Freud's renunciation of the seduction theory. Steele rather echoes Peet's arguments about Polanyi. Referring to recent developments in cultural and feminist approaches to memory, he sets out how Freud and Schachter's accounts illustrate the ways in which history as well as memory is inscribed within personal and cultural narratives which embody certain notions of male authority and female victimisation.

Estelle Barrett explores the idea that bodily processes activated through artistic and creative practices are intrinsic to reparation and healing. Creative practice, argues Barrett, involves an integration between mind and body, language and materiality. In that sense then, the argument mirrors Johnson's concern with the problem of boundaries between mind and body, creative practice, emotional work and the embodied production of alternative knowledges and subjectivities. Taken together, the papers in this section present the reader with an important set of tools for going beyond psychology's mind/body dualism and some important pointers to new theoretical approaches and methodological tools.

The previous issue of the journal was dedicated to a theoretical exploration of the notion of counter stories – those academic political narratives which challenge dominant structures, practices and ideologies. The last section in this issue represents the final 'set' among our counter stories. These three essays, authored by William Cross, Linda Powell and Anne Marie Tupuola, trouble the academy and its relation to community, indigenous knowledge and domination. William Cross writes through the wisdom of 'fiction' a story that invites us to problematise 'where' we teach. He questions the university as the privileged site for knowledge production/consumption, as he introduces spaces in communities – in this case, the black barber shop – where wisdom grows and politics flourish. Linda Powell takes us inside the belly of university life – a course on group relations for school administrators – to examine critically 'how' we teach. In this paper she challenges readers to consider the unconscious text that so fundamentally shapes any classroom, but particularly those classrooms that aim to teach 'management' and authority. Powell dares to challenge the rationality and hierarchy that organise, indeed contain, such classrooms; as she reveals the terror embodied in such pedagogical repression. Anne Marie Tupuola takes on not the pedagogy of higher education but the core of what constitutes knowledge, that is, 'what' we teach. Through the seemingly narrow window of theorising Samoan adolescence, Tupuola opens up large questions about Western colonialism as it globalises, universalises and bleeds across the psychological canon. Together these three essays disrupt conceptions of 'where' we teach, 'how' we teach, 'what' we teach – and who is 'we' – at just the historic moment when the academy confronts fundamental crises in legitimacy in a global, post modern world.[1]

The opinion and commentary section of the issue contains a discussion by John Cromby and David Nightingale of what they characterise as the limits of the usefulness of social constructionism for critical psychology. This is an important discussion not least because, as they point out, it crosses a number of debates about types of discourse analysis, realism and relativism. What is at stake, I suggest, is a way beyond the polarisations, accusations and counter-accusations towards the development of new tools for understanding both the place of psychology, discourse and the production of subjectivity within a politically engaged practice.

The issue ends with three book reviews. Martha Michailidou reviews Couze Venn's 'Occidentalism: modernity and subjectivity'; Patrick Leman discusses Wetherell, Taylor and Yates' 'Discourse theory and practice: a reader'; and Ian Hodges reviews Elizabeth Wilson's 'Neural Geographies: feminism and the micro-structure of cognition'.

I cannot conclude this editorial without remarking that 11 September occurred while we were putting this issue together. We called for commentaries on the important issues that followed from it. People responded with so many pieces that we decided to devote the entire next issue to the topic. I do hope therefore that this and future issues of the journal continue to be a source of important and fruitful ideas in these troubling and difficult times.

Notes

1. With thanks to Michelle Fine for providing this paragraph in relation to counter stories. Professor Fine and Anita Harris were Guest Editors for Issue 4: *Under the Covers: Theorising the Politics of Counter Stories.*

Fleshly (dis)figuration, or how to make the body matter

Nikki Sullivan

The dermagraphic focus on the mark of fleshly disfiguration as an index to the truth of the subject, is apparent in many psychological theses on bodily inscription. In such works the scar, cut, tattoo, are read as images of self-mutilation; as signs of a psychological disorder which impels the subject to disfigure the body. The skin, according to this model, functions as a communicative border between inside and outside, on which psychologically relevant themes are portrayed. Consequently, the role of the dermal diagnostician is characterised by a movement from surface to depth; from a focus on the image of disfiguration, to the disorder which 'causes' it. In effect, such analyses involve a movement from the material to the immaterial, from the fleshly to the conceptual. The body comes to matter only in so far as its matter or materiality is veiled over in and through the clinical extraction of abstract and essentially immaterial 'truths'.

This essay critically analyses the unquestioned assumptions which inform such theses and argues that they problematically reduce the other to an Economy of the Same. Drawing on the work of Lyotard – in particular the notion of figuration as that which affects both the articulation and disarticulation of meaning – I demonstrate that the matter of the body matters since it is this which complicates any attempt to fix the fleshly image, and allows a consideration of the duplicity of bodily inscription. Thus this paper endeavours to move beyond the limitations of dermagraphism which, as Didi-Huberman claims, produces a sentence which controls the destiny of the marked other and which incarnates the corporeal to corpse, by exploring the intertextual affect of fleshly writing.

> Open the so-called body and spread out all its surfaces: not only the skin with each of its folds, wrinkles, with its great velvety plains, and contiguous to that, the scalp and its mane of hair, the tender pubic fur, nipples, nails ... the light frills of the eyelids, set with lashes – but open and spread, expose the labia majora, so also the labia minora with their blue network, bathed in mucous, dilate the diaphragm of the anal sphincter, longitudinally cut and flatten out the black conduit of the rectum, then the colon, then the caecum, now a ribbon with its surfaces all striated ... ; as though your dress-maker's scissors were opening the leg of an old pair of trousers, go on, expose the small intestines' alleged interior ... ; armed with scalpels and tweezers, dismantle and lay out the bundles and bodies of the encephalon; and then the whole network of veins and arteries ... the lymphatic network, and the fine bony pieces of the wrist, the ankle, take them apart and put them end to end with all the layers of nerve tissue which surround the aqueous humours, and the cavernous body of the penis, and extract the great muscles, the great dorsal nets, spread them out like smooth sleeping dolphins (Lyotard 1993: [1]).

So begins Jean-Francois Lyotard's *Libidinal Economy*. But how are we to engage with, understand, or respond to, this repugnant yet compelling image of what at first glance appears to be a graphic account of dissection or corporeal mutilation? Perhaps more importantly, what would we expect to dis-cover if we carried out Lyotard's bidding? In peeling away the skin, the membranes, the muscles, would the speculative gaze render transparent the essence of the body or the subject who supposedly animates it?

In a paper entitled 'Psychodynamic Implications of Tattoos', published in the *American Journal of Orthopsychiatry* in 1983, Gerald Grumet, whose aim is to finetune the clinical task of 'dermal diagnosis', claims that 'the human flesh has proven itself a suitable canvas on which to portray psychologically relevant themes' (1983: 487). The task of the dermal diagnostician, at least as Grumet sees it, is to interpret images of 'self-mutilation' – whether they be scars, burns, cuts, or tattoos[1] – as signs of a psychological disorder which compels the subject to disfigure his or her body. This task is characterised by a movement from surface to depth; from a focus on the image of disfiguration to its source; from the fleshly to the conceptual; from the material to the immaterial. True knowledge *is* attainable, it seems, when surface is peeled away (whether literally or metaphorically) to reveal an essential depth (Taylor 1997: 17). Such a relation between surface and depth, phenomena and noumena, representation and reality, is an all-pervasive presence in Western ontology, but like Yukio Mishima, I want to consider why it is that 'thought, like the plumb-line, concern[s] itself exclusively with vertical descent' (Mishima cited in Lingis 1994: 84). 'If the law of thought is that it should search out profundity ... then it seem[s] excessively illogical to me that men should not discover depths of a kind in the "surface" ... Why should they not be attracted by the profundity of the surface itself?' (Mishima cited in Lingis 1994: 84-5).

But it seems that not everyone is obsessed with a logics of vertical-descent, which is why, when we follow Lyotard's account of dissection, we find that what appears to be depth supporting surface is perhaps nothing more than an endlessly complex (con)figuration of surface(s). So what if, as Lyotard claims, the skin is a surface without depth, which is why 'when we open [the body] we affirm only that which is, the vast coiled skin, where slits are not entries, wounds, gashes, openings, but the same surface following its course after a pocket-shaped detour' (Lyotard 1993: 21-2). If the body is not, as Grumet assumes, the surface expression of an inner essence, then is knowledge (of the body) any longer possible? If the response to this question is negative, then what we find ourselves faced with is the problem of writing or speaking *after* – as Lyotard puts it in *The Differend* – that is, the problem of writing or speaking without any pre-given rules.

The task of this essay is to critically examine the dominant psychological model of self-mutilation or fleshly (dis)figuration as I want to call it, as a *figure* for the understanding of understanding. In so far as the term 'understanding' implies the grasping of that which stands under[2] – of depth or essence – then any attempt to critique a representational model of the body and of subjectivity necessarily involves a (re)consideration of the production of knowledge and the textual effects such a process generates. What I hope is already clear at this point is that dominant ontological accounts of the body and of subjectivity and social relations are (in)formed by, and (in)form, binary oppositions such as the distinction between surface and depth, representation and reality, mind and body, self and other, and so on. Rather than simply reiterating the postmodern claim that dualisms are inherently problematic, my aim is to analyse how and why this might be so; to discuss the lived implications of the logics of this particular language game[3] or discourse, at least as they function in regards to attempts to respond to fleshly (dis)figuration.

The essay is divided into three sections. The first section examines the psychological representation of self-mutilation as a form of disfiguration. In the second section I turn to the work of Lyotard, in order to consider the notion of *figuration* as that which disrupts representation but is not opposed to it. The final section evokes the figural within the psychological representation of disfiguration and thus disfiguration becomes (dis)figuration; that is, the 'unknowing' of knowledge as truth, as abstract, static, disembodied and graspable.

Disfiguration

In an interesting analysis of various body-modificatory practices and the ways in which they are understood in psychiatry and in other cultural contexts, Armando Favazza raises the issue of self-mutilation and illustrates – albeit inadvertently – the difficulties involved in the application of classificatory and evaluative terms. Favazza defines self-mutilation as 'the deliberate destruction or alteration of one's body tissue without conscious suicidal intent' (1996: xviii-xix). In the introduction to his text Favazza claims that unlike Kraft-Ebing's *Psychopathia Sexualis*, *Bodies Under Siege*, which he describes as his magnum opus, 'goes beyond mere description to search for meaning' (1996: xix), and herein lies its value, since as he sees it, 'the first steps in doing something about a problem are giving it a name and a classification' (1996: 232). And this is exactly what Favazza proceeds to do.

Favazza begins his analysis by dividing self-mutilation into two types, the first of which he refers to as culturally sanctioned self-mutilation. This includes practices such as eyebrow plucking and ear piercing, and cultural or community specific rituals such as circumcision and, for example, the Sun Dance of the Plains Indians in which young braves gaze at the sun and struggle until the skewers that have been inserted under the muscles of their chests and backs break free. The second type of self-mutilation he refers to as deviant or pathological self-mutilation. Favazza then divides this latter phenomenon into three categories: namely, major self-mutilation which he associates with psychosis; stereotypic self-mutilation which he claims is often a symptom of acute psychosis, schizophrenia, autism and congenital disorders such as Retts disorder, Tourette Syndrome, Lesch-Nyhan Syndrome and so on; and moderate or superficial self-mutilation. This last category – which includes practices such as scratching, cutting, burning, and carving – appears he claims, as a symptom or associated feature of a great many disorders including impulse control disorders, obsessive-compulsive disorder, anxiety disorders, post-traumatic stress disorder, disassociation disorders, depression and personality disorders. And it is this category which is of interest to me in this essay.

In his obsessive compulsion to know Favazza not only compiles a list of possible causes or factors which influence fleshly disfiguration, but goes on to plunder the depths of these disorders themselves for that which presumably causes them. What he finds is a combination of childhood abuse, infantile illnesses and biological under-pinnings such as low levels of serotonin. To cut a long and rather dry story short, Favazza, like Grummet, believes that 'the skin may ... be thought of as a sort of message centre or billboard' (Favazza 1996: 148). In both accounts the (self-mutilating) subject is assumed to be the origin of writing, and the body-text is read as a form of corporeal confession. Moreover, writing is understood and/or constituted as 'a message passing from an addressor to an addressee both of whom are independent of it' (Lyotard 1988: 11). I will return to these points in due course.

Taking a similar approach Janice McLane, in a paper entitled 'The Voice on the Skin: Self-Mutilation and Merleau-Ponty's Theory of Language', defines self-mutilation as 'the deliberate cutting, burning, or otherwise injuring of one's body in reaction to psychological and/or physical trauma'. It is primarily done, she claims, 'by women, and its practitioners are usually survivors of some kind of childhood abuse' (1996: 109).[4] McLane suggests that self-mutilation can be understood as an inaudible form of speaking one's pain. She says:

> When hidden pain starts to speak, it will speak silently. Its voice may appear as a cut on the leg, a burn on the arm, skin ripped and scratched repeatedly. There will be no sound, not any, only unfelt and silent pain which makes its appearance in another pain, self-inflicted, and when that second, collateral pain emerges, it will articulate in blood and blisters the open definition you desire, although it may not be in a language you care to see. This, it says, is pain, and this is real in any language you care to speak (1996: 111).[5]

For McLane, then, self-mutilation is 'the creation of a voice on the skin' (1996: 115); the creation of a mouth-like wound which can speak what the actual physical mouth has been forbidden to utter. She describes the bizarre and disfiguring expression of the lived contradictions of abuse in this way:

> The voice is so appalling that even the self speaking in wounds cannot stand to hear it. For who can really bear to be their own torturer? Who can look into their own eyes and see the three-headed-baby nature of themselves, such a freak that they carve their own body into wounds? Some people can look into a mirror and call their own wounding tattoo-art, body piercing, religious ecstasy, a drug trip ... But these terms themselves are an artful arranging of cooked bits on a plate to disguise the fact that one is eating pieces of bloody dead animal ... The voice is too terrible to contemplate. *But we must* (McLane 1996; 111, emphasis added).

As McLane sees it, the wound tells the story of the subject's history, of her psychosomatic state, the uncontrollable and chaotic nature of which she cannot bear to face, or to speak, directly. According to McLane, whilst the pain of abuse is impossible to discern as such, it nevertheless (in)forms the psychophysical integrity of the so-called abuse survivor, and creates an enforced silence which must be broken if 'healing' is to be possible. Drawing on the work of the phenomenologist Maurice Merleau-Ponty, she argues that the possibility of an openness to others and to a world, which is the pre-condition of (inter)subjectivity and of communication, is what recedes when a person is silenced in and through abuse. Both the corporeal schema and the structure of the world are 'experienced' as pain. Yet pain, and thus the abuse survivor's sense of self, are impossible for her to discern as such, and therefore to express. However, McLane argues that the abuse survivor's bodily being-in-the-world, her corporeal and psychological schema, is a lived expression of her embodied history. She says:

> a primary pain is absorbed into itself and becomes the living body ... A spine of bone becomes a spine of pain. A beating heart, which looks like any other heart, becomes an injury-circulating mechanism. Sometimes it is a vulva which goes from dimly sensed body-part to the dimly remembered site of cruelty; sometimes it's a mouth which was meant for ice-cream and becomes bloody (1996: 110).

Due to the lived contradictions of abuse, the subject cannot openly communicate her dilemma, not even to herself, and thus 'through her body, [must] learn to speak again' (McLane 1996: 110), since in McLane's reading of Merleau-Ponty's theory of language, 'speech is a lived structuring of what is new' (McLane 1996: 109); the possibility of an openness to others and to a world – hence McLane's characterisation of self-mutilation, irrespective of the form it takes, as 'the creation of a voice on the skin'; a mouth-like wound which 'can speak what the physical mouth has been forbidden to utter' (McLane 1996: 115). This bodily-speaking, it seems, both articulates – albeit silently – the carnal 'experiences' of the abuse survivor, and at the same time literally rewrites the material (existence), or psychophysical schema, of the body-subject. Thus McLane sees self-mutilation as an ambiguous 'speaking through the body' which does not simply *express* subjectivity, but more importantly, (re)formulates bodily-being. In other words, McLane is wary of the tendency to unthinkingly pathologise fleshly disfiguration, and instead, attempts to reconceptualise it as a less than negative practice which, in a perhaps unconventional way, has emotional and political import. On the one hand then, McLane moves beyond a simple positing of the subject of self-mutilation as pathological, and attempts to elaborate an anti-essentialist analysis of the constitution of subjectivity and experience. At best, her analysis demonstrates, firstly, that the subject does not precede experience, but rather, is constituted in and through it, and secondly, that experience is what we seek to explain and thus is complicit in the production of knowledge rather than being the origin of knowledge. On the other hand, McLane's assumption that self-mutilation is the effect of some kind of childhood abuse, and that the abuse-survivor is in need of 'healing', tends to impose limits on the possibility of critically exploring the ways in which knowledge is produced, and the culturally and historically specific assumptions which inform its production.

According to McLane, the creation of a voice on the skin as a disfiguring form of corporeal confession functions as a quasi-therapeutic attempt to reinstate what she describes as 'a unified lived structure for the abuse survivor' (1996: 112), which it achieves, she claims, in three connected ways. Firstly, self-mutilation (re)establishes the difference between pain and the pain-free by localising pain in one particular injury 'thus allowing the rest of life to stand in temporary contrast as that which does *not* have wounds or pain' (McLane 1996: 112).

Secondly, self-injury reinstates the boundary between the existence and non-existence of the self since it constitutes an act which renders the subject's existence present to itself: *I cut, I feel, therefore I am.* Thirdly, fleshly disfiguration distinguishes self from other by a literal carving-out of self-possession: it is the self, rather than another, that mutilates the self. In effect then, the disfigured subject heals her 'self', becomes unified, through the (re)construction of her 'self', the world, and the relation between them, in terms of dualities: self/other, pain/non-pain, existence/non-existence and so on. In short, self-mutilation as the creation of a voice on the skin is therapeutic insofar as it generates 'the possibility for another, more *authentic* voice [to] emerge' (McLane 1996: 117, my emphasis).

In each of the analyses briefly outlined, fleshly disfiguration could be said to be understood as a form of corporeal confession. Cuts, scars, burns, tattoos and so on, are read ideographically. That is, as graphics which tell the story or the 'truth', of the subject's psychic interiority. This is not, however, to suggest that the analyses are theoretically identical. Unlike Grumet and Favazza, McLane does not 'forget' the corporeal engagement of the body in the production of meaning and in the constitution of identity and sociality. Indeed, her reading of Merleau-Ponty's notion of gesture as the basis of language, and at the same time as that which is distinct from language, allows her to claim that the flesh is voice – a corporeal voice which does not speak in language, but vibrates in wounds, cuts, burns, tattoos. However, whilst this voice is literally inaudible – which is not to suggest that it cannot be sensed – it metaphorically, and by a process of substitution, makes heard what the physical mouth has been forbidden to utter, what has been silenced by abuse – that is, the abuse survivor's embodied history, her subjectivity, the uncontrollable and chaotic nature of which she cannot bear to face, or speak, directly. Thus, whilst for McLane the marked body is not simply a canvas on which psychological themes are intentionally expressed, it is nevertheless the site of a confession, albeit a complex and ambiguous one.

These various renderings of the body of the other as readable, and the interiority of the other as an object of knowledge, involve a number of connected assumptions that, I would argue, are highly problematic. Firstly, as I've already suggested, subjectivity is assumed 'to consist in a sort of [autonomous] inward depth, which can be seen exteriorised, expressed, on the articulations of the body' (Lingis 1983: 25).[6]

Secondly, and connected to the first point, the body is conceptualised and/or constituted as nothing more than the site of an expression 'moment by moment, of an inward spirit, or a person belonging to him [or her] self' (Lingis 1983: 25). The role or function of the marks of fleshly disfiguration then, are merely to *signify*, 'to efface themselves [and thus the body] before the meaning, or ideality, or logos' (Lingis 1983: 23). Thus the body comes to matter only insofar as its matter or materiality is veiled over in and through the clinical extraction of abstract and immaterial truths. Moreover, this effacing of the materiality of the body in the pursuit of truth is a structural necessity, for as Mark Taylor points out in a critique of Hegelian dialectics, it is '[o]nly when the body is under-stood as being finally grounded in spirit [that] knowledge becomes secure' (1997: 18). Lastly, implicit in each of the accounts discussed is the assumption that it is imperative that we listen to the voice on the skin, that we read the textual body of the self-mutilator, interpret it, and pronounce judgements upon it. I will return to this point in the final section of the essay.

Figuration

In *Discourse, figure*, published in 1971, Lyotard elaborates an analysis of the relation between what he calls discourse, and figure. For Lyotard, discourse is the 'condition of representation to consciousness by a rational order or structure of concepts' (Readings 1991: xxxi). Concepts operate as monads antithetically defined by their position and relation within a 'textual' system, and reason is the tool used to calculate such relational positions. Discourse grasps things solely in terms of the rules, linkages and conventions of representational logic, as '*meanings* or significations that discourse may *speak*' (Readings 1991: xxxi). The figural, on the other hand, is the unassimilable heterogeneous other at work within and against discourse; it is that which disrupts representational logic, and which every representation must forget. Like 'the jews' and/or *le différend*[7] the figural is within representational logic and, simultaneously, resists this logic; it is 'what never ceases to open the wound of the unaccomplished' (Lyotard 1990: 22). In other words, the figural is *not* opposed to discourse, but rather, provides the very grounds of its (im)possibility. It takes place at the limit of representation, yet 'persists not so much at the limits but rather at the heart of representation' (Lyotard 1990: 5), and consequently 'wounds' discourse, opening up the system of representation to a radical heterogeneity, 'a difference which cannot be rationalised or subsumed within the rule of representation' (Lyotard 1971: 4).

Since the discursive and the figural are inextricably bound – despite the fact that the former's status as knowledge is dependent on the disavowal or 'forgetting' of figurality – then the relation, as Lyotard formulates it, is one of *duplicity* rather than *duality.*[8] As Readings stresses, if it is *not* the case that representation is bad or erroneous, whilst figuration is good or true, then the task of reading is not simply to dis-cover the meaning of a text – in this case the marked body – but rather, to refuse to allow claims to know the truth of a 'thing' to forget the duplicity, the differences, that figurality raises (Readings 1991: xxxi-xxxiii).

Lyotard's critical analysis of structural linguistics as the overlooking of the sensible in and through a focus on the textual, as the suppression of seeing by reading, exemplifies this task. Lyotard argues that Saussure develops an account of textual space as two dimensional, a space of absolute opposition. The process of reading, according to this model, is simply one of decoding, effected by a switching between the system of oppositions and the linguistic term.[9]

Drawing on the work of Merleau-Ponty, Lyotard claims that vision appears as a *figure* in the textual conception of space.[10] Visibility, he argues, consists of something more than an active subject that looks, and a passive object that is looked at. Rather, the seeing eye participates in the world it views and vice versa. Seeing entails being a body that is itself capable of being seen. As Merleau-Ponty puts it in *The Phenomenology of Perception:*

> [H]e who looks must not himself be foreign to the world that he looks at. As soon as I see, it is necessary that the vision ... be doubled with a complementary vision ... myself seen from without, such as another would see me, installed in the midst of the visible ... He who sees cannot possess the visible unless he is possessed by it, unless he is of it (1962: 134-5).

This corporeal intermingling is what Merleau-Ponty refers to as the chiasmatic imbrication of subject and object in perception. Both the self and the world are affected in and through this intertwining. The self is always already bodily and as Merleau-Ponty puts it, 'the body is neither subject nor object, neither *in-itself,* nor *for-itself*' (1962: 212-3);

it is 'a gaping wound' (1962: 101), a liminal (non)site in which 'opposites' join and separate. The body, then, for Merleau-Ponty, can never be apprehended since it is less an object than an interlacing, a 'structure of implication' (Merleau-Ponty 1962: 149). In *The Visible and the Invisible,* Merleau-Ponty continues this line of thinking via the concept of 'flesh', a term providing the preconditions and the grounds for the distinction between subject and object, self and other. Here he states that 'we must not think the flesh starting from substances, from body and spirit – for then it would be the union of contradictions – we must think it as ... the concrete emblem of a general manner of being' (1968: 193). Whilst 'flesh' does not simply displace perception as the object of Merleau-Ponty's later theoretical investigations, it has been described by Elizabeth Grosz as 'a more elementary ... term ... the [pre]condition of both seeing and being seen, of touching and being touched, and of their intermingling and possible integration, a commonness in which both subject and object participate' (1994: 95). Furthermore, in *The Visible and the Invisible* the world is described by Merleau-Ponty, as 'universal flesh' (1968: 137); that is, an affective network of sensuous relations in which everything is intertwoven – but not conflatable, nor entirely distinguishable, and thus not reducible to an Economy of the Same. As Mark Taylor has noted, the intertwining of universal flesh produces a text(ure), a weaving together that 'is' visibility (Taylor 1987: 72-3). Given this, it is not so much, as common-sense logic would have it, that seeing precedes reading in a linear sense, but rather, that reading and seeing are inextricably bound: thus vision could be thought of as exemplifying the co-existence of mutually constitutive yet incommensurable terms, of the discursive and the figural.

What this suggests is that our sense of what reading the body might entail needs to move beyond the dominant understanding of reading as a process of cognitive recognition, in which the sensible, the corporeality of that which reads and that which is read (and the two are never separate), is veiled over and/or reduced to mere signification. Reading need not, as it does in the work of Grummet, McLane and Favazza, simply claim to dis-cover the hidden meaning of the text or the other who supposedly authored it. Rather, 'reading must pose itself as an act which sets the text to work, as a work which deconstructs textual oppositions to testify to figural differences' (Readings 1991: 52).

This sort of logic informs *Libidinal Economy* in which Lyotard develops the notion of the libidinal band, the Möebian skin. The libidinal band is not so much a 'real' thing which Lyotard attempts to represent in order to counter the depth model of the body and of subjectivity, but rather, is a befitting fiction if you like, that allows Lyotard to gesture towards what is excluded by representational thinking; namely, the unassimilable, the figural. Unlike the dermal diagnosticians discussed earlier, Lyotard states that libidinal economists 'are suspicious of the separation allowed between inscription and its site' (1993: 16). It is necessary, he claims, that we

> strengthen our ... palpative potential ... until we forge the idea of an intensity which, far from setting itself up on a producer-body, determines it; the idea of a passage over nothing, which produces, one instant beyond countable time, the being of its proper passing, its *passage* ... Therefore not a surface first, then a writing or inscription over it. But the libidinal skin of which, *after the event,* one will be able to say that it is made up of a patchwork of organs, of elements from organic and social bodies, the libidinal skin initially like the *track* of intensities, ... *the surface crossed and crossing* (1993: 16-17).

What this suggests is not that there is *a* body that is written on or with, that disfigures or is disfigured, but rather, that 'the body' comes into being in and through processes that posit it as an object separate from that which surrounds it (ie represents it), but which at the same is indeterminate insofar as it retains the trace of the other, of heterogeneity or figurality, as that which it is defined in opposition or relation to, and therefore, as that which is internal to it but not reducible to it.

(Dis)figuration

In a paper entitled 'The Figurative Incarnation of the Sentence: Notes on the "Autographic" Skin', Georges Didi-Huberman (1984) provides a critique of what has come to be known as 'dermagraphism'; a clinical procedure associated with the work of nineteenth century clinicians such as Charcott, Barthelemy and Dujardin-Beaumetz. Didi-Huberman claims that dermagraphism was associated with patients suffering from delusions, problems of vision, sensitivity to hypnosis, and hysteria (1984: 69). Didi-Huberman tells how in 1893 Barthelemy noted a pattern in which 'the patient suffers a crisis of vision, "falls" into vertigo, and produces a text which "surfaces" into the visible' (Barthelemy cited in Didi-Huberman 1984: 69). But not only did the clinicians concerned read these texts, but more importantly, they also attempted to reactivate this process by inscribing the bodies of their patients in various ways. Dermagraphic experimentation, for example, involved the writing with a rubber stylus of a doctor's name upon the body of a woman during hypnosis, and issuing suggestions such as the following one: 'This evening at 4pm ... you will bleed from the lines that I have drawn on your arm' (Barthelemey cited in Didi-Huberman 1984: 69). The anonymous patient discussed by Barthelemy did indeed bleed, if we are to believe his account, and the words, we are told, remained visible for more than three months. What we find in this and other accounts of dermagraphism is that the patient's body is appropriated as a 'work'; it becomes the (textual) product and possession, the voice if you like, of the subject (the clinician as author), and functions to reaffirm both his sense of self in opposition to the improper (body of the) other, and his status – as the subject of knowledge – within the clinical context.

The infliction of the clinician's palm upon the patient's flesh was another method used and discussed by Barthelemy. The following quote from Barthelemy makes apparent the violence endemic to the extraction of meaning and/or truth from the body of the other. He says: 'If one lightly touches the patient, the dermagraphism does not always manifest itself. If, however, one gives a quick slap or flick to the skin, one soon sees the entire finger or hand take shape as a swelling' (cited in Didi-Huberman 1984: 69). Dermagraphism then, as this quote suggests, is both the name given to the process of reading the textual body of the other, and the term given to the textual mark that is written upon the patient's body and which in turn is read by the clinician. What I want to suggest is that rather than dis-covering the truth or essence of the other, this form of reading writes the body of the other as the expression of the story of the other that it desires to read, that it authors or authorises. As the examples discussed show, dermagraphism does this literally by inscribing the name of the clinician, or his hand-print, upon the textual body of the patient. It is possible to conclude from this, I would argue, that the subject does not precede writing, but rather is constituted in and through processes of reading and writing, the distinction between which is far from clear. Thus neither addressee nor addressor (assuming that we can any longer posit such a distinction) is independent of the 'message' which passes 'between' them. Thus we can conclude that dermal diagnosis is as much a (re)writing of the self as it is a reading/writing of the body of the other. But it seems to me that this is precisely what is forgotten in psychological attempts to represent the subject of self-mutilation.

It is my contention that such forms of analysis dis-figure the body of the other, *not* because they distort the 'reality' of that body, but because they apprehend – that is, read and write – the body, solely in terms of meanings that discourse can speak; they disavow materiality, the carnal, *inter*textuality and/or the figural, and thus in supposedly rendering audible the voice of the other, they in fact silence or forget radical difference rather than testifying to the *différend*.[11] This is perhaps what Didi-Huberman means when he concludes that '[d]ermagraphism produces … a kind of *thanatography*, a sentence which controls [or attempts to control] the destiny of the patient [the other], and which incarnates the corporeal to corpse' (1984: 70). Given this, we might perhaps describe the work of Grumet, Favazza and McLane as exemplifying what Nietzsche has described as 'the hand that in a considerate fashion – kills' (1984: 73).

Whilst dermagraphism may no longer be a popular or acceptable clinical procedure, the assumptions on which it was founded are still apparent (as I have suggested) in psychological and/or dermal diagnostic attempts to extract abstract truths from the depths of the so-called disfigured body. Rather than either validate this approach, or simply dismiss it as erroneous, my aim has been to demonstrate that fleshly (dis)figuration can be seen as performing the role of the figural in the understanding of understanding. Like McLane, I too believe that 'we must listen' to the voice on the skin, to fleshly (dis)figuration. But unlike McLane, for whom the imperative to listen is in order to hear, to make audible the truth that has been silenced, to know, to cure, to produce closure, I want to listen to the unspeakable voice of the other at work within and against the psychological representation of the disfigured body. This 'we must', then, is not so much a command to undertake a Heraclesian journey into the underworld in order to return with the head of that which was once too monstrous to face directly, but rather, an ethical invocation in the Levinasian sense. For Levinas this 'we must' – at least if it is understood as an ethical response-*ability* which is affected in and through exposure to the other – is something which engenders being(s) rather than something which can be reflected upon by a subject(ivity) that pre-exists it, and/or is external to it. Such an encounter with carnality, with the flesh, 'is not only indicative, [and] informative but simultaneously, vocative and imperative' (Lingis 1986: 227). Lingis describes the ethical event or relation, which exceeds the sphere of cognition, and in and through which self and other are mutually constituted, in the following way:

> In his flesh I see ... the demanding insistence of his being. Skin is not hide nor covering, camouflage, uniform, adornment. It is a surface of exposure, zone of susceptibility, of vulnerability, of pain and abuse. In the skin inscribed with its own wrinkles, one ... read[s] ... the vulnerability of what is other. One's eyes touch it lightly, affected by the susceptibility of [the other] ... In this exposedness the other does not affect me as another substance that solidifies under my hold, that sustains and supports. His face is not the surface of another being. It is flesh of no identifiable colour that does not hold its shape. There is want of being in all flesh; what faces is not something whose identity I can grasp. The anonymity of fingers, legs, genitals is not that of implements utilizable by anyone but the unrepresentable importunity of a want, the inapprehendable movement of a contestation, the unmeasurable force of a question that badgers and disrupts (1989: 138).

Or to put it more simply, the carnal materiality of the other 'weighs on me' (Lingis 1989: 137), questions me, contests me, disturbs my perspectives, and the law that governs or gives life to them.

On the one hand then, it may be and in fact is possible to read the body of the other as a canvas upon which psychologically relevant themes are portrayed, as Grumet has suggested, but at the same time what such practices presuppose, and what disallows closure, is the vocative and imperative force of the fleshly encounter, in and through which both self and other are continuously (re)constituted, (re)read and (re)written: mark and are marked.[12]

My conclusion then is that fleshly (dis)figuration remains duplicitous, because, like 'my' bodily being, the bodily being of the other both affects, and is affected by, a trace of what Levinas calls the Other-in-me.[13] 'The body' (as text) is not an object that can be apprehended, but rather, is a 'gaping wound' (Merleau-Ponty, 1962: 394); an openness onto the world which figures the unassimilable. It is the site of an excess that is at the heart of representation and yet is forgotten in and through representation; that generates the possibility of reading, writing, knowledge, and simultaneously interrupts it.

The question which remains unaddressed in my analysis is what the implications of this critique might be for clinical practice – a question that is difficult to answer and yet unavoidable given the context in which the essay finds itself. I concede that I do not have an answer, which is not to suggest that a response is not possible. Whilst on the one hand, I am wary of what I see as normalising attempts to read, represent, and/or judge fleshly (dis)figuration, I do not on the other, presume myself to be 'safe and sound' (Lyotard 1990: 26), to somehow be beyond representational logic and its inherent limitations. Thus it seems to me that the question is not so much whether or not to write/read the inscribed body, but rather, *how* to read fleshly (dis)figuration so as not to forget the figural; how to make possible a response rather than an answer.[14] What I hope this essay has managed to do is to provide a response, to testify to the figural, and thus to show that writing can bear witness to ethical response-*ability*. 'Instead of being the description of an experience, conducted by an "I" in quest of self-knowledge ... writing is the testimony of a fracture, of the opening onto the other ... its aptitude for hearing a call' (Lyotard 1988: 113).

An ethics of reading/writing then, is not a hermeneutic method, but rather, is the affective insistence of 'reading as a *crisis of judgement*' (Readings 1991: 128). And insofar as an ethics of reading/writing could be said to engender the performative effect of 'provoking further discussion' (Readings 1991: 37), then it is neither an absolutist approach to textuality, a form of relativism which promotes a refusal to judge, nor a pluralist claim that all judgements are of equal value. Rather, an ethics of reading fleshly (dis)figuration allows for a critical exploration of the ways in which reading and writing might be complicit in the production of knowledges, identities, and social relations.

Notes

1. For a similar analysis of the marked body that focuses in more detail on tattooing, see Sullivan (1995).
2. See Taylor (1997: 17).
3. In *The Postmodern Condition* (1984) Lyotard, following Wittgenstein, uses the term 'language games' to refer to the rules, linkages, conventions and possible 'moves' associated with particular discourses and discursive practices.
4. This position is shared by Sheila Jeffreys who, in an article entitled 'Sadomasochism, Art & The Lesbian Sexual Revolution', argues that tattoos, piercings, scars and so on, are forms of self-mutilation which abuse

non-survivors often employ. For a critical response to Jeffreys' claims see Sullivan (1997).

5. Sections of McLane's article, such as the one quoted here, are written in italics, although the reason for this is never given.
6. For a well-developed critique of this understanding of subjectivity which he sees as exemplifying classical philosophy and its theoretical limitations, see Lingis (1983: 19-46).
7. For Lyotard the term *le différend* refers to, but does not represent, the unassimilable or unnameable that is at the heart of representation, and yet which every representation necessarily forgets.
8. See *Libidinal Economy,* (30-1).
9. For an extended discussion see Readings (1991: 11).
10. At the same time, Lyotard claims that textuality appears as a figure in the phenomenological understanding of perception, thus he avoids reaffirming a dualist tendency to posit one theoretical perspective as good, right or true, and the other as its opposite.
11. In *The Differend,* Lyotard states that '[t]he *différend* is signalled by [the] inability to prove. The one who lodges the complaint is heard, but the one who is a victim, and who is perhaps the same one, is reduced to silence' (1988: 10).
12. For a similar critique of the tendency to overlook the vocative and imperative characteristics of intersubjectivity in the focus on meaning and intentionality, see Sullivan (1997; 1999).
13. For Levinas, the ethical encounter, the trace and the response-ibility it evokes, occurs as a past that cannot be re-presented; a past 'more ancient than every representable origin, a pre-original and anarchial *passed*'; ... 'a past which was never present' (1978: 9, 24).
14. See Lyotard (1990: 60).

References

Bennington, G. (1988) *Lyotard, Writing the Event*, New York: Columbia University Press.

Didi-Huberman, G. (1984) 'The Figurative Incarnation of the Sentence: Notes on the Autographic Skin', *Journal* 47:5, 66-70.

Favazza, A. (1996) *Bodies Under Siege: Self-Mutilation and Body Modification' in Culture and Psychiatry* (2nd Edition), Baltimore and London: Johns Hopkins University Press.

Grosz, E. (1994) *Volatile Bodies: Towards a Corporeal Feminism*, Sydney: Allen & Unwin.

Grosz, E. (1990), 'Inscriptions and Body-Maps: Representations and the Corporeal' in T. Threadgold and A. Cranny-Francis (eds), *Feminine Masculine and Representation*, Sydney: Allen & Unwin, pp62-74.

Grumet, G. (1983) 'Psychodynamic Implications of Tattooing', *American Journal of Orthopsychiatry* 53:3, 482-92.

Jeffreys, S. (1994) 'Sadomasochism, Art & the Lesbian Sexual Revolution', *Artlink* 14:1, 19-21.

Levinas, E. (1978) *Otherwise Than Being or Beyond Essence*, A. Lingis (trans), The Hague: Martinus Nijhoff.

Levinas, E. (1969) *Totality and Infinity*, A. Lingis (trans), Pittsburgh: Duquesne University Press.

Lingis, A. (1994) *Foreign Bodies*, New York: Routledge.

Lingis, A. (1989) *Deathbound Subjectivity*, Albany: State University of New York Press.

Lingis, A. (1983) *Excesses: Eros and Culture*, Albany: State University of New York Press.

Lyotard, J.F. (1993) *Libidinal Economy*, I. Hamilton Grant (trans), Bloomington and Indianapolis: Indiana University Press.

Lyotard, J.F. (1990) *Heidegger and 'the jews'*, A. Michel and M. Roberts (trans), Minneapolis: University of Minnesota Press.

Lyotard, J.F. (1988) *The Differend: Phrases in Dispute*, G. Van Den Abbeele (trans), Minneapolis: University of Minnesota Press.

Lyotard, J.F. (1984) *The Postmodern Condition: A Report on Knowledge*, G. Bennington and B. Massumi (trans), Minneapolis: University of Minnesota Press.

Lyotard, J.F. (1971) *Discours, figure*, Paris: Klincksieck.

McCance, D. (1996) *Posts: ReAddressing the Ethical*, Albany: State University of New York Press.

McLane, J. (1996) 'The Voice on the Skin: Self-Mutilation and Merleau Ponty's Theory of Language', *Hypatia* 11:4, 107-18.

Merleau-Ponty, M. (1968) *The Visible and the Invisible*, A. Lingis (trans), Evanston: Northwestern University Press.

Merleau-Ponty, M. (1962) *The Phenomenology of Perception*, C. Smith (trans), New York: Routledge and Kegan Paul.

Nietzsche, F. (1984) *Beyond Good and Evil*, R.J. Hollingdale (trans), Harmondsworth: Penguin.

Readings, B. (1991) *Introducing Lyotard: Art and Politics*, London and New York: Routledge.

Sullivan, N. (1999) 'Queer Pleasures: Some Thoughts', *Social Semiotics* 9:2, 251-6.

Sullivan N. (1997) 'Fleshing Out Pleasure: Canonization or Crucifixion', *Australian Feminist Studies* 12:26, 283-92.

Sullivan, N. (1995) 'Illustrative Bodies: Subjectivities, Sociality, Skin Art', *Social Semiotics* 5:1, 143-58.

Taylor, M.C. (1997) *Hiding*, Chicago: University of Chicago Press.

Taylor, M.C. (1987) *Altarity*, Chicago: University of Chicago Press.

Without or with condoms? AIDS and the male sex drive

Nicole Vitellone

This essay critically examines the take up of Wendy Hollway's (1984) analysis of the male sex drive in an AIDS culture. In particular it considers this take up of the male sex drive thesis in analyses of heterosex in AIDS culture. While this thesis informs many such analyses, nonetheless this essay shows how such understandings of heterosex in AIDS culture conflate the male sex drive discourse with the male body. Through an analysis of objects, and in particular via a discussion of the object of the condom in both AIDS research on heterosexuality and safer (hetero)sex campaigns I show how such a narrow focus on male bodies negates the ways in which sexuality – and in particular a male heterosexual sex drive – may have sources other than that of the literal male body. I suggest that current interpretations of the male sex drive, especially feminist analyses of heterosexuality, take for granted consumer culture and more specifically the performativity of objects.

> And I note what may be yet another instance of vicissitude, an ironic turn in our cultural history from the 1970s to the 1990s: that the stubborn drive – Freud's 'basic instincts' – dismissed by constructionists, feminists and postmodernists ... has come back in through the window of the popular media to haunt once again our public and private fantasies (de Lauretis 1998: 877).

It is often argued that what is key for understanding the practice of unsafe heterosex is the male sex drive discourse. So strong is this reading of unsafe sex as concerning the male sex drive and as key for the constitution of hegemonic heterosexual masculinity that it is commonly assumed that safer heterosex is a very unlikely event. Indeed, even the proliferation of the image of the condom in popular HIV/AIDS advertisements, such as the long-running Australian 'If it's not on, it's not on' poster campaign, and eroticised media representations of condom use, are understood not to change heterosexual men's resistance towards condom use. However, in this essay, through tracing the debates on the male sex drive in analyses of heterosex and HIV/AIDS, I question this dominant interpretation. In particular, through a consideration of the object of the condom not as exterior to heterosex, but rather as constitutive, I suggest that recent research findings from Australia on increasing rates of repetitive heterosexual male condom use point to a hydraulic safer male sex drive. In so doing, I also question the dominant focus in analyses of heterosexuality on literal body parts, especially the penis/phallus. This essay therefore suggests that the condom and indeed cultural objects more generally are overlooked in analyses of gender and heterosexuality.

Sexology and the beginnings of the male sex drive

The construction of sexuality by sexologists in the last decade of the nineteenth century was according to Weeks (1985, 1986) premised on the notion of hydraulic sexual instinct. For example, through the use of metaphors such as 'overpowering forces, engulfing drives, gushing streams and uncontrollable spasms' (Weeks 1986: 46), sexologists figured sexuality as an instinctual force. At the centre of this figuring of sexuality was the male body and male sexual practices. In particular, in the writing of sexologists instinctual metaphoric references were employed in relation to the penis. Thus it was the penis which came to be referenced as an unstoppable biological force. Moreover, this social construction of the male sex drive – as a capacity of the biological penis – became normalised, since as Weeks (1986: 46) notes such discourses have proliferated and 'dominated the western discourse on sex'.

Through her reading of Foucault, Wood (1985) also understands the dominant depiction of sexuality as 'governed by biological processes' (Wood 1985: 156) to constitute sexuality as an 'instinct (Wood 1985: 157). And for Wood what is key in the constitution of sexuality as an instinctual force is the discourse on heterosexual sex itself. As she points out:

> ... this sexual instinct is not, by and large, portrayed as purposelessness energy, but as an instinct invested with a biologically ordained *aim* (intercourse) and *object* (usually a person of the opposite sex) (Wood 1985: 156-157).

Thus according to Wood (1985: 157) the discourse of (male) sexuality as a biological drive concerns the portrayal of 'how the instinct functions' in the context of (hetero)sexual sex. Bland (1996) has further argued that sexological discourses normalised and naturalised penetrative heterosexual sex:

> In the early twentieth century and into the inter-war years, while sexologists ... *extended* the definition of the 'sexual', the definition of 'sex' itself was narrowed down into 'penetration' (and 'normal sex' into 'heterosexual penetration') ... Non-penetrative sexual activity was simply not 'real' sex (Bland 1996: 93).

This sexological definition of 'normal sex' and 'real sex' as 'heterosexual penetration' has also been interpreted by feminists as unnatural and coercive for women. Jeffreys (1990) for instance has argued:

> Sex was the act of coitus in which a man penetrated a woman's vagina with his penis. It was the job of the sexologists to inculcate this knowledge into the resistant or inadequate multitude (Jeffreys 1990: 19).

Thus in naturalising and normalising the meaning of heterosex as coitus – via the discourse on penile/vaginal penetration – the sexologists are not only perceived by Jeffreys to have constructed men's hydraulic sex drive as an instinctual biological truth, but also, in inculcating women with the meaning of heterosex as natural, sexological discourses are understood to have incited women to perform such acts. The construction of heterosexual penetration as normal by the sexologists has been interpreted by Jackson (1984) as simultaneously naturalising for some women their coercive experience of heterosex. For example, she argues that the 'science of sex constitutes above all an apology for and justification of precisely that form of male sexuality ...

based on uncontrollable urges, power and violence' (Jackson 1984: 53).

Moreover, in her research on convicted rapists Jackson (1978) found that the effects of such an apology for male power by the sexologists constitute a legitimation of violent male sexual behaviour, a legitimation which she found to be mobilised by rapists to justify and neutralise act(s) of rape. This contention is also borne out in Smart's (1989) investigation of the legal trial of rape whereby the discourse of the male sex drive was found to be utilised by the defendants as a technique to legitimise and thus neutralise sexual acts of violence. As Smart puts it:

> ... being a sexual predator is regarded as normal, even desirable for men ... The rape trial will not allow any criticism of this 'natural' activity (1989: 42).

Such a normalisation of the act of rape is thus widely perceived to be a justification of male heterosexuality as 'naturally predatory'. And, as Edwards (1996) suggests the construction of the sexual predator as normal in the legal trial of rape also reflects a wider cultural belief that the male sex drive is 'readily aroused at any time and can become dangerous if not regularly satisfied' (Edwards 1996: 185).

Whilst these feminist analyses of the hydraulic model of male (hetero)sexuality (Jackson 1978; 1984; Smart 1989; Jeffreys 1990; Edwards 1996) suggest that the male sex drive discourse concerns gendered power relations, Hollway's (1984) analysis of male sex drive calls into question such analyses. Hollway recognises that these kinds of feminist interpretations of heterosexuality do indeed challenge the construction of male sexuality as a hydraulic force. But she also suggests that such analyses of the male sex drive as concerning male (hetero)sexual power and female insubordination put in place another monolithic understanding of gender, one where a biological determinism is replaced by a social determinism. Hollway writes:

> True we have challenged men's 'natural sexual drive'. But we have replaced it with an idea of the power of the penis/phallus which, in another guise, grants men's sexuality a monolithic power over us (Hollway 1984: 63-64).

Hence for Hollway, such feminist accounts of heterosexuality point to the meaning of the penis in the act of heterosex as producing a phallic body part which is constitutive of gender power relations.

Ramazanoglu and Holland (1993) suggest that the power of the penis in the act of heterosex can not however so easily be separated out from a socio-cultural analysis of gender. Thus, in response to Hollway's claims that interpretations of the male body and in particular the body part of the penis in certain feminist analyses of heterosexuality have now become (over)defined by a rigid understanding of heterosexual male power as phallic, they argue:

> There is the question of how far the power of the penis is also a material power, a gendered difference in embodiment which leaves a woman at physical risk regardless of what discourses they produce ... (Ramazanoglu and Holland 1993: 248).

Moreover, Ramazanoglu (1995) in the article 'Heterosexuality, Biology and Why Men Stay on Top' goes on to suggest:

> If we rule out the grounded, material body out of knowledge of gender relations, and so out of theories of power, the wider problems of where power lies and why men exercise so much power over women remain (Ramazanoglu 1995: 38).

To begin to think through whether the issue of male power concerns the 'material body' and in particular the 'physical' body part of the penis, I want to turn to analyses of the male sex drive discourse in relation to HIV/AIDS. In particular, I want to focus on feminist interpretations of safer (hetero)sex campaigns to think through, firstly, Hollway's claims that analyses of male power give too much power to the penis/phallus, and secondly, Ramazanoglu's (1995) concern that current moves to rule 'the grounded material body out of knowledge of gender relations' ignore the biological reasons as to why 'men stay on top'. To begin, I draw on my previous work (Vitellone 2000) where I analysed interpretations of the object of the condom in mainstream safer sex campaigns. There, I pointed out the way in which the discourse of the (heterosexual) male sex drive has been understood by HIV/AIDS researchers and social and cultural theorists of HIV/AIDS to concern the hydraulic performance of the body part of the penis – without condoms – in the act of unsafe (hetero)sex.

Without condoms

By drawing on the research and analyses of safer (hetero)sex practice by feminist and medical sociolologists, psychologists, as well as queer and cultural theorists discussing HIV/AIDS, I discussed how within contemporary analyses of heterosexuality and in particular male (hetero)sexuality, there is a common understanding of popular AIDS campaigns promoting heterosexual condom use as running counter to the normative male sex drive discourse. Indeed, the object of the condom itself is widely considered to threaten heterosexual men's performance of the culturally constituted male sex drive. For instance, the practice of penile–vaginal penetration with condoms is perceived to be especially problematic, because as Wilton (1997: 33) argues (following Richardson, 1993), 'it is in direct contradiction of the dominant social scripting of male sexuality, namely that it is uncontrollable or barely controllable force'. Moreover, what stands out from such feminist analyses of the 'social scripting of male sexuality' in relation to popular safer sex discourse is that the performance of hydraulic male heterosexuality – as an 'uncontrollable or barely controllable force' – is understood to be at issue only in relation to the everyday practice of unsafe (hetero)sex, that is via the *absence* of condoms.

The perception of heterosexual male condom use as contradicting the normative male sex drive discourse is also, I argued, linked to an association of condom use with the other, homosexuality (Vitellone 2000). Lupton (1994: 317) for instance suggests, 'the discourse of homosexuality and deviance have converged upon condoms', since, 'condoms signify homosexuality' (Lupton 1994: 315). Moreover, in Patton's (1990, 1993, 1994) analysis of safer sex discourse, this elision of homosexuality with condoms, and heterosexuality with unsafe sex is perceived to be constitutive of a hierarchy of sexual identities. That is to say, Patton understands the construction of heterosexual penetration as 'safe by nature' (Patton 1993: 257) – and therefore in no need of protection – to be produced by a homophobic logic which positions non penile/vaginal (hetero)sexual practices as not normal, not natural, and therefore not safe. Thus in both Patton and Lupton's analysis of the object of the condom (see also Wilton and Aggleton 1991; Redman 1996), what is considered to be at issue for heterosexual men in the act of safer heterosex (with condoms) is not only the constitution of a sexed male body as an uncontrollable, unstoppable force, but also the performance of a normative *heterosexual* self-identity.

Whilst such interpretations of male heterosexuality imply that Hollway's (1984) definition of a 'biological sex drive' may have immediate purchase for analysing the configuration of gender and sexual identity in relation to HIV/AIDS, I want to consider some of the issues raised by Hollway (1984) in her analysis of feminist accounts of the male sex drive. In particular, I want to consider Hollway's claims that in deconstructing the 'biological sex drive' model of male sexuality feminist writers concerned with the configuration of gender relations often substitute an analysis of hydraulic sexuality with corporeal male power which emphasises the social power of the body, and in particular the body part of the penis. In considering Hollway's claims, I also want to address the somewhat oppositional stance taken by Ramazanoglu (1995), who argues that feminists must engage with the corporeal male body in their analyses of male power in order to understand the constitution of gender relations. Thus, I consider whether such corporeal interpretations of hegemonic male (hetero)sexuality adequately address the configuration of the male sex drive, especially in relation to HIV/AIDS. In so doing, I also consider whether current understandings of male heterosexuality – as concerning the hydraulic performance of the body part of the penis in the act of heterosex *without* condoms – conflate an understanding of identity formation and gender relations with a literal male body, and thus assume that such processes occur in juxtaposition to the object of the condom.

This assumption regarding the literal male body is for instance apparent in Kippax, Crawford, Waldby and Benton's (1990: 538) analysis of the male sex drive in relation to HIV/AIDS and heterosexuality, especially when they suggest: 'the power relations which describe the terms of the male sex drive discourse render negotiation unintelligible'. So pervasive is this particular interpretation of the discourse of the male sex drive – as concerning the practice of heterosex without condoms – that Kippax et al (1990: 542) have also suggested that the ability to negotiate (with men) the practice of safer heterosex (with condoms) is often difficult for women to achieve.

Such a view is also at issue in Stewart's (1994) analysis of her Australian research findings conducted on young women in Victoria when she concludes that the issue of safer sex negotiation for young heterosexual women in relation to condom use 'remain[s] the focus of a number of tensions and contradictions, *because it calls upon women to go against the male sex drive discourse*' (Stewart 1994: 29, my emphasis).

Here then, the construction of male heterosexuality as a hydraulic instinct is understood to concern the performance of the male body, and in particular the body part of the penis. Stewart thus takes for granted that the male body part of the penis is imbued with power. Consequently, Stewart simply assumes that a consideration of the penis is important for understanding male power. This assumption is for example evident in her claims that the male sex drive discourse has a negative impact on young women's attempts to make men wear condoms. The conflation of power with the body part of the penis in the act of heterosex is also evident in the following comment whereby a discussion of gender relations takes place in juxtaposition to the object of the condom:

> Whilst safe-sex initiatives have attempted to instigate more powerful, self-determining modes of femininity via slogans such as 'Tell him if it's not on it's not on' they have done so at the exclusion of recognising the broader social relations of gender (Stewart 1999: 382).

Although this analysis of the safer sex discourse 'If it's not on, it's not on' positions the object of the condom as outside of 'broader social relations of gender' and the 'male sex drive', it also suggests that women's ability to negotiate the practice of safer (hetero)sex with men challenges normative gender relations. Such a view is further evident in the work of Richardson when she argues that the construction of normative female sexuality as 'passive and male as "active" ... [is] threatened by the allocation of responsibility for negotiating sexual practices to women and the demand they take active control over the sexual encounter' (1996: 174). In this sense, the discourse of condom use in safer sex campaigns, such as the Australian 'If it's not on, it's not on' AIDS education campaign, is considered to challenge the social construction of male sexuality as a powerful hydraulic force as well as the definition of female sexuality as responsive to men's culturally constituted uncontrollable biological sexual instincts. But whilst Richardson (1996), Stewart (1994, 1999) and Kippax et al (1990) all understand the object of the condom in the discourse on safer(hetero)sex to question and potentially subvert the social construction of men's natural sex drive (see also Holland, Ramazanoglu, Sharpe & Thomson 1998; Patton 1994; Thomson and Holland 1994; Wilton and Aggleton 1991 and Wilton 1997), they also consider, along with Waldby, Kippax and Crawford (1990) women's ability to negotiate with men the practice of safer (hetero)sex to be significantly undermined by the dominant male sex drive discourse.

In measuring gender in this way, that is through men's performance of unsafe (hetero)sex, these feminist analyses of HIV/AIDS can therefore be seen to put in place an understanding of the male sex drive as a fixed and inherent feature of dominant *male* sexuality. In other words, because structuralist and poststructuralist feminist accounts of unsafe (hetero)sex in relation to HIV/AIDS suggest that the male sex drive can be understood as either concerning a gendered social structure (Holland et al 1998; Richardson 1996; Stewart 1994, 1999; Wilton and Aggleton 1991; Wilton 1997), or a discursive social construction (Kippax et al 1990), in both these accounts of (hetero)sexuality there is a conflation of the male sex drive with a corporeal male body. Moreover, since these current discussions of male power rely on an understanding of men as reluctant to practice safer (hetero)sex, these analyses can also be seen to produce – via a discussion of condom use – the concept of mechanical sexuality as concerning the performance of the corporeal body part of the penis. Such feminist interpretations of heterosexuality may therefore paradoxically reproduce the sexological definition of hydraulic sexuality as a naturally occurring biological male instinct, and the act of unsafe (hetero)sex as a normal sexual practice.

In this sense, if we return to Hollway's (1984) consideration of feminist theories of male power in relation to the male body, especially her concern that contemporary social analyses of heterosexuality map a universal model of gendered power relations onto the body part of the penis, then it seems that such a mapping may indeed be at play in current analyses of heterosex practice (without condoms). For instance, in a recent discussion of male heterosexuality and condom use Jackson and Scott (1997) suggest that the inability of heterosexual men to make a transition from the normative mechanical performance of unsafe (hetero)sex to safer (hetero)sex practice is an effect of socially constructed gendered inequalities:

> ... getting men to use [condoms] was not so simple. Public discourse around safer sex in this period can be understood within a post-Fordist frame, with a focus on re-skilling and increased flexibility. Heavy male sex work, with the emphasis on performance, seemed to be of less value

> and female negotiating skills came to the fore. Meaningful negotiation, however, requires an equal starting point and *most health advice has ignored the inequalities within the gendered dynamics of heterosexuality* (Holland et al 1990) ... In the end, this public discussion has taken a form which offers minimal challenge to male sexuality ... (Jackson and Scott 1997: 564-565, my emphasis).

Here, by claiming that public discussion of condom use 'offers minimal challenge to male sexuality' – since the discourse of safer sex which encourages women to negotiate with men safer (hetero)sex practice 'ignores the gendered dynamics of heterosexuality' – the authors suggest that the constitution of heterosexuality, and in particular hegemonic gendered relations, are, firstly, embodied in the performance of 'heavy male sex work' (without condoms) and secondly, can be known in advance of the 'public discourse of safer sex'. Pringle (1992) however, is critical of such moves when she argues:

> Bodies have a meaning only to the extent that they are already situated within discourse ... contemporary theorists largely take for granted that we make sense of the world through discourse. Identities, whether as sexed, sexual or gendered are not pre-given. They have to be constructed, articulated and maintained: they do this using the discursive framework available to the time and culture (Pringle 1992: 100).

In making the argument that contemporary theorists of culture and social differences must take into account 'the discursive framework available at the time' in order to understand the meaning of bodies and the constitution of identities, Pringle's work can thus be seen to contrast with the analysis of heterosexuality and the male body offered by Jackson and Scott (1997). In particular, by foregrounding the significance of the discursive framework as opposed to broader structural inequalities for interpreting the meaning of bodies and the social construction of gender and sexual identities, Pringle's work implies that the performance of 'heavy male sex work' as discussed by Jackson and Scott in relation to the practice of unsafe (hetero)sex, may not necessarily pre-exist the public discussion of HIV/AIDS and condom use, but rather may be constituted in and by the discourse of safer sex itself. Indeed, Waldby (1996: 10) makes this point in her discussion of the previously mentioned Australian 'If it's not on, it's not on' safer sex campaign, when she suggests 'heterosexual men remained unmarked, the unspecified force which women are asked to control'. In this sense, the male sex drive is perceived to be constituted by the popular discourse of condom use in AIDS prevention campaigns which convey the message that heterosexual men are reluctant to engage in the practice of safer (hetero)sex. Waldby's analysis of men's culturally constituted uncontrollable sexual urges therefore contrasts with analyses of the male sex drive which suggest that the configuration of hydraulic sexuality can be known in advance of such campaigns.

With condoms

Whilst the discourse of men's reluctance to use condoms in the Australian safer sex campaign 'If it's not on, it's not on' is considered by Waldby (1996) to construct as normative heterosexual men's uncontrollable hydraulic sex drive, recent research findings suggest that the practice of safer heterosex may be a more common occurrence. For instance, research findings from Australia suggest that condom use by heterosexual men for the practice of safer heterosex is rather high and increasing. Whilst there are limitations to the method of self-report, these findings nevertheless repetitively suggest that younger adolescent men are increasingly wearing condoms. In Lindsay, Smith and Rosenthal's (1997) survey of 3500 Australian secondary students, for example, the use of condoms by young year ten (fifteen to sixteen-year-old) heterosexual young men was found to be a normative act, with 74 per cent of the 171 male respondents surveyed in 1997 claiming that in the previous twelve months they 'always' used condoms when engaging in (hetero)sex (Table A5, figure 5.4: 30). And in a smaller study of 244 young people aged between fifteen and eighteen in Victoria, Rosenthal, Smith and de Visser (1997) also found high levels of condom use amongst high school students. In this study, 81 per cent of the 244 respondents claimed to have practised safe sex in their most recent sexual experience. Similarly, in this research project it was found that more young men (93 per cent) than young women (70 per cent) used a condom during their most recent sexual experience. In addition, the researchers discovered that 'if a condom was used, it was more likely to be provided by the male than the female partner' (Rosenthal et al 1997: 103). These particular findings, which point to both heterosexual men's initiation of condom use and the normative experience of safer heterosex practice, were similarly found by Smith and Rosenthal (1997). In their study, the researchers investigated young Australian men's (seventeen to eighteen-years-old) sexual practices during 'Schoolies Week'. Here, the majority of the male respondents expected to have sex while on their end-of-school holidays in Queensland (80 per cent), with 83 per cent expecting to use condoms and two-thirds of the young men actually practicing safer sex with casual partners (Smith and Rosenthal 1997: 175). Further research on levels of condom use in Australia by Roy Morgan Research for Ansell condoms also confirms the findings of the above studies. Results from a 1998 survey, for instance, suggest an increase in the number of young people purchasing condoms, with 70 per cent of sixteen to nineteen-year-olds having used condoms in the three months prior to having being interviewed, an increase of 28 per cent on the 1997 figures. Interestingly, whilst the survey findings point to an increase in condom use for the practice of (safer) heterosex, these findings also point to a decrease in the number of young women using condoms, with a drop from 47.3 per cent in 1996, to 37.8 per cent in 1998 (*The Canberra Times*, 24 August 1998: 3). Thus, the act of condom use by young heterosexual men for the practice of safer (hetero)sex may have become somewhat of a normative occurrence in the context of heterosexuality.

Together these findings call into question analyses of popular safer sex advertisements, such as the 'If it's not on, it's not on' campaign. In particular, these findings question the often made assumption that condom use for heterosexual men is problematic since the object of the condom interferes with the performance of men's spontaneous and uncontrollable sex drive. Moreover, the above findings which point to 'it' – safer (hetero)sex – as normative, suggest that Patton's (1996: 144) discussion of the constitution of normative heterosexuality as involving 'its' 'claim to naturalness' may now involve not heterosexual men's dis-identification with the object of the condom in safer sex campaigns as Patton claims, but rather an identification with 'it' – the object of the condom – in the discourse of safer (hetero)sex.

Turning to the work of Butler (1990) on gender as performatively constituted and Lury (1996) on the social life of objects in consumer culture, I want to suggest that the above findings on heterosexual male condom use may indicate, on the contrary, that gender identity is currently constituted by the performativity of the object of the condom. First, I want to consider Butler's definition of gender as concerning 'the repeated stylisation of the body, a set of repeated acts within a highly rigid regulatory frame that congeal over time to produce the appearance of substance, of a natural sort of being' (Butler 1990: 33) in relation to HIV/AIDS research. Specifically, although Butler does not consider the performativity of objects, if we take into account the findings on safer (hetero)sex practice, then the object of the condom in the safer sex discourse 'If it's not on, it's not on' could be read as constitutive of a set of repeated acts that produce over time the appearance of male (hetero)sexuality as a natural instinctual and hydraulic force. And in this sense it seems that analyses of the male sex drive in relation to HIV/AIDS which suggest that the practice of safer (hetero)sex is an unnatural act and the object of the condom in safer sex discourse is outside of the constitution of the male sex drive, may therefore take for granted the nature of objects. For as Lury suggests 'the object is ... simultaneously a natural and a cultural object' (1996: 16), and its appropriation is 'more often than not both a moment of consumption and production, of undoing and doing, of destruction and construction' (1996: 1). Thus, I want to reconsider Pringle's (1992) claims that the way in which identities are 'constructed, articulated and maintained' in contemporary AIDS culture concerns the situating of *bodies* in discourses. And in response to this claim I want to suggest that such a literal emphasis on the corporeal overlooks the way in which gendered, sexual and sexed identities may currently be made through the performativity of objects. For instance, if we reconsider analyses of the safer sex campaign 'If it's not on, it's not on' – especially in relation to interpretations of the male sex drive as concerning the performance of unsafe (hetero)sex without condoms – the focus on the body, and especially the body part of the penis, in these analyses relies on a taken for granted assumption that the construction, maintenance and articulation of a heterosexual masculine self-identity concerns the corporeal male body. Moreover, the logic at play in these analyses concerns the performativity of the natural male body as opposed to the cultural object of the condom, an object which is perceived to interfere with the dominant male sex drive discourse. In this sense, it seems that whilst feminist post-structuralist readings of the discourse of the male sex drive as socially constituted deconstruct essentialist understandings of male heterosexuality, these interpretations of hydraulic sexuality – as concerning the performativity of the male body (as opposed to the condom) – may also as Kirby (1997: 5) suggests 'retur[n] us to the very nature/culture, body/mind divisions that are so politically insidious'.

Some of the findings from Waldby, Kippax & Crawford's (1993) study, for instance, suggest that condom use may not involve a disruption to the performance of the male sex drive discourse as is often assumed. As one male respondent in Waldby et al's study commented:

> I finally went out with someone where it was incorporated in and it felt good, it felt *natural* and it became part of the process and now for me it is *part of the process* and it's not like going against the *flow* at all ... sometimes the woman would put it on me, sometimes not ... it feels nicer, you're both doing it, you don't actually stop ... (Waldby et al 1993: 253, my emphases).

The idea that the condom 'felt good', 'natural', 'is part of the process' and was 'not like going against the flow', for this male respondent in this particular experience of safer (hetero)sex, thus suggests that the phenomenon of the male sex drive – as an unstoppable mechanical hydraulic force – may now concern the eroticised object of the condom. In a similar study of heterosexual condom use, Browne and Minichiello (1994: 236) also found that 'when the condom was used as part of eroticism, informants found it was not "interfering" and that they were able to remain aroused without severe disruption to the flow of pleasurable sex'.

The above findings thus contradict the dominant interpretation of the male sex drive discourse in relation to HIV/AIDS. In particular, such findings call into question analyses of heterosexual male condom use – for the practice of safer (hetero)sex – as breaking the flow and not natural. In this way, Grosz's description of 'animal sex':

> When eroticism is considered a program, a means to an end ... a mode of conquest, a proof of virility ... an inner drive that periodically erupts, or an impelling attraction to an object that exerts a 'magnetic' force (ie, as actively compelling ...), it is reduced to versions of this hydraulic model (1995: 294)

may be understood to concern the performativity of objects, rather than the performativity of literal body parts. In other words, what I am suggesting here is that Grosz's interpretation of hydraulic sexuality as one that concerns 'a means to an end', a 'proof of virility' and an 'inner drive that periodically erupts' seems to concern not the male subject's corporeal body, but the condom itself.

Research findings from Tanner and Pollack's (1988) study of thirty-six heterosexual couples attending a US university indeed suggest that eroticised representations of condoms may be the key for the constitution of mechanical safer (hetero)sex practice. In their research, which involved a comparative study of the effects eroticised representations of condoms have for producing a shift towards safer heterosex practice, Tanner and Pollarck found 'a significant change in attitudes towards condoms took place in those couples who were instructed to incorporate the condom into erotic pleasuring' (Tanner and Pollack 1988: 539-540). Such representations constituted an 'enhancement of positive attitudes towards condoms' and 'increas[ed] pleasure' (Tanner and Pollack 1988: 540). In addition, research findings from Lupton and Tulloch's (1996: 42) Australian study suggest that such positive responses to eroticised representations of condoms may be gendered. For example, in this study of 1005 year twelve secondary school students and mass media portrayals of HIV/AIDS, considerably more men (52 per cent) than women (28 per cent) responded favourably to the question 'The [TV] Sex show, like a porno magazine can draw people in they'll learn about AIDS from that'.

Porn, condoms and the male sex drive

For Altman (1992) and Watney (1987) this successful conflation of 'exciting and satisfying' sex with the image of the condom in popular TV representations is considered to be the fundamental factor in producing the shift from unsafe to safer sex:

> ... we so urgently need to enlarge and expand our sense of the sexual, in order to incorporate condoms as new stage props into the theatre of our desiring fantasies ... We need a massive television campaign about the use of condoms targeted at all constituencies of desire which actually make up the population (Watney 1987: 133).

Thus in arguing that the eroticisation of the condom would 'change and expand our sense of the sexual' Watney's analysis suggests that the meaning of heterosexual pleasure may be made by the representation of the condom itself. In addition, the metaphoric description of the condom in Watney's analysis as a 'new stage prop in our desiring fantasies' may further be read as suggesting that the cultural object of the condom in popular media campaigns may be constitutive of an active desire for safer (hetero)sex practice. Indeed, Lupton (1994) makes this point explicit when she argues:

> Until condoms are associated with wickedly exciting and satisfying heterosexual activities, and presented in such a way in popular media, it is doubtful that their use will ever be accepted by those who identify themselves as heterosexual and sensual (Lupton 1994: 317).

But whilst Lupton along with Watney and Altman perceive such attempts to transform sexuality, especially heterosexuality, to accommodate the use of condoms to be an outcome of media campaigns which eroticise the condom, Wilton (1994, 1997) takes opposition to such claims. In particular, Wilton takes opposition to analyses of eroticisation which suggest that representations of 'hot' safer (hetero)sex will produce a shift in heterosexual men's sex practices towards condom use (see Adelman 1992; Altman 1992; Lupton 1994; Patton 1989, 1991; Watney 1987; Waldby et al 1990, 1993). For instance, she argues:

> The pornographic vernacular, which locates sexual desire and agency in the male and constitutes the female body as the object of the desiring male gaze, is complicit in the discursive structuration of precisely those gendered relations of power which *impede the adoption of safer heterosex* (Wilton 1997: 129, my emphasis).

In other words, Wilton does not perceive sexualised representations of the condom to be constitutive of an active desire for hydraulic safer (hetero)sex practice. Rather, for Wilton sexualised images of heterosex with condoms are considered to 'impede the adoption of safer heterosex'. Moreover, according to Wilton, it is 'the location of sexual desire and agency in the male' and the objectification of the female body – for the 'desiring male gaze' – in such representations of safer (hetero)sex practice which are considered to work against the take up of condom use by heterosexual men. This understanding of the constitution of sexuality in the context of porn – as concerning the representation of bodies – ignores how objects like the condom may be key for the making of heterosexual desire and heterosexual male agency.

Whilst Wilton's thesis on the sexualised representations of condoms is clearly dissimilar from Watney (1987), Altman (1992) and Patton's

(1991) analyses of the eroticised object of the condom, in the sense that for these authors such representations of the condom are seen to change and not impede the adoption of safer (hetero)sex, Wilton (1997) nevertheless appears to have a similar position to Patton (1989, 1991) and Watney (1987), in that she also has a utopics of the condom or what might be termed a *condom utopics*. That is, because Wilton considers the object of the condom as 'feminising' of hegemonic heterosexual masculinity (Wilton 1997: 34) and the practice of safer sex as 'simply dissonant with the construction of the male sex "drive"' (Wilton and Aggleton 1991: 155), her analysis of gender here suggests that if heterosexual men were to practice safer (hetero)sex, the dominant gendered construction of hydraulic male (hetero) sexuality would be transgressed. Patton (1993: 259) makes a similar move when she comments 'heterosexual identity can only be reconstructed as truly "safe sex" when heterosexual men are just *queer* enough to wear a condom'. Here then, the use of the condom by heterosexual men is perceived by Patton to be utopic in the sense that the object of the condom is understood to transgress the binary distinction between a normative 'safe' heterosexual identity and pathologised unsafe homosexuality. Thus, according to Patton 'to fuck without a condom is the new, all-American fantasy of heterosexuality rescued from queerness' (Patton 1996: 155).

Condoms and the making of hydraulic (hetero)sexuality

But Gamson (1990: 266) has argued, 'the condom ... always carries with it ... some connotation of sexual intercourse'. And according to Moore (1997: 449) 'male condoms are the one latex technology used in safer sex with a prior history that signifies sexual activity'. Moreover, this connotation of sexual intercourse in relation to the male condom may further be read to invoke connotations of the male body part of the penis. Sedgewick (1993), for instance, points out:

> Notoriously, if sex means penetration and penetration means penis, then there's no sex in the absence of a penis or *penis prosthesis* and no sex between or among women except insofar as we simulate having the phallus (Sedgewick 1993: 98, my emphasis).

Thus if we return to the representation of the condom in popular safer (hetero)sex discourse such as the Australian 'If it's not on, it's not on' campaign, the object of the condom may not be considered to as simply constituting a departure from the hydraulic model of male heterosexuality produced by the sexologists at the turn of the century. That is to say, the object of the condom in safer sex campaigns may be understood not to undo the male sex drive, but rather always carry with it a connotation of hydraulic sexuality. Indeed Teifer (1997) has suggested that there has been a turn towards an intensification of a technical model of hydraulic sexuality in medical discourse. Although Teifer herself does not discuss the specific object of the condom in her analysis of the contraceptive revolution and the medicalisation of sexuality, she nevertheless suggests that this process has 'only reinforced a limited script for heterosexual sexual life – arousal, intercourse, performance, false universals, technical focus' (Teifer 1997: 112). And this point seems on my reading to have much significance for understanding the object of the condom in the 1990s discourse of safer sex in the sense that the condom may be understood to constitute and be constitutive of a technical focus in relation to heterosex. In short, safer sex culture concerns a technically imagined heterosex. That is to say, the condom itself in a HIV/AIDS context makes a hydraulic model of heterosexuality. Read in this way, Altman's (1995: 105) understanding of 'the condom ... as an emblem of sexuality in the modern world' may therefore be called into question. For it seems that rather than representing a universal sign of sexuality, the popular object of the condom in safer (hetero)sex discourse, such as the Australian 'If it's not on, it's not on' campaign concerns an emblem of heterosexual (male) pleasure and identity figured in terms of a technical performance.

References

Altman, D. (1992) 'AIDS and The Discourses of Sexuality', in R.W. Connell and G.W. Dowsett (eds), *Rethinking Sex: Social Theory and Sexuality Research*, Melbourne: Melbourne University Press, pp32-48.

Altman, D. (1995) 'Meanings and Identities in the Time Of AIDS', in J. Gagnon and G. Parker (eds), *Conceiving Sexuality: Approaches to Sex Research in a Postmodern World*, New York and London: Routledge, pp97-109.

Adelman, M. (1992) 'Sustaining Passion: Eroticism and Safe-Sex Talk', *Archives of Sexual Behaviour* 21 (5): 481-494.

Bland, L. (1996) 'The Shock of the Freewoman Journal: Feminists Speaking on Heterosexuality in Early Twentieth-Century England', in J.Weeks and J.Holland (eds), *Sexual Cultures: Communities, Values and Intimacy*, London: Macmillan pp75-97.

Browne, J. and Minichiello, V. (1994) 'The Condom: Why More People Don't Put One On', *Sociology of Health and Illness* 16 (2): 229-251.

Butler, J. (1990) *Gender Trouble*, New York and London: Routledge.
de Lauretis, T. (1998) 'The Stubborn Drive', *Critical Inquiry* 24: 851-877.
Edwards, A. (1996) 'Gender and Sexuality in the Social Construction of Rape and Consensual Sex: A Study of Processes and Outcome in Six Recent Rape Trials', in J. Holland and L. Adkins (eds), *Sex, Sensibility and the Gendered Body*, London: Macmillan, pp178-202.
Gamson, J. (1990) 'Rubber Wars: Struggles over the Condom in the United States', *Journal of the History of Sexuality* 1 (2): 262-282.
Grosz, E. (1995) 'Animal Sex: Libido as Desire and Death', in E. Grosz and E. Probyn (eds), *Sexy Bodies*, London and New York: Routledge, pp278-300.
Holland, J., C. Ramazanoglu, S. Sharpe and R. Thomson (1998) *The Male In The Head. Young People, Heterosexuality and Power*, London: The Tufnell Press.
Hollway, W. (1984) 'Women's Power In Heterosexual Sex', *Women's Studies International Forum* 7 (1): 63-68.
Jackson, M. (1984) 'Sexology and the social construction of male sexuality (Havelock Ellis)', in M. Jackson, S. Jeffreys, L. Kay and P. Mahony (eds), *The Sexuality Papers: Male Sexuality and the Social Control of Women*, Melbourne: Hutchinson Publishing Group.
Jackson, S. (1978) 'The Social Context of Rape: Sexual Scripts and Motivation', *Women's Studies International Forum* 1: 27-38.
Jackson, S. and S. Scott, (1997) 'Gut Reactions to Matters of the Heart: Reflections on Rationality, Irrationality and Sexuality', *Sociological Review* 15 (4): 571-574.
Jeffreys, S. (1990) *Anticlimax*, London: The Women's Press.
Kippax, S., J. Crawford, C. Waldby and P. Benton (1990) 'Women Negotiating Heterosex: Implications for AIDS Prevention', *Women's Studies International Forum* 13 (6): 533-542.
Kirby, V. (1997) *Telling Flesh: The Substance of the Corporeal*, London and New York: Routledge.
Lindsay, J., A. Smith and D. Rosenthal (1997) *Secondary Students, HIV/AIDS and Sexual Health*, Centre for the Studies of Sexually Transmissible Diseases, Monograph Series No. 3, Carlton: La Trobe University.
Lupton, D. (1994) 'The Condom in the Age of AIDS: Newly Respectable or Still a Dirty Word? A Discourse Analysis', *Qualitative Health Research* (4) 3: 304-320.
Lupton, D. and J. Tulloch, (1996) '"Bringing home the reality of it": Senior school students' responses to mass media portrayals of HIV/AIDS', *Australian Journal of Communication* 23 (1): 31-45.
Lury, C. (1996) *Consumer Culture*, Cambridge: Polity Press.
Moore, L.J. (1997) '"It's Like You Use Pots and Pans to Cook. It's the Tool": The Technologies of Safer Sex', *Science, Technology and Human Values* 22 (4): 434-471.
Patton, C. (1989) 'Cindy Patton on Safer Sex, Community and Porn', *Rites* 5 (10): 10-12.
Patton, C. (1990) *Inventing AIDS*, London and New York: Routledge.

Patton, C. (1991) 'Safe Sex and the Pornographic Vernacular', in Bad Object-Choices (ed), *How Do I Look?*, Seattle: Bay Press, pp1-33.

Patton, C. (1993) '"Safe by Nature": Reconstructing Heterosexual Identity Under the Sign of AIDS', in S.Wilkinson and C. Kitzinger (eds), *Heterosexuality*, London: Sage pp257-261.

Patton, C. (1994) *Last Served ? Gendering the HIV Pandemic*, London: Taylor and Francis.

Patton, C. (1996) *Fatal Advice: How Safe-Sex Education Went Wrong*, Durham and London: Duke University Press.

Pringle, R. (1992) 'Absolute Sex? Unpacking the Sexuality/Gender Relationship', in R.W. Connell and G.W. Dowsett (eds), *Rethinking Sex: Social Theory and Sexuality Research*, Melbourne: Melbourne University Press, pp76-101.

Ramazanoglu, C. and J. Holland (1993) 'Women's sexuality and men's appropriation of desire', in C. Ramazanoglu (ed), *Up Against Foucault: Explorations of Some Tensions Between Foucault and Feminism*, London and New York: Routledge, pp239-264.

Ramazanoglu, C. (1995) 'Back to Basics: Heterosexuality, Biology and Why Men Stay on Top', in M. Maynard and J. Purvis (eds), *(Hetero)sexual Politics*, London: Taylor and Francis, pp27-42.

Redman, P. (1996) '"Empowering Men to Disempower Themselves": Heterosexual Masculinities, HIV and the Contradictions of Anti-oppressive Education', in *Understanding Masculinities*, Buckingham: Open University Press, pp168-179.

Richardson, D. (1993) 'Sexuality and Male Dominance', in D. Richardson and V. Robinson (eds), *Introducing Women's Studies: Feminist Theory and Practice*, London: Macmillan.

Richardson, D. (1996) 'Contradictions in Discourse: Gender, Sexuality and HIV/AIDS', in J. Holland and L. Adkins (eds), *Sex, Sensibility and The Gendered Body*, London: Macmillan, pp161-178.

Rosenthal, D., A. Smith and R. de Visser (1997) 'Young People's Condom Use: an Event Specific Analysis', *Venereology* 10 (2): 101-106.

Sedgwick, E.K. (1993) *Tendencies*, London: Routledge.

Smart, C. (1989) *Feminism and the Power of the Law*, New York and London: Routledge.

Smith, M.A. and D. Rosenthal (1997) 'Sex, Alcohol and Drugs? Young People's Experience of Schoolies Week', *Australian and New Zealand Journal of Public Health*, 21 (2): 175-180.

Stewart, F. (1994) 'Young Women, Safe Sex and Health Promotion: Why It's Not On to Tell Him', *Australian Feminist Studies* 20 (summer): 25-34.

Stewart, F. (1999) '"Once You Get a Reputation, Your Life's Like ... Wrecked": The Implications of Reputation for Young Women's Sexual Health and Well-Being', *Women's Studies International Forum* 22 (3): 373-383.

Tanner, W.M. and R.H. Pollack (1988) 'The Effect of Condom Use and Erotic Instructions on Attitudes Towards Condoms', *The Journal of Sex Research* 25 (4): 537-541.

The Canberra Times (1998) 'Condom use up but women not so keen: survey (by Roy Morgan Research for Ansell condoms)', 24 August 1998: 3.

Thomson, R and J. Holland (1994) 'Young Women and Safer (Hetero)Sex: Context, Constraints and Strategies', in S. Wilkinson and C. Kitzinger (eds), *Women and Health: Feminist Perspectives*, London: Taylor and Francis, pp13-33.

Tiefer, L. (1997) 'Medicine, Morality and the Public Management of Sexual Matters', in L. Segal (ed), *New Sexual Agendas*, London: Macmillan, pp103-133.

Vitellone, N. (2000) 'Condoms and the Making of "Testosterone Man": A Cultural Analysis of the Male Sex Drive in AIDS Research on Safer Heterosex', *Men and Masculinities* (3) 2: 152-167.

Waldby, C., S. Kippax and J. Crawford (1990) 'Theory in the Bedroom: A Report from the Macquarie University AIDS and Heterosexuality Project', *Australian Journal of Social Issues* 25 (3): 177-185.

Waldby, C., S. Kippax and J. Crawford (1993) 'Research note: Heterosexual men and "safe sex" practice', *Sociology of Health and Illness* 15 (2): 246-256.

Waldby, C. (1996) *AIDS and the Body Politic. Biomedicine and Sexual Difference*, London and New York: Routledge.

Watney, S. (1987) *Policing Desire: Pornography, AIDS and The Media*, Minneapolis: University of Minnesota Press.

Weeks, J. (1985) *Sexuality and Its Discontents*, London: Routledge and Kegan Paul.

Weeks, J. (1986) *Sexuality*, London: Ellis Horwood/Tavistock Publications.

Wilton, T. and P. Aggleton (1991) 'Condoms, Coercion and Control: Heterosexuality and the Limits to HIV/AIDS Education', in P. Aggleton, G. Hart and P. Davies (eds.), *AIDS: Responses, Interventions and Care*, London: The Falmer Press, pp149-156.

Wilton, T. (1994) 'Feminism and The Erotics of Health Promotion', in L. Doyal, J. Naidoo and T. Wilton (eds), *AIDS: Setting A Feminist Agenda*, London: Taylor and Francis, pp80-95.

Wilton, T. (1997) *Engendering AIDS*, London: Sage.

Wood, N. (1985) 'Foucault on the History of Sexuality: an Introduction', in V. Beechey and J. Donald (eds), *Subjectivity and Social Relations*, Milton Keynes: Open University Press, pp156-175.

Thinking beyond the brain: embodiment and the psycho-somatic

Lawrence Johnson

When mind and body are in dispute, desire arises for stable points of reference like disciplinary boundaries. This essay contends that the sense of the integrity of a 'body' of thought or of a critical textual corpus is not a spatial-corporeal metaphor, but is an aspect of the way in which disciplinarity represents modes of being in the world, which, like all human activity, involve actualisation of the mind and body. Such actualisation is described here as 'embodiment', which is defined as the ways in which the unconscious posits its exterior. Critical theorising about mind and body must include an account of the relationship between 'theorising' mind and body and 'being' embodied. This essay makes this point by using 'polytextual' readings of texts that discuss phenomena (such as phantom limbs) which render problematical the intuitive understanding we have of our minds and bodies.

> It is no more incumbent upon science to find a soul in the body than to find God in the world. True, science does not tell the whole story. But, alas, it is a story that cannot be *told* except *per speculum in aenigmate*.
>
> Zeno Vendler, 'The Ineffable Soul' (1996: 328)

In an episode of the popular television science series *Ultrascience* (Discovery Channel, Foxtel, 26 March 1999) results of tests to determine the viability of implanting silicon chips into the brain were described as 'surprising'. When placed on a silicon chip, the elementary stuff of which brains are made (neurons) gravitated toward electronically stored information, as if driven by an instinctual compulsion to 'talk to each other'. The neurons behaved as though their primary instinct is not to preserve their own kind but to follow all paths toward complexity. Thus, they were said to demonstrate constructive and communicative drives, a characteristic backed up by the observation that isolated neurons tend simply to stop, as though they had 'programmed themselves to die'. The presenter declared that such discoveries emerge 'as powerful new brain technologies unlock more of the mind's secrets'.

From a critical psychological perspective the claims made in texts intended for popular consumption, such as this one, may seem all too easy to grasp as a substitute for 'hard' scientific research and just as easy to dismiss as so much popularised hyperbole. This 'critical psychological perspective' includes arms of psychology which have developed a common interest in reflexively interrogating psychological practices and exploring possibilities for dialogue with other disciplines. As this simple definition suggests, the various schools of critical psychology are also characterised by a fundamental belief that their critical activity proceeds from a sufficiently stable point of reference to enable self-reflexivity, and that this point of reference is organised around a framework that enables demarcations between one's own and 'other' disciplines.

This sense of disciplinary propriety is what might ordinarily prompt psychologists to prick up their ears at the claims made in popular science texts that 'powerful new brain technologies' are only now unlocking the secrets of the mind. Such a claim obviously threatens the sensibilities of those who feel that the 'secrets' of the mind are properly the domain of the psychological rather than the physical sciences. Critically-minded thinkers may at least pause over the unquestioning conflation of the *brain* with the *mind* at the core of these claims, as though no measure is taken of the long-standing debate that has come to be known as the 'mind-body problem'. Of course, it is unlikely that many psychologists would feel the need to respond to a popular science programme, for reasons that will probably range from a refusal to engage in dialogue with physical science (imagined to be equally stubborn in its refusal to entertain core philosophical questions) to simple disregard for 'unimportant' or 'naive' products of popular culture.

The point I want to make here is that this sense of disciplinary propriety is what may be at stake in debates over the mind-body problem.

I do not mean simply that these debates place disciplinary borderlines in dispute, although the uncertainty surrounding these boundaries provides a starting point. My broader argument will be that when *mind* and *body* are in dispute, in particular, a stark desire emerges for stable points of reference like disciplinary boundaries or fields of discourse among the disputants. This argument will be constructed upon a premise that the sense of exteriority and interiority, or of the integrity of a 'body' of thought, or of a critical textual corpus, are not simply spatial-corporeal metaphors defining a discipline. Rather, they are aspects of the way in which disciplinary activity functions as a *mode of being in the world*, which, like all human activity, is linked to the processes actualising human minds and bodies. For the purpose of this argument, I shall consider these processes *in toto* under the blanket of a single term: *embodiment*. Although my understanding of the term shall become more apparent, I will define it loosely here as *the ways in which the unconscious posits its own exterior*.

As I have indicated, the mind-body problem throws the uncertainty of the disciplinary boundaries of those involved in the debate into sharp relief. If there is an unwillingness on the part of psychologists to respond to popular scientific texts which oversimplify or conflate notions of mind and body, another reason may be that the mind-body problem has been debated in an increasingly closed forum; an index of the reluctance of those involved in the debate to broadcast the fact that they have a problem which they seem unable to collectively resolve. In *The Mind-Body Problem: A Guide to the Current Debate*, Richard Warner and Tadeusz Szubka (1996) survey the state of the debate, suggesting that there are too many schools of thought involved, and the stakes are too high, to expect that something like a unified mind-body theory is attainable. The editors claim that what is at stake is no longer the *answer* to the relation of mind and body, but what status to give to the *questions* we ask: what is at stake, then, is the 'explanatory adequacy' of any discourse to account for the mental.

Several of the contributors to this collection argue that we may indeed never be able to account for mental or non-physical phenomena from the standpoint of a discourse of the physical.[1] Colin McGinn (1996), in particular, claims that the problem cannot be solved, yet that such insolubility is precisely the condition of uncertainty with which the mind is positioned in relation to its physical origins. Using formal propositional logic, McGinn demonstrates that conscious reason is inherently incapable of accounting for itself (*qua* consciousness) in regards to its physical status. Yet he concludes that we may only talk about the relation of mind to body in terms of observable physical effects, a problem for neuroscience (*not* philosophy). This conclusion follows logically from the premise with which his argument commences, that minds 'are biological products like bodies' (McGinn: 100). While I do not wish to rail against this physicalist approach, I shall pursue a parallel argument, based on McGinn's own claims about the condition of uncertainty which surrounds the origins of consciousness. Thus, I question whether the corollary that consciousness has biology as its only source can be stated with any degree of certainty.

In a postscript to his essay, McGinn admits that he was wrong to have assumed that the limits appertaining to conscious reason applied equally to all representational systems, and he adds that genetic coding and subconscious brain representations may 'contain the kind of philosophical information denied to conscious reason' (115). His aim is to wrest initiative in the mind-body debate away from the proper domain of reason (philosophy) and situate it with the physical sciences (such as genetics or brain science). Yet McGinn realises that to satisfy demands of 'explanatory adequacy', he must appeal to philosophy in qualifying the kinds of information that physical sciences should be able to extract from genes or brain matter. After all, genes or brain matter (neurons) are not seen as adequate in themselves to account for the origin of consciousness, but when we view them as systems of representation or codes, unconstrained by the limits of conscious reasoning, they begin to fit the criteria for explanatory adequacy. I argue here that we might just as adequately consider the *unconscious* as containing precisely the kind of philosophical information denied to conscious reason. Furthermore, as we shall see, investigations into unconsciousness account for the formation of representational systems by reckoning the condition of representation *per se*.

Importantly, however, I do not pretend that this argument provides any kind of solution to the mind-body problem. Like McGinn, I suggest that the problem is insoluble, and I propose merely an alternative account of why such insolubility emerges inevitably from how, in everyday life as thinking social beings, we conduct and construct ourselves in the world. To enable discussion of the relations between disciplines in these terms, I will use the concept of 'critical polytextualism' developed by Rex and Wendy Stainton Rogers in *Stories of*

Childhood (cited in Morss 1996: 138-41). Critical polytextualism refers to the 'multiplicity of interpretations' always in operation in any social or critical practice, suggesting that these multiple interpretations mark themselves *textually* as one text among others within the category of interpretation.

Rather than dismiss the popular science television programme on the grounds of ignorance, irrelevance or naiveté, I want to provide a polytextual reading to illustrate the utility of the concept here. To do this, I will briefly compare the claims made in the episode of *Ultrascience* with Sigmund Freud's development of the concepts of *eros* and *thanatos*. This comparison provides a minimal and somewhat reductive example of a polytextual reading, yet this reduction will help to isolate the key problematic of the 'explanatory adequacy' of a discourse when this adequacy is defined in terms of the inadequacies of other discourses. This is not to suggest that an explanatory method that is self-aware about its own inadequacies is necessarily closer to the truth of its object than one that believes itself to be thoroughly adequate; it is rather to suggest that the truth we find is a product of our methods for finding the truth. If our method is defined (polytextually) in opposition to another discourse, the truths we find will be defined in the same way. By definition, two people looking at an object from different perspectives will not see the same object, and neither will see the whole of this object, yet we may learn more about the people than the object itself by looking closely at the perspectives from which each sees the object.

In the episode of *Ultrascience*, tests into the viability of new brain technologies revealed two related types of activity from neurons: attraction to electronically charged inorganic matter and the inability to continue to function in isolation. Moving from observation to explanation, these types of activity are labelled 'behaviours' to which a particular type of motivation can be attributed. Attraction to electronically charged matter is described as a constructive, communicative impulse, a description aided by calling the charge 'information'. The inability to function in isolation is then cast as the negative side of this same impulse: when it is unable to 'talk' the neuron will 'die', as if 'programmed' to do so. Of course, this movement from observation to explanation provides the ground for the claim that these new brain technologies (as the instrument of observation) are unlocking secrets of the mind (emerging in explanation).

More than a century earlier, in his 'Project for a Scientific Psychology' (1895), Freud posited three types of neurones (ö, ø and ù), corresponding to the functioning of the nervous system – he called these the 'agencies' [*Instanzen*] of the psychic apparatus in the *Interpretation of Dreams* (1900) – mediating between sensory perceptions and the treatment (cathexis) of internalised material. Yet even as he was finishing his 'Project', Freud was concentrating his thoughts less on defining the types of neurons than on mapping the functions to which they corresponded. From *Interpretation of Dreams* onwards, he formulated his topography of the psychical apparatus: the conscious, pre-conscious and unconscious, subdivided by imperatives of the id, ego and superego, and serving competing interests of the life drive (*eros*) and death drive.

Elizabeth Wilson (1998) provides a compelling case for reading the Freudian canon and its topography in a way that suggests he never altogether abandoned his neurological 'Project' (133-44). She points out that in Freud's model for a scientific psychology, neurons are unable to carry the origin of consciousness except inasmuch as they provide the agencies for the differences between endogenous and external excitations of Qn (quantity). Thus, he 'dislodge(s) a strict biological essentialism from the neuron', on the path to critiquing neuropsychological localisation (Wilson: 143). Freud's 'Project' does not recruit the physical science of neurology in order to render the psyche intelligible: it inverts this trajectory 'and uses the psyche to render traditional neurology intelligible' (144). The unpublished model for a scientific psychology was therefore a blueprint for Freud's metapsychology, in which the relation of neurology, biology or physiology to the psyche are viewed with ambivalence, but never fully disregarded. As a result, for Wilson, the 'Project' manifests 'a certain dilemma (of mind and body, neurology and psychology) that a hundred years later is no closer to being addressed properly inside psychology' (139).

Returning momentarily to the episode of *Ultrascience*, I suggest that the way in which its conclusions are drawn can be compared with Freud's theoretical investigations into the drives on at least two levels. On one level, the two drives that are attributed to the neurons – constructive and destructive – may seem uncannily similar to the primary drives around which Freud formulated and then revised his hypothetical topography of the psychical apparatus. On another level, these drives are identified according to the logic of reductive biologism:

physical science is recruited in order to render the secrets of the mind intelligible. The popular science programme uses observation of the brain to mark explanations of mental processes as properties of the object rather than as products of interpretative discourse.

That these two discourses could mirror each other so closely with respect to their object (neurons) and explanations (two primary drives), yet represent diametrically opposed standpoints (reductive biologism versus a direct inversion of the same), is an example of the 'critical polytextualism' identified by the Stainton Rogers. As I have indicated, in my understanding of this term, polytextualism suggests not only the multiplicity of critical interpretations in operation in any practice but also the *relativity* of these interpretations to each other, intertextually. Contradictory interpretations of the same phenomenon are adequate in themselves, in so far as they are true to their perspective, yet no interpretation is ever fully adequate with respect to the phenomena they purport to explain. Such inadequacy arises not simply from the status of *representations of things*, but also from the degree to which representations (*as texts*) refer to *other texts*. Understanding the polytextualism of a critical text enables us to consider its relation to the broader body of texts – its *corpus* (a deliberate metaphor, to which I will return) – to which it belongs. For the Stainton Rogers, such consideration leads to further and more elaborate explanations by taking measure of the range of interpretations available. What thus emerges from an understanding of critical polytextualism is not a replacement of one inadequate explanation with a more complex explanation that is better only in so far as it is aware of its inadequacy; rather, in the words of John Morss (1996), it is the rejection of all pretensions to realism which makes this approach 'closer to literary styles of analysis such as deconstruction' (141).

This suggestion is not intended to unduly privilege literary styles of analysis over other interpretative practices. Rather, it is intended to highlight the problems confronting the disputants in the debate over mind and body, given the need to present their arguments textually – that is, to engage with the polytext produced by the discourses in dispute – and to produce a corpus or body of texts of one's own. For this reason, I have been quite deliberate in my choice of texts for use in the first example of this mode of reading: two discourses which may seem in some degree irrelevant to the debate proper, yet which provide extremely strong positions (in opposition) on the concepts of mind and body.

What I want to do now is open this minimal polytextual reading out by introducing the concept of embodiment, which I have already defined loosely as the ways in which the unconscious posits its own exterior. I am aware that this is not a definition of the term with which many will have immediate agreement. Yet it strikes me that the reason for this may be that there have been few attempts to actually produce a clear definition of embodiment in spite of the fact that issues of the body have been prominent in critical theory and feminist theory for decades and, of course, in the terms of the mind-body problem for centuries. For some schools of thought, there would be no need to develop a definition beyond that provided by common usage: to make corporeal or incorporate (as in, to include in a body). For some, as we have seen, the solution to the mind-body problem is no more nor less than *to incorporate the mind*.

For my part, the need to define embodiment emerges alongside the considerations of critical psychologists and feminist theorists who continue to interrogate the received 'truths' about being human inside a human body. In summarising the writings of Rosi Braidotti, Elisabeth Grosz and Moira Gatens, among others, Kathy Davis points out that theorising about the body is all too often a 'disembodied activity' much in need of an account of individuals' (including the theorist's own) embodied experiences:

> Understanding what embodiment means to individuals depends upon being able to sort out how sexual, 'racial' and other differences intersect and give meaning to their interactions with their bodies and through their bodies with the world around them. Conditions of embodiment are organized by systemic patterns of domination and subordination, making it impossible to grasp individual body practices, body regimes and discourses about the body without taking power into account. By assuming that the theorist is also embodied, feminist theory opens up possibilities for exploring new ways of doing theory (1997: 14).

I will argue in what follows that critical psychological theorising about the mind and the body must recognise (or indeed proceed from) an account of the relationship between *theorising* mind and body and *being* embodied. The argument hinges on a further series of polytextual readings of texts that discuss phenomena, such as phantom limbs, which render problematical the intuitive understanding we have of our minds and bodies.

A recent episode of another popular science series, *Mystery of the Senses* (Lifestyle Channel, Foxtel, 21 March 1999), discussed the degree to which the brain was the extra-sensory source of what we otherwise sense as reality. Referring to phantom limbs, the presenter explained that perceptions of reality do not devolve from the physicality of the outside world (through the senses) but come from 'within here' (he was pointing to his head). For the presenter, this 'here' referred to the brain, to which he added that electrical stimulations by electrodes on the surface of the brain are not registered by the subject as sensations on or in the brain but elsewhere on the body (as an itch on the nose, or a twitch in a finger, for example). The implication is that our sensory relation to the external world is determined by electrical activity in the brain rather than by what is given from without – in any case, we find that the question of our status in the world is only for the physical sciences to address.

The claims made in this program may simplify the case, but they do seem to reflect the prevailing views of many scientific researchers into phantom limb phenomena at least until the last decade of the twentieth-century. Peter Lloyd stated that, among the different approaches to the mind-body problem, physicalism, the view 'that the mind is really a physical phenomenon going on inside the brain', was the prevailing view (1993: 17). In terms that are similar to those expressed in *Mystery of the Senses*, Lloyd first presents a case for physicalism based on some simple 'tricks': damage to nerve fibres may cause the brain to construe pain in the area of the body where the incoming nerves are rooted, unaware that these signals originate somewhere along the damaged fibres *en route*; the phantom limb sensations of amputees clearly do not originate in the missing limb itself; and electrical stimulation of an incoming nerve will cause the brain to project sensation onto that part of the body from which that nerve impulse should have originated (18). The conclusion to be drawn from these 'tricks' is straightforward enough: 'What this shows us is that the mind is not really dispersed throughout the body but is centralised in the brain. The brain constructs an illusory distribution of mental sensations over the body' (18).

Lloyd's simplistic presentation of the physicalist approach may echo the presenter who points to his head to designate the origin of sensory perceptions, yet his purpose is quite different. He also presents detailed evidence of 'actual experiments on living brains' to examine the physical correlates of the conscious mind and finally to dismantle identity theory which posits a one-to-one relationship between locations on the brain and mental phenomena. Lloyd's strategy is effective: the more straightforward the physicalist argument seems to be, the more compelling becomes the concrete evidence of actual experimentation in arguing against these ideas. Of course, Lloyd does not reject all the tenets of physicalism, only the push toward localisation in identity theory. The point is to demonstrate that the mind and the brain are not identical, but to also show that there is a more direct relationship between the mind and the brain than between the mind and the rest of the body.

Such claims prompt the following question: how are we to distinguish between the brain and the rest of the body? For neurology, in particular, the question has unnerving – I use the term deliberately – consequences. At what point do we consider that the networks of nerve fibres, which extend throughout the body, can be distinguished from the brain or the body in our understanding of their functions? If the nervous system is understood as a function of the way in which brain processes control and respond to bodily stimuli, is it possible to think of a 'body' that is not already contained by our thinking about brain processes? Significantly, one of the effects of asking these questions – the explanatory adequacy of which can be measured in the degree to which brain and body are defined in their interrelationships – is that the imperative to consider the mind seems to fall by the wayside.

Wilson (1998) provides a comprehensive account of how an account of the human psyche can be restored to the agenda of neurological science, by deconstructing the dilemma of mind and body, neurology and psychology, which, as we have seen, can be attributed to Freud's 'Project for a Scientific Psychology' from over a century ago. The advantage of the Freudian model, particularly via the deconstructive approach Wilson takes into consideration, is that its defining characteristic is not the location of neurons but the *relations between* them. Thus, the key to understanding the relation of mind to body is not in locating the mind but in coming to terms with the forces that animate biological matter on the path to cognition. The neurological science to which Wilson adheres is connectionism, a group of relatively new theories of cognition based on models 'sometimes referred to as neural networks or parallel distributed processing (PDP) models', since these theories privilege the connections between units in attempts to understand cognitive functioning (Wilson 1998: 5-6).

My interest is in Wilson's synthesis of deconstructive and psychoanalytical modes of analysis together with the neurological science from which Freud took his initial steps on the royal road to the unconscious. Returning to phantom limb phenomena, I think this synthesis can be mobilised within the much older tradition of conceptualising mind and body as an embodied practice. At the very foundation of dualism, for example, the phantom played a crucial role, since it was with the example of the phantom limb that Descartes attempted to divorce the mind from the brain by linking the former with the entire body rather than one of its higher organs. Nevertheless, as Elizabeth Grosz states, Descartes's psychophysical dualism situates the interaction of mind and body in the brain, as it is in this organ that 'movements' resulting from peripheral stimulations are centred (1994: 63). Descartes thus clings to the brain as the primary surface upon which the mind and body interact. It is as though the founder of dualism wanted to render problematical the relation of mind and body based on the example of accounts of non-physical phenomena (phantom limbs), but found that if he reasoned empirically the phenomena only make sense by recourse to explanations in terms of the physical effects of non-physical phenomena and the degree to which these effects are located (perhaps, originally) in the brain.

Yet even at the foundation of the dualism of mind and body, Descartes problematises this distinction in a way that can be understood if we read the Cartesian text *as a text*. In Descartes, as Gary Shapiro has argued (after Jean-Luc Nancy), the program of anatomising mental phenomena is not only theorised but actively *thematised*, such that the discourse itself can be seen to constitute the corporeality of the represented body:

> 'While I am writing', writes Descartes in his *Rules for the Direction of the Mind*, as he implicates an entire apparatus and instrumentality by which he realizes himself as the one whose thoughts are embodied by being written and being read. In 'Dum Scribo' Nancy traces how far Descartes' (who perhaps should not be called a Cartesian here) 'mind and body take form together – in writing which is imprinted.' Descartes' word for body, of course, is *corpus*. Descartes can be reread and rewritten in his corporeality, as a thinker who fantasized his body as a pen and for whom the prosthetic language in which he describes his bodily activity is not a mere metaphor (1994: 61).

Beyond empiricism, then, Descartes *performs* the textuality of the body by inscribing in and through the written word the corporeality of the text (*corpus*). Even at the inception of dualism, the performativity of the critical text thus hints at a corporeality that inheres in something other than flesh and bone. Descartes' 'prosthetic language' is not simply a metaphor, precisely because it presents a written text as an extension of the corporeal, whereby inscription equals embodiment. In other words, Descartes' text is also his own phantom limb.

This equation of body and text, of embodiment and inscription, also emerges inevitably from clinical studies into phantom limb phenomena. During the last decade, the most prolific experimenter and theorist of phantom limbs has been Vilayanur Ramachandran, whose recent *Phantoms in the Brain* (with Sandra Blakeslee 1998) contains accounts of much of this past research. Ramachandran has collected many further examples of the sorts of 'tricks' to which Peter Lloyd referred in 1993, yet his focus remains on clinical applications of these phenomena. Perhaps the most famous of his experiments is the use of a mirror in a box to enable amputees to 'see' the phantom limb – they see a reflection of their surviving limb in the same location as the phantom limb. What this enables the patient to do is overcome the resilient 'body image', the result of which is that residual pain or paralysis associated with the phantom limb dissipates. The key to success in such experiments is attributed to the illusory nature of the view we have of ourselves, which Ramachandran calls 'perceptual plasticity': 'All our perceptions – indeed, maybe all aspects of our minds – are governed by comparisons and not by absolute values' (1998: 167).

Importantly, this plasticity poses a dilemma from an empirical standpoint, since we are unable to determine an objective correlate for the body image (an 'absolute value') that can be measured and verified scientifically. Yet the claim that perceptions, maybe even all aspects of our minds, are governed by comparisons *is* amenable to a deconstructive (or at least a somewhat analytical) approach to psychical phenomena. It is no surprise to find that Ramachandran describes the brain functions that produce phantom limbs and similar phenomena as part of a process akin to Freudian defence mechanisms. Rather than develop a composite neurological theory of repression, however, Ramachandran's primary interest remains the clinical possibilities for a physiological approach to these phenomena. Indeed, in an earlier paper he proposes that a physiological intervention, 'left ear coloric stimulation, may eventually be used actually to replace psychoanalysis as a device for reviving repressed memories and for producing insight' (1994: 330).

Responding to Ramachandran's work on phantom limbs, Gail Weiss reiterates the point that the success of these experiments is not a triumph of body over body image but 'the construction of a new morphological imaginary, one that offers new sites of projection and identification and new bodily possibilities' (1999: 37). Weiss emphasises the plasticity of the body image itself as much as the perceptual faculty through which it is realised. The notion of a body image has frequently in the past been used as an index of the unity of a blueprint that we possess within ourselves of the whole of our bodies. Under the rubric of such terms as 'schemata', 'homunculus', 'neuromatrix', 'genego' (genetic ego) and others, a number of models have been developed to account for a map of our bodies to which our brain refers in making sense of external stimuli or perceptions.[2] For Weiss, Ramachandran's clinical evidence supports the long-standing philosophical tradition from Descartes to modern phenomenology, which does not deny the materiality of the body but designates the 'imaginary' as the overarching domain within which the whole of our perceptual life is played out. By understanding this domain *morphologically*, we form a picture of that aspect of the body image, governed by comparison, which can be analysed: that is, we can begin to analyse the mechanisms, rules and limits to change.

Summarising various accounts of phantom limb experiences, Grosz notes that the phantom is not really an image or recollection of the absent limb, since it is often distorted (1994: 71). Such distortions – the phantom may be lighter, more sluggish, or larger or smaller than the missing limb – are only measurable *as distortions* by referring in the past to properties and dimensions of the missing limb. Thus, distortion expresses a 'nostalgia for the unity and wholeness of the body, its completion' (73). The phantom experience is 'a memorial to the missing limb, a psychical delegate that stands in its place ... the narcissistic reassertion of the limb's presence in the face of its manifest biological loss, an attempt to preserve the subject's narcissistic sense of bodily wholeness' (73). Phantom limbs manifest or intensify, after partial loss, a narcissistic function of embodiment: the degree to which our body image exceeds the container of the flesh, or to which 'reality' merely extends corporeality via the body-text or *corpus*.

Perhaps the relationship between the corporeal and the textual, when referring to body image theorising, is still difficult to express in such concrete terms as these. Yet we may need to look no further than the testimonies supplied as clinical evidence by the *subjects* of the experiments that we have been describing, to find a compelling expression of the relationship I am attempting to elaborate. Invariably, under experimental conditions or in tests relating to phantom limb phenomena, the principal determinant for the presence and behaviour of the phantom is the verbal report given by the test subject. Certainly, observers cannot determine the presence of the phantom in the same way other intact organs or limbs can be observed, measured, probed or scanned in their (scientifically) detached entirety. The phantom thus represents an excess, for it exceeds the observable boundary (the skin) by which the body appears to be limited, and its reality cannot be ascertained with reference to this boundary. The appropriate phrase for referring to the phantom is nothing like 'take my hand' or 'how many fingers do you see'; instead, it is only with 'take my word for it' that the individual who possesses a phantom can bear witness to its presence and to the quality of the sensations or movements the phantom registers.

The reliance by those testing for the (absent) presence of phantom limbs on individual testimonies is worth noting here because it suggests that accounts of phantom limbs are not merely diagnostic ('tell me if this hurts' and such like) but core features of reality testing in the actualisation of a phantom for both the subject and the observer. Thus, we may presume that in normative functioning of the body image, our sense of our own corporeality *as well as that of others* is inextricably linked to a mode of representation. Weiss refers to embodiment in these terms as 'intercorporeality', inasmuch as every body image is always an image of a particular body, 'a body that is different from all others and that is lived in idiosyncratic ways', yet which is negotiated and changing since it occurs 'among body images, body image ideals … and the cultural imaginary that actively supports them' (1999: 66). The discursive practices by which we theorise the body image do not take place independently from these processes, for they contribute to the establishment of particular ways of thinking about the body.

One implication of the studies into phantom limb phenomena is that the way in which we assume our selves to be embodied *in toto* is contingent upon a textualised body image that only coincides *through expression* with the physical surface of our bodies. What remains to be shown here is how theorisations of mind and body may access the morphological imaginary governing this coincidence. My suggestion is that we might usefully discuss this possibility by considering how issues of embodiment relate to a psychoanalytical understanding of mind and body. Consideration of psychoanalytical uses of the terms 'psyche' and 'soma' will allow us a chance to glimpse (if only awry, in a sense) the unconscious source of embodiment, by thinking of a textualised body image that is at once concurrent with consciousness and the outer surface or limit that the unconscious imposes upon itself precisely so that it will be closed off from external phenomena and from consciousness.

My use of the term *psychosomatic* will not be diagnostic, in the sense that a physician may classify a particular physical condition as psychosomatic where a psychical source for physical symptoms may be assumed in the absence of any apparent physical source. Julia Kristeva has concisely stated that a 'psychosomatic condition' – just like wounded 'narcissisms', 'false personalities' or 'borderline states' – derives from 'the inability to represent' (1995: 9). As a psychoanalyst herself, Kristeva may seem justified in reclaiming the category of the psychosomatic from the field of medicine which has taken the term for its name.[3] Yet this focus on the 'inability to represent' is a *response* to the pressures upon psychoanalysis that Kristeva sees as having accompanied the 'recent advances in neurobiology and pharmacology' (1995: 30). By this I mean that Kristeva's theorisation of the psychosomatic condition contributes to her push for psychoanalysis to develop broader relevance, beginning with a reconsideration of the concept of the drive as a response to new brain technologies. The drive, in Kristeva's terms, 'is a pivot between "soma" and "psyche," between biology and representation – the highest level of organization and permanency to which Freudian listening and theory can aspire'; with 'biology' defined by Kristeva as 'drives and energy, if you wish, but always already a "carrier of meaning" and a "relation" to another person, even though this person may be yourself' (1995: 30).

When Kristeva describes the psychosomatic condition as an inability to represent, then, she is responding to the diagnostic practices of analysts and physicians for whom bodies are merely biological entities with which things commonly go wrong. I understand that for most people the term 'psychosomatic' means (at best) a non-existent complaint that is simply imagined, or (at worst) madness. No longer does the expression 'in the head' cover the terrain of the psychosomatic in the popular imagination now that science has told us that it is only the brain (*qua* the mind) that we find if we look inside our heads. Kristeva reminds us, however, that a diagnosis of a psychosomatic condition is to both 'psyche' and 'soma' what a diagnosis of a heart condition is to a normally functioning heart. The normative status of the psychosomatic is precisely the opposite of its status in diagnostics – if the psychosomatic 'condition' is understood as an inability to represent then the normative function of the relationship between psyche and soma must be the very condition of representation itself. This claim responds to the problems perceived by Kristeva by invoking the drive's pivotal role *between* biology and representation.

Yet the lesson of critical polytextualism now comes clearly to the fore: it is simply not sufficient for our purposes here to arrive at the conclusion that the relationship between psyche and soma constitutes the condition of representation, if we arrive at this point by way of negating a diagnostic discourse. Why, then, should we privilege the Freudian drive or the psychoanalytic understanding of the psychosomatic over those bodies of texts to which Kristeva responds? The point to be made is that Kristeva recognises that the drive is 'always already' a 'carrier of meaning' even if it is understood biologically, in terms of the carriage of energy. To be understood psychoanalytically – in terms of that which is radically unavailable to conscious reason – the terms 'psyche' and 'soma' have been subjected to what Nicolas Abraham (1994) has called 'designification.'

For Abraham, the terms used in psychoanalysis do not acquire new meanings, because 'they do not strictly speaking signify anything, except the founding silence of *any act of signification*' (1994: 84). This is to say that psychoanalysis strips words of what they may signify to conscious reasoning, thereby addressing (although, by definition, never expressing) the unconscious source of representations. 'Psyche' and 'Soma' pass into psychoanalytical understanding by being stripped of the meanings attributed them by 'naive empiricism' or phenomenology:

> The *somatic* must be something quite different from the body proper, which derives from the psychic as one of its functions, the psychic having been described by Freud as an exterior layer, an envelope. The

> *somatic* is what I cannot touch directly, either as my integument and its internal prolongations or as my psyche, the latter given to the consciousness of self; the somatic is that of which I would know nothing if its representative, my fantasy, were not there to send me back to it, its source as it were (Abraham 1994: 87)

Abraham notes that one term exempted from designification is the term for what passes between psyche and soma in their interrelation: 'only the *representative*, the mediator between the two poles x, seems to have preserved its meaning, inasmuch as it is a term known by comparison with a known relation of mediation' (86).

What is inherent in the relation of the psychic to the somatic is therefore nothing more nor less than the very fact of this relation, as it inheres in a representation of the somatic in the psychic and the psychic in the somatic. By designifying the term 'psychosomatic' via the form of the term 'Psycho-Somatic', Freud's anti-semantic discourse identifies the representative (Kristeva's 'carrier') as that which is 'always already' anterior to meaning. The 'meaning' may vary – a memory trace, a body image, a partial object, a compulsion … in short, the psychical 'reality' – but the fact of the representative remains constant. We now begin to arrive at an understanding of the everyday psychical necessity of embodiment. If the carrier is constant, then there would seem to be no end to its carriage. This seeming endlessness is just the character that Freud ascribed to the drives, for which the goal is never so important as the getting-there – philosophically, this is called desire; in biological terms, this represents 'energy' animating flesh. Of course, the drive is necessarily driven-toward, for which purpose a goal is *inscribed in* the principle of getting-there – representation presupposes its object, which the drive posits irreducibly as an exteriority to itself. As a result, the principle of an exterior limit to the drive is included in its very movement. For Abraham, this limit is manifested in the first instance in the formation of an interior-exterior layer – the two directions toward which the limit extends – of the psychical enclave of the unconscious. The relations between the somatic and the psychic are embedded upon this nucleus, in a series of peripheries, of which the outermost formation (or envelope) is the ego.

We should not forget, of course, that for Freud the ego which envelops the psychical apparatus is 'first and foremost, a bodily [*körperliches*] ego; it is not merely a surface entity [*Oberflächenwesen*], but is itself the projection of a surface' (in Anzieu 1989: 85). While the somatic is not understood psychoanalytically as the body proper, we do find that in the ego the surface of a body is represented as the exterior limit of the psychical. Embodiment as I have been describing it in this essay is the realisation of the Freudian ego, which we now understand to be the outermost layer posited by the unconscious. Importantly, this process is at once bodily and psychical, with the drive creating the very need for layers to be posited equally capable of being understood as both desire (philosophically) and energy (physiologically).

I also want to emphasise that for Abraham the formation of the ego – this projection of the bodily surface at the limits of the psyche – is the same process as acquisition of the metaphorics of word-formation. Reviving Sandor Ferenczi's definition of introjection as the 'process of broadening the ego', Abraham and Maria Torok (1994) explain that in libidinal attachment the child confronts its own inability to internalise the exteriorised object through the mouth, for which it compensates by filling the mouth with word sounds. Word-formation is thus inseparable from embodiment, each constituting one side of the formation of the ego. To conclude, then, the corpus of psychoanalysis locates the terms with which we might *represent* embodiment as the same process in which realities are constituted in words and thoughts – *as representations*. For psychoanalysis, the shaping of the ego takes place in the process by which the subject first acquires words in forming a metaphorical relation with the outside world. Conscious reason is carried out within this relation, and it is therefore coterminous with the projected surface that the interior posits as its outer limit.

I suggest that the disciplinary boundaries or fields of discourse that generate the sense of propriety that I discussed at the beginning of this essay are products of this drive toward an exteriorised limit. As we have seen, this is the same as saying that disciplinary limits are in some sense a function of the process of embodiment. Interrogations of the mind-body relation take place within discourse, and are therefore embodied practices in their own right. Yet interrogations of the other side of representation risk getting under the skin of the text, as it were, and forcing us to abandon the critical corpus or body of texts (that is, the polytext) marking out the surface upon which our discourse inscribes itself and those of us who speculate within this domain. What is at stake is not simply the opening out of the boundaries of one discipline in response to a challenge presented by another; rather, it is the radical abandonment of all boundaries that have traditionally separated one discipline from another, one corpus from another, or one body of ideas from another. If we find that we are still protective of this body of ideas, it may only be because we are still too attached to the idea of the body.

This essay expands on a paper presented at the Millennium World Conference in Critical Psychology at the University of Western Sydney, Nepean, on 1 May 1999.

Notes

1. See, for example, Galen Strawson, 'The Experiential and the Non-experiential' (69-86); Steven J. Wagner, 'Supervenience, Recognition, and Consciousness' (87-98); and Colin McGinn, 'Can We Solve the Mind-Body Problem?' (99-120); and the editors' summaries of these essays (3-5).
2. For discussion of these terms see, for example, the following: on Frederic Bartlett's 'schemata' see Wilson (1998: 171-77); on the traditional 'homunculus' see Damasio (1996); on 'neuromatrix' see Melzack (1993); and on the 'genego' see Hearne (1999).
3. On the history of psychosomatic medicine, see Graeme Taylor (1987: 1-38).

References

Abraham, N. (1994) 'The Shell and the Kernel: The Scope and Originality of Freudian Psychoanalysis', in N. Rand (ed and trans), *The Shell and the Kernel: Renewals of Psychoanalysis*, Chicago: University of Chicago Press, pp79-98.

Abraham, N. and M. Torok (1994) 'Mourning *or* Melancholia: Introjection *versus* Incorporation', in N. Rand (ed and trans), *The Shell and the Kernel: Renewals of Psychoanalysis*, Chicago: University of Chicago, pp125-38.

Anzieu, D. (1989) *The Skin Ego*, Chris Turner (trans), New Haven: Yale University Press.

Damasio, A.R. (1996) 'Making Images and Creating Subjectivity', in R. Llinas and P.S. Churchland (eds), *The Mind-Brain Continuum: Sensory Processes*, Cambridge, Mass: Massachusetts Institute of Technology Press, pp19-27.

Davis, K. (ed) (1997) *Embodied Practices: Feminist Perspectives on the Body*, London: Sage Publications.

Freud, S. (1895) 'Project for a Scientific Psychology', in J. Strachey (ed and trans), *The Standard Edition of the Complete Psychological Works of Sigmund Freud*, 1, London: Hogarth Press and the Institute of Psycho-Analysis, 1953-1974, pp295-397.

Freud, S. (1900) 'Interpretation of Dreams', in J. Strachey (ed and trans), *The Standard Edition of the Complete Psychological Works of Sigmund Freud*, 4-5, London: Hogarth Press and the Institute of Psycho-Analysis, 1953-1974, pp1-627.

Grosz, E. (1994) *Volatile Bodies: Toward a Corporeal Feminism*, Bloomington: Indiana University Press.

Hearne, K. (1999) 'The Concept of the Virtual Self', Positive Health On-Line 44, <http://www.positivehealth.com/permit/Articles/Mind%20Matters/hearne44.htm>

Kristeva, J. (1995) *New Maladies of the Soul*, R. Guberman (trans), New York: Columbia University Press.

Lloyd, P.B. (1993) 'Is the Mind Physical? Dissecting Conscious Brain Tissue', *Philosophy Now* 6: 17-21.

McGinn, C. (1996) 'Can We Solve the Mind-Body Problem?', in R. Warner and T. Szubka (eds), *The Mind-Body Problem: A Guide to the Current Debate*, Oxford: Blackwell, pp99-120.

Melzack, R. (1993) 'Pain: Past, Present and Future', *Canadian Journal of Experimental Psychology* 47.4: 615-629.

Morss, J.R. (1996) *Growing Critical: Alternatives to Developmental Psychology*, London: Routledge.

Ramachandran, V.S. (1994) 'Phantom Limbs, Neglect Syndromes, Repressed Memories, and Freudian Psychology', *International Review of Neurobiology* 37: 291-333.

Ramachandran, V.S. and M. Blakeslee (1998) *Phantoms in the Brain: Human Nature and the Architecture of the Mind*, New York: William Morrow.

Shapiro, G. (1994) 'Jean-Luc Nancy and the Corpus of Philosophy', in J. MacCannell and L. Zakarin (eds), *Thinking Bodies*, Stanford: Stanford University Press, pp52-62.

Taylor, G.J. (1987) *Psychosomatic Medicine and Contemporary Psychoanalysis*, Madison: International Universities Press.

Vendler, Z. (1996) 'The Ineffable Soul', in R. Warner and T. Szubka (eds), *The Mind-Body Problem: A Guide to the Current Debate*, Oxford: Blackwell, pp317-28.

Warner, R. and T. Szubka (eds) (1996) *The Mind-Body Problem: A Guide to the Current Debate*, Oxford: Blackwell.

Weiss, G. (1999) *Body Images: Embodiment as Intercorporeality*, New York: Routledge.

Wilson, E.A. (1998) *Neural Geographies: Feminism and the Microstructure of Cognition*, New York: Routledge.

Embodiment and commitment in scientific inquiry: recovering Polanyi's sense of personal agency

Christopher Peet

Within contemporary science studies there is a lacuna around the notion of agency. Michael Polanyi's sense of the personal agency of the scientist addresses this lack. Polanyi articulates agency around the two foci of embodiment and commitment. I situate Polanyi's articulation against the better-known and more influential work of Thomas Kuhn. I argue that Kuhn appropriated Polanyi's notion of tacit knowing in a manner that confused and occluded Polanyi's focus on agency. Recovery of Polanyi's sense of agency within scientific inquiry substantiates our understanding of science, and complements already-existing, ideological critiques of science.

In this essay I argue for a recovery of Michael Polanyi's understanding of scientific inquiry. Polanyi's conception of scientific inquiry in terms of personal knowledge contains throughout a sophisticated articulation of human *agency*. Polanyi articulates agency around two foci: that of 'tacit knowing', which for Polanyi is a fundamentally embodied activity, and that of the person as committed, a fundamentally existential, moral activity that defines the person within his or her social, historical, and universal situation. Within the burgeoning field of science studies, there is a lacuna around precisely these issues of personal agency, embodiment, and moral commitment. A recovery of Polanyi's work such as I propose here serves, then, to address a neglected facet of science studies.

The constellation of reasons for the neglect of agency within science studies is complex and unclear. Consideration of the relation between Polanyi and Thomas Kuhn is illuminating in this regard, because Kuhn's appropriation of Polanyi occludes and ultimately confuses the issue of personal agency. Kuhn's enormous impact has overshadowed Polanyi's work, entrenching a perspective on science that tends to bypass and ignore the potential focus on agency Polanyi raises. Recovering Polanyi's work not only addresses the neglected issue of agency, but also redresses an imbalance of perspective within science studies.

I propose to pursue this redress according to the following scenario. Science studies, post-Kuhn, follow his lead in offering sociological, anthropological, and historical analyses of science. I characterise these analyses as external, ideological critiques. In contrast, Polanyi's emphasis on the person serves as an internal critique of science that *complements* the ideological analyses. Contrary to sociological or historical emphases on the impersonal and supra-personal factors determining the working of science – which marks their critiques as 'external' – consideration of agency emphasises personal factors, making such a critique of science 'internal'. The personal focus of an internal critique on responsibility and commitment has a consequent conservative, tradition-affirming potential, that complements the supra-personal focus on power of external critiques and their consequent revolutionary, transformative potential (hence my characterisation of these as ideological). The complementarity of these different types of critique should therefore not be understood as one of comfortable fit, but rather of persistent and recurring tensions. I am not sure it can be otherwise.

To make my case I locate Polanyi in relation to the better-known and more influential Kuhn. Focusing on shortcomings of Kuhn's position in terms of agency, I summarise Polanyi's articulation of personal knowledge. This articulation divides within the context of Polanyi's work into the themes of embodiment and commitment.

Science Studies: Kuhn and the dismantling of the traditional view

Science, whether conceived as a diverse set of social practices or a body of knowledge, or even as a culturally-instituted heritage of modern

Europe, is still far from being understood. Critiques of science are in their infancy. The aim of these critiques is to assist in bringing about positive transformations of science's practices, knowledge claims, and its functioning as a cultural institution. The burgeoning field of science studies is a much needed development along these lines, and there is now a proliferation of anthropological, feminist, historical, and sociological analyses of science.[1] It is appropriate to make two points here, which are, I think, also related: first, that the impetus for these studies can be traced back to the enormously influential work of Thomas Kuhn, specifically *The Structure of Scientific Revolutions* (1970). Second, that there has *not* been a corresponding explosion of psychological studies of science (see Gholson, Shadish, Neimeyer and Houts 1989). I understand the second as in part an effect of the first, in that the ideological, external configuration of Kuhnian-inspired studies systematically neglects the personal, agentic aspects of science. However, the explanation for the second point runs deeper. The neglect of agency is not restricted to science studies nor to a fledgling psychology of science. The deeper problem resides in that psychology in general has no sophisticated, coherent notion of agency, much less a theory of the person. Such a notion or theory is precisely wherein psychology could make its distinctive contribution to science studies. Although a good argument could be made for a potential psychology of science to be in principle more encompassing than the focus on agency I am concerned with here, my claim is that psychology's contributions to science studies will remain piecemeal and meagre until the issue of agency is addressed.[2] The cross-disciplinary neglect of agency emphasises the crucially historical nature of the problem. Within psychology, historical and theoretical studies of the discipline demonstrate that the neglect of agency is a subset of larger problems intrinsic to psychology (see for example Danziger 1990, 1997; Koch 1976, 1999; Taylor 1989).

Kuhn helped dismantle the myth of science as a purely rational and progressive project. The Popper-Kuhn debate occupied the philosophy of science scene in the 1960s and 1970s (Lakatos and Musgrave 1970). While Popper (1958, 1933) made drastic revisions to the logical positivist vision of science, these revisions amounted to a logical extension of their program of rationally reconstructing science, culminating in Popper's (1967) proposal for an 'epistemology without a knowing subject'. This program devolved on the assumption that the objective content of scientific knowledge was independent or detachable from its context. What Kuhn and Polanyi go to great pains to establish is the nontrivial contribution of *the situation* to scientific knowledge; put differently, the inescapable context-dependence of the knowledge content.

Paradigms, confusion, and occlusion

What was so influential about Kuhn's work, as is well known, were his novel and interrelated concepts of normal science, revolutionary science, and paradigms. His notion of paradigm proved compelling to many in spite of, or perhaps because of, its exceeding vagueness. (Masterman, 1970, charts twenty-one uses.) What is not so well known, however, is that his notion of paradigm derives in large part from the work of Michael Polanyi.[3] I will confine myself to two observations that highlight a confusion within Kuhn's thinking that takes on an ironic significance in comparison to Polanyi's understanding. In the process of Kuhn's confusing Polanyi's notion of agency, he simultaneously occludes it as well.

First, Kuhn's attempted clarification of his initial formulation of paradigm shows clearly the idea of 'tacit knowing' – Polanyi's concept – to be central and that Kuhn has misappropriated it in a confusing fashion. Kuhn (1970, 1962) makes the following two claims: 'First, if I am talking at all about intuitions, they are not individual. Rather, they are the tested and shared possessions of the members of a successful group ... Second, they are not in principle unanalysable' (p191). The second claim brings Kuhn to the 'essential point' he wants to make, that this 'shared group intuition' is 'a process' that is 'potentially fully explicable in terms of neuro-cerebral mechanism' (p192). Kuhn proposes the psychologistic reduction of a social phenomenon to 'neuro-cerebral mechanism' in order to avoid the charge of individualism! That this strange move bypasses both the person as agent, and the very embodiment that the concept of tacit knowing was meant to illuminate, speaks to the depth of Kuhn's misappropriation of Polanyi.

My second observation involves an equal degree of strangeness and irony. Polanyi brings this point out by way of commentary on a Kuhn paper. Polanyi (1961) criticises Kuhn's distinction between normal science and revolutionary science as well as the proffered explanation for the transition from the former to the latter in terms of the scientist's 'discriminating' between 'essential anomaly' and 'mere failure' (pp376-8). Polanyi argues that Kuhn is missing the point of what is involved in the scientist's discrimination. Discrimination is the ongoing exercise of the scientist's personal judgement. Throughout all scientific work, normal or revolutionary, the scientist is perpetually appraising the noteworthiness of results, occurrences, unexpected phenomena, and anomalous effects. The criticism is in large part historical: Polanyi is claiming that in science it is only ever possible to decide on what is normal and what is revolutionary, and therefore which anomalies become 'essential' and which are simply never accounted for, *after the fact*. Kuhn is then reading in ahistorical fashion that hindsight back into the history. The criticism is a historical one that assumes a taking on of the agent's perspective, which does not have the advantage of hindsight. Kuhn's response continues his anti-individualist stance, albeit with dubious reasoning, and attempts to avoid Polanyi's criticism by raising sociological issues instead. In the turn to sociology, Kuhn bypasses not only Polanyi's criticism, but passes over the notion of agency as well.

In summary, my claim is that Kuhn's notion of paradigm is essentially a sociological notion that relies uncertainly on an untenable psychologism that is Kuhn's version of 'tacit knowledge'. Neither the sociological nor the psychologistic level address the issue of personal agency, whether construed in terms of embodiment or in moral terms of commitment. While the notion of commitment is central to Kuhn's work, as it is for Polanyi's, it is clear that Kuhn understands commitment solely in a cognitive sense that is determined by the social context and reducible to neurology. Further, Kuhn's account resides on a basic ahistorical premise that provides the link between his interrelated conceptions of normal science, revolutionary science, and paradigms. Polanyi, on the other hand, understands the person as always necessarily historical and social, and as practically and morally embodied. He explicitly does not allow for a reduction of the person – or knowledge, or the psychological – to 'neuro-cerebral' explanation. To grasp this argument requires a more comprehensive recovery of Polanyi's position.[4]

Recovering Polanyi

The division of Polanyi's position thematically into embodiment and commitment follows naturally the chronological division of his work into a first and second period. In the first period Polanyi is primarily concerned with articulating science as a social organisation, the history of its development, and the moral, political and sociological implications of that form of social organisation. For this period, the fundamental principle upon which Polanyi's argument relies is that of commitment.[5] The transition to the second period occurs in *Personal Knowledge* (1958), in which he begins to work out his insights into tacit knowing. In his second period Polanyi attempts to consolidate his initial work through developing a consistent theory of knowledge that, in grounding the notion of commitment in embodiment, links in an indissoluble way the person to tradition in the very development and exercise of a personal agency. It is this second period for which Polanyi is best known, and the fundamental principle upon which his arguments could be said to rely here is that of embodiment.[6]

My strategy for recovering Polanyi's work is in three parts: 1) outline briefly the relations of embodiment to commitment within scientific inquiry; 2) explicate Polanyi's most advanced notions of tacit knowing and embodiment, from his second period, and 3) concluding with the more general conception of commitment of his first period. My purpose for this strategy is on the one hand due to his earlier work being better comprehended conceptually in terms of his later articulation. On the other hand, the trajectory Polanyi follows is revealing for conceptualising agency for science studies in general and also more specifically for an incipient psychology of science. Polanyi's later thinking around embodiment elaborates his thinking around commitment through making explicit his understanding of personal agency which formed the basis, implicit but assumed, of his first period.

1) Embodiment and commitment in scientific inquiry

Polanyi along with Kuhn argues for the context-dependency of all scientific knowledge, over and against the rationally reconstructed, abstract conception of a context-independent objectivity put forward by the logical positivists and Karl Popper. Unlike Kuhn, Polanyi's emphasis on scientific inquiry departs more radically from philosophy of science (a term Polanyi never uses to describe his own work). Polanyi develops his conception of personal knowledge through a sustained critique of the myth of a value-free, impersonal objectivity, a critique that depends in large part on his reconstrual of the stronghold of scientific objectivity: method. Every step of this reconstrual aims at retrieving the inarticulate and informal, and potentially inarticulable and unformalisable, moments of personal decision and responsibility on the part of the scientist in his or her application of the method. On this account, scientific method is more precisely described as a set of discursive and technical practices, employing various technologies, instruments, measurements, theories, and assumptions in a complex interplay of magnification, exclusion, enhancement and distortion of a subject matter in order to derive highly specified facts which fit into some systematic ordering. These practices, however, do not exist *as such* outside of their use by persons. They are integrated, in use, into the person of a scientific investigator. This use is skilful; a skill learned by doing. Such skill cannot be reduced to rules, as this begs the question of the personal application of the rules, but comes closer to an artistic activity in which rules are more aptly described as maxims. Through this skilful use, these various technologies, instruments, measurements, etc., are incorporated into the body, extending particular capabilities.

In integrating these practices in one's person, in learning and refining the skills that accomplish this integration, and in incorporating the techniques and technologies into one's body, one has – usually unwittingly – already embarked on a particular course of commitments. Polanyi describes these commitments as existential; they are not taken up after rational deliberation, pre-meditated choice, or carefully considered judgement. Rather, they are the commitments necessarily made in order to constitute that position which makes deliberating, choosing, or judging possible at all. Our bodily inhabiting of the world is an inescapable prejudice, for which we need not apologise except to those who have *impossibly* escaped a point of view. These types of commitments are existential precisely insofar as Polanyi understands our form of being, or consciousness, to be always and inescapably an embodied condition. The corollary to this existential committing, which Polanyi (1958) describes variously as 'pouring ourselves' into things, 'assimilating' them, 'dwelling in' them (p59), and so forth, is emotional and moral: there is a risking and hazarding of one's self, for what one has committed oneself to cannot be determined prior to the commitment. The commitments, then, prior to reason or criticism, are not merely embodied in some neutral way, but are infused with a passion; any existential commitment of oneself is a passionately embodied act. Polanyi accomplishes through this articulation a way of relating embodiment, as the ground or active site of the person's moral, existential sense, to commitment. As he had already worked out an understanding of science based on commitment in his first period which precedes this articulation, it only remains for him to clarify his notion of embodiment, which he does in terms of the body as a bi-polar, 'from-to' structure of knowing.

2) Embodiment: the 'from-to' structure of knowing

Technologies, techniques, and symbol systems, as bodily extensions, not only enhance bodily ability, but are also integrated into a background of possibilities against which a specific actualised figure can stand out. Polanyi's utilisation of the Gestalt dynamics of figure/ground leads to the crucially important implication that, as background, those existential, embodied commitments that make up this background are simultaneously occluded and overlooked. One's commitments are rendered invisible, tacit or absent for the sake of something to be made visible, explicit or in some wise present. In Polanyi's terms, in attending *from* the background particulars *to* what they conjointly bear on, one has subsidiary awareness of the particulars and focal awareness of what they bear on. This double effect, of the disappearance of what enables the appearance, of a becoming invisible in rendering something visible, of tacit operations that support the explicit, is the fundamental characteristic of bodily activity, of perception, of what it means to know something. Polanyi calls this the 'from-to' structure of knowing. Perception, which provides the prototype for this structure of knowing, is then the taking up of a particular stance within the world by a resolution of the world's essential ambiguity. Analytically, the world is not *given* so much as *presupposed*; the inescapable supposition being that it is continuous prejudicial activity of the body in the world that provides a coherence necessary for knowing. The integrating of the subsidiaries *from* which we know is a personal partaking and participating in the world, with the focal entity *to* which our subsidiary knowledge bears being the achievement of that participation. The import of this conception of knowing as a from-to structure, that Polanyi realises clearly, consists in its thorough-going preclusion of a subjective-objective dichotomy: although knowledge is both personal and particularised it never leaves the 'objective' world to become 'subjective'. This point is crucial for any conception of agency, in defence against the inevitable accusations of subjectivism. Further, the double effect of knowing as a from-to structure – a bringing into focus simultaneously with a rendering subsidiary – proffers an explanation as to the success of the subjective-objective dichotomy. The roots of the dichotomy in undifferentiated, embodied experience, in both self and world, fade from focal, explicit consciousness in the very act of constituting focal, explicit consciousness. Either extreme, of complete subjectivity or total objectivity, prove to be inadequate abstractions, incomplete parts of a greater whole, figures disavowing their grounds.

Significant as the opposition to the subject/object distinction is, the type of exploration that would do the topic justice falls outside the scope of this essay. In this connection it is worth mentioning, however, that Polanyi's account bears many similarities to phenomenology, in particular to the phenomenology of Merleau-Ponty. Taken together, they combine to form a profound alternative conception of the body, of perceiving and knowing, that consistently precludes subjectivist or objectivist extremes. They seem to have derived their points of view independently, despite strong convergence.[7] Merleau-Ponty (1962, 1945) gives the most extensive treatment of what I have been calling the double effect in perceiving and knowing, of the simultaneous rendering subsidiary of various bodily operations for the sake of some focus. Merleau-Ponty (1964) revisits these themes later, re-examining the body in perception and in knowing and exploring the implications of the non-homogeneity of invisibility. Polanyi and Merleau-Ponty contribute originally and richly to understanding the role of the body in the constitution of experience: both stand at the end of positivism prior to the various conceptual turns that underwrite, more generally and across disciplines, the postmodern.

Polanyi's consistent emphasis on scientific method in terms of the embodied practices of the scientist, an embodying that structures scientific knowing in particular ways, provides the grounds for the strong claim that the workings of science are inexplicable without an understanding of the scientist's agency. The basis for agency is constituted, tacitly and bodily, through the scientist's active appropriation, in doing, of those discursive and technical practices that make up the scientist's tradition. Formulating agency in these terms might suggest that the very notion is illusory, as it is determined by tradition, by supra-personal factors of the social, historical, cultural, and contingent context. Recalling Kuhn, agency can be bypassed as it is fully determined by the paradigm. Polanyi, however, argues that what is determined by the tradition are those initial conditions on which basis the scientist's agency is initially formed and then developed. These initial conditions provide an orientation and starting point that is supra-personally determined, but from this it does not follow that therefore all of the scientist's actions are also determined. A basis is not equivalent to a determinant. One could substitute person here for scientist, to generalise the theory, as arguably becoming a person consists of actively appropriating one's traditions into which one is born, like one's body or one's language. This appropriation is not explicit, and in fact never need be made explicit. According to the logic of Polanyi's argument this appropriation is, despite its tacit, inarticulate status, a valid form of knowledge and is ultimately the reservoir of knowledge from which *all* our explicit, formal, highly specified knowledge draws. In Polanyi's oft-cited phrase: we know more than we can tell.

Three features of this account recommend it: first, it feasibly suggests a nondeterministic but interdependent relationship between the tradition and the person that locates the person historically even as it explains that person as an independent agent. Second, it demonstrates how the person's appropriation of the tradition is concealed in the very act of appropriation, offering an explanation of how Popper or Kuhn could, given an excessive rationalist emphasis or sociological preoccupation, consistently overlook what Polanyi argues is most essential to science. Third, it initiates a hermeneutics that, although in this instance applied specifically to scientific investigators within the context of scientific work, generalises well to psychological theorising (on this point see Koch 1976; Campbell 1989). Polanyi's account immediately translates into a starting point for a psychology of science. For example, the explicit self-descriptions of scientists need to be placed into the practical and historical context of their particular research tradition. Where those descriptions invoke ideals or abstractions, they are not to be bypassed, but understood as a particular manner of orienting a mostly embodied, mostly inarticulate, practice. The *explicit* self-understanding of a scientist's sense of agency has to be weighed against its *tacit* background, which underlies and supports the self-understanding and composes the body – literally – of the scientist's *sense* of agency. The components of the tacit background consist in, on the one hand, the practising community of scientists of which the scientist is part, and on the other, the history of his or her scientific tradition and therefore, by implication, the broader cultural tradition in which the scientific tradition is situated. Again, an implication here is that agency is in actuality illusory, that the entire sphere of the personal reduces to social, historical, and cultural constituents, and therefore the notion of person or agency can be done away with in terms of, for example, paradigms. However, this conclusion assumes only one pole of the bi-polar, from-to structure of knowing; while the background of subsidiaries is essential for there to be a focal figure at all, the focal entity itself, in becoming the coherent integration of particulars it is, thereby becomes irreducible to its parts. What confers this irreducible status upon the focal pole of knowing composes the second theme of agency Polanyi is concerned with, that of commitment, understood as a primarily existential, moral activity. In examining Polanyi's articulation of this aspect, we also examine more closely the relation of the personal to the social, historical, and cultural traditions in which the person is constituted.

Agents vs paradigms: the personal in the social

I want to pause here momentarily to recall the critique of Kuhn: the emphasis on the sociological, as based on an ultimately psychologistic reduction, bypassed the person of the scientist as an active agent. What does Polanyi offer by contrast? Polanyi describes the scientist's active appropriation of the tradition as a 'plunging' and 'groping': learning by doing means an uncritical, or more accurately, an a-critical acceptance of those various techniques, assumptions, and instruments upon which scientific work is based. What is interesting here is that this a-critical mode is itself a form of knowledge or way of knowing, albeit non-explicit; that is, it is a tacit knowing, known in and by the body. Tacit knowing, although perpetually absenting itself in rendering itself subsidiary for the sake of some focal or explicit awareness, is not therefore inaccessible to the scientist, but is in principle available to some extent – unlike Kuhn's appeal to 'neuro-cerebral mechanism' for an explanation – upon *reflection*. An a-critical commitment, made tacitly, can be made explicit and considered critically. In the person's a-critical, bodily taking up of tradition, it becomes possible through reflection to read commitment into this action, a commitment which catalyses the integration of those particular practices and defines not only those practices and the tradition in certain ways but also the person. The implication here, which I want to countenance, is that the personal is constituted in the social by means of commitment to pre-existing social practices, but that precisely due to this commitment and the capacity to reflect on it the person defines him or herself as a self-determining agent who is therefore irreducible to the social. The most insightful clue to getting clear on this complex reflexivity is that for Polanyi the domain carved out by the agent's constitutive commitments is at base the *moral* domain, a clue to which I return below.

In terms of a critique of science, the implication is that to understand scientific method as some impersonal, value-free procedure which insures objective results by keeping out subjective distortions (like values or personal commitments) is dead wrong; to the contrary, 'scientific method' is dead and ineffectual save when animated by a personal commitment which for the most part is embodied tacitly, in doing, by the scientific investigator. This is the *endpoint* of Polanyi's philosophy. It emerges in its fullest complexity with the articulation of embodiment in his second period. His philosophy followed a persistent trajectory from its origins in his first period that described scientific inquiry in terms of commitment, origins that took the social aspects of science into account before concluding with an articulation of the personal.

3) The commitment to freedom: the autonomy and social organisation of science

That Polanyi's thinking culminates in a focus on the scientist as an embodied, committed agent was neither premeditated nor even foreseeable in its beginnings. Polanyi leaves his career in chemistry behind and turns to philosophy in the 1930s and 1940s in order to deal with pressing social and political issues. Specifically, Polanyi is opposing Marxist-inspired proposals in England calling for state planning of science based on the model of the Soviet Union. More generally, he sees this proposal as symptomatic of a widespread destructiveness manifesting across Europe, in every sphere of life, which was not to be attributed to any particular nation, state, or event. European civilisation was destroying itself through war, totalitarianism, and nihilism. These were the logical consequences of the misunderstanding and malpractice of its own tradition. Polanyi understands the misapplication of science to be a crucial contributor to this self-destructiveness, an understanding based on his own experience as a scientist, powerful intuitions concerning the role of science in society and in politics, and the particulars of his personal background that throw him continuously into the confluence of these destructive processes.[8]

Polanyi's enterprise in this early period can be described specifically as an argument for the autonomy of science and more broadly as a defence of traditional formulations of European social and political practices in terms of ideals and principles. Science as a body of knowledge and as a social organisation exemplifies a particular way of embodying ideals, upholding tradition, and preserving Europe's free, democratic civilisation. Ultimately, Polanyi's goal is to protect freedom, particularly freedom of thought, from the self-destruction afflicting so much else. At the heart of Polanyi's enterprise, although it takes a prolonged effort over decades to uncover, is his assumption of personal agency as the locus of freedom. The person, as agent, is therefore also the locus of responsibility, and the linchpin about which the successful functioning of science, and in turn a free society, turns. The scientist's exercise of freedom and responsibility takes place within a particular social organisation – the community of scientists – which itself must be autonomously self-regulating in order to provide to its members appropriate support, space, and constraints. Polanyi's appeal for autonomy in science cuts both ways: autonomy sets limits to science's authority, even as it allows a freedom for scientists within those limits. The Marxist argument for state planning denied that science was ever truly autonomous, but was always and fully determined by social and economic factors. To plan science was to make this truth explicit and take conscious control of this truth. That the Marxists appealed to the scientific basis of historical materialism as informing the truth of their own arguments was the prime example, for Polanyi, of science overstepping its bounds: the implications of its theory aimed to destroy the very premises which, according to Polanyi, the theory had to presuppose in the first place. This vicious circularity becomes self-fulfilling in its logical consequences, for with its premises destroyed science becomes unlimited in its application. The premises for science at the level of social organisation are the basis for its autonomous functioning within society; without these premises, science loses its freedom. That these premises rely on personal agency, which in turn also becomes suspect, means that the political implication of an unrestrained application of science is the loss of personal freedom. Government becomes totalitarian.

Polanyi counters with an argument for autonomy in science that he claims is also therefore an argument for a free society. Scientific knowledge, claiming both universal validity and normative status, sets up as its authority a relation to a universal and normative truth that lies outside not only particular special interests, but also outside and above political powers, such as the state's. Science as an institution and a community serves as a power check on potential excesses. Science, in combination with other democratic institutions embodied in the different political bodies, the legal system, organised religion, the education system, and so on, asserts a presence that limits state power. An infringement on the autonomy of any of these institutions, such as state control and planning would effect, is an infringement on democracy. What is essential for making this reciprocal relationship of state to institution work inheres in the subservience of both to standards oriented to supra-institutional, supra-political ideals taken as authoritative: ideals of truth, justice, equality, freedom, and so on.

To argue for autonomy for science is to argue for its freedom from state intervention. This is not an unconditional freedom, for the very conditions that support freedom also constrain science as an institution by means of responsibility. Science demands freedom on the basis of standards that define it as a science and to which it holds itself accountable. The entire process of upholding these standards through the interplay of education, training, funding, promotion, peer review, publication methods, conferences, invisible colleges, and so on, becomes according to Polanyi a self-organising system too complex to be overseen by some executive centre. It is self-organising in terms of lateral controls exerted through collegial discussion and criticism; scientists are constantly engaged in assessing the validity of findings and the consequent acceptance or rejection of hypotheses, explanations, and theories. Obviously these judgements are not made on an ad hoc basis but according to prevailing standards. As such, Polanyi concedes science is inherently dogmatic but claims that this is unavoidable: to relax the standards will invite correspondingly inferior quality. To allow freedom for science demands an expectation of responsibility from scientists, and an extension of trust from the rest of the society of which the scientists are part accompanied by all the risks and hazards such trust entails. There is neither guarantee of this trust nor proof against risk. But the scientists are accountable to certain standards, on a particular basis, which is the basis for science's autonomy as a self-organising social institution. This basis is personal agency. It is only on the basis of personal agency that scientists' accountability to others, and hence their own personal sense of responsibility, can make any sense at all.

Personal agency and universal intent

Polanyi's thought followed, from his first principled arguments for the tradition of science, to his examination of science as a social organisation, to the political implications of that form of social organisation, a trajectory that depended throughout on the assumption of personal agency. That it takes the time and thought it does for this assumption to become explicit is testimony to the complexity and depth of Polanyi's intuitions and the problems he faced. The argument for freedom, in science particularly but more generally in thought, is an argument for an orientation to universal ideals – of which freedom itself is one – that devolves on some centre from which responsibility cannot be further deferred, and this centre proves to be the person. The exercise of personal agency takes place within a framework of universal intent, the comprehensiveness of which forms the basis for understanding tradition, the social, the political, and ultimately, moral questions around the true and the good. Freedom manifests at the political level in democratic practices; at the level of social organisation, it manifests in autonomy; while at the individual level, it manifests in personal agency. And therefore, just as the argument for autonomy in science is two-sided: setting limits to science and securing freedom within those limits, so the argument for personal agency is also two-sided: demands and obligations are set upon the scientist, within which his or her freedom is constituted. In this articulation of the two-sidedness of agency, the first inkling of a possibly profound psychology within Polanyi's work emerges, too.

In the simultaneous affording of freedom and placing of responsibilities upon the person, the whole range of a person's resources (moral, emotional, intellectual and spiritual) is mobilised. For neither freedom nor responsibility can be experienced neutrally, impassively or non-committally, but these are always experienced as involving one's very person, as evaluative of one's very self: that is, existentially. This existential sense of involvement or evaluation begins from, and/or against – but always *within* – one's social context. The individual's social context sets the parameters and outlines the conditions in which his or her sense of freedom, responsibility and self, develop, and it does so through providing the tacit background of practices, standards, norms, values, and mores, that make the existential commitments meaningful. The development of one's person and agency is inescapably a moral process actualised through commitment. The person emerges as an independent moral centre through inculcating the standards implicit or explicit in the background. Polanyi will later come to articulate this background as forming the tacit, subsidiary pole of the bi-polar structure of knowing: what the individual *knows from*. Agency – experienced in, and as, freedom and responsibility – is defined within an orientation to supra-personal standards that the person cannot 'know' in any explicit, formal, or critical sense, but to which he or she inarticulately and existentially has already committed *in order to know*. These supra-personal standards, in turn, do not only define the person in relation to the social: they define the social and the personal in relation to the universal. That is, these standards are not upheld by the community or society, or person, as conventions, but as ideals that (are presumed to) hold universally. (In fact, according to the logic of commitment laid out here, to expose some collectively held standard as 'mere convention' presupposes a broader background that situates the standard and defines it as convention; the greatest breadth ascribable to any such background would be one of universal proportions.)

The ideals as 'standards', then, are standards of orientation, which 'orient' a person not primarily in any cognitive, rational or explicit sense, but through demanding one's deepest and hence most inarticulate commitments. If the person is oriented to the highest of ideals, such as truth, goodness, and justice, he or she is put into the position of always at best trying to live up to them. The ideal is never exhausted by a person's actual performance. In making these existential, a-critical commitments one defines oneself in relation to ideals to which one's commitments always fall short. But through these acts – a striving that defines through falling short – one both exercises agency and sets its limits. These acts of commitment, of striving and defining, presuppose a passion animating them even as they also simultaneously set the conditions for the realisation of the moral. Just as an autonomous democratic institution in service to the particular ideals it holds to be universal and normative serves as a check on the power of the state, so too at the personal level does an orientation to higher ideals serve to form and check the range and application of our morality and our passions.

What the person acts from in making these commitments, and what charges the very stuff of these commitments so that they are existential for one's person, experienced as passionate, and moral in their supra-personal implications, are the supra-personal standards of his or her social tradition without which he or she would have no basis for an orientation to higher ideals. The possibility of realising the universal is always and necessarily inescapably personal, a personal that always presupposes pre-personal social particulars. The universal and the particular, as embodied in the person, are not opposed but inextricable. The inescapability of particularity as the basis for universal intent does not invalidate the notion of universal, but underscores that the intent is always precarious and hazardous, always carrying the risk of failure to realise its intent. The notion of the universal is not invalidated because if it were, neither it nor the notion of particularity would make sense, and this would in effect undercut the very basis for having any coherence, for making any sense, at all.

Conclusion

Given this three-part recovery of Polanyi, I think we are now in a position to appreciate some of the scope and implications of his sense of personal agency. Polanyi's defence of freedom in science, and by extension freedom in society, depends on an ascription of responsibility to some autonomous centre from which responsibility cannot be further deferred. This centre proves to be that of the scientist, and by extension the person in general, as a free and responsible agent. The scientist's agency is actualised through commitments, moral and existential, to ideals held to be universal, from social standards that orient the commitments. It is only within this framework of universal intent that commitment, and by implication agency, makes sense. Commitment is actualised bodily in terms of the bi-polar structure of knowing, wherein the person knows from a tacit background of subsidiary particulars to a focal entity that is their integration. For Polanyi the experience of this achievement, which is in most cases an explicit achievement, is that personal knowledge of the scientist that is both the foundation of science and that aspires to universality. Within the framework of universal intent, such personal knowledge risks failure and challenges scientific normativity in its potential; through its acceptance, it affords reflection and criticism even as it re-instates a new normativity.

To adequately assess or address personal knowledge claims made within a framework of universal intent, then, requires more than either ideological, external critique, or sociological or 'neuro-cerebral' explanation, as Thomas Kuhn suggested. For regardless of whether the claim realises its universal intent or not, and therefore transforms its conventional status into the *question* of its universal status – within the person, this would mean transforming one's community conventions; within a social setting, this would mean transforming its cultural conventionality; within a tradition, this would mean transforming its historical conventionality – the assessment of the claim in terms of its success or failure requires a recognition and exploration of the scientist's active sense of agency. This results in an internal critique of science that complements the external critiques and redresses a lacuna within science studies around issues of agency. This would also be an important step in developing an incipient psychology of science that also lacks an adequate thematisation of the person in terms of agency. Retrieval of Michael Polanyi's sophisticated sense of agency articulated around the foci of embodiment and commitment affords a profound starting point for such an internal critique, a starting point that deserves renewed attention and deeper exploration.

The author would like to thank Leendert Mos and Natalia Shostak for their comments on this paper, and the Social Sciences and Humanities Research Council of Canada for their funding of this research through a Doctoral Fellowship Grant (No. 752-99-1198).

Notes

1. A brief but representative list of the literature I have in mind here: Barnes (1974), Bloor (1976), Haraway (1991), Harding (1986), Knorr-Cetina & Mulkay (1983), Latour (1993), Latour & Woolgar (1979), Shapin and Schaffer (1985), Woolgar (1988).
2. For example, Grover (1981) offers a cognitive psychology perspective; Keller (1985) approaches science from a feminist psychoanalytic base.
3. Kuhn (1961) explicitly acknowledges Polanyi's providing 'the most extensive and developed discussion I know of ... my apparently strange usage [of paradigm]' (p392), later relegating this acknowledgement unobtrusively to footnotes (Kuhn 1970, 1962), and yet later making a single mention of Polanyi on an unrelated note (Kuhn 1977). Other important influences are also offhandedly acknowledged by Kuhn; most prominently, Mannheim (1936, 1929) and Fleck (1979, 1935).
4. The sad and strange neglect of Michael Polanyi's work in the latter half of the twentieth century requires attention in its own right, but as it is a topic tangential to this paper I do not address it here. The fundamental difficulty Polanyi presents the reader is an originality of perspective outside traditional disciplines and vocabularies. A superficial exposure to his eclectic and idiosyncratic approach to science and social theory can serve to distract

from the insight and profundity of his thought. The strategy I adopt in this paper to offset this initial disadvantage is a simple, two-fold thematic breakdown of his work around the focus on agency in order to best suggest the scope and coherence of Polanyi's thinking. A more particulate reading would better delineate my own gloss from Polanyi's work proper, but at the risk of losing the broad scope. Consequently I eschew citation in favour of overview in the hope that what is gained outweighs what is lost.

5. What I am designating as Polanyi's 'first period' in terms of years covers approximately two decades, from the mid-1930s until the mid-1950s. In terms of texts, this period is covered by Polanyi (1940, 1941, 1946, 1951).
6. Polanyi's 'second period' covers the last two decades of his life, from the mid-1950s until the mid-1970s (Polanyi 1959, 1966, 1969). Deserving especial mention for refinement of his articulation of embodiment are Polanyi (1966) and the lattermost essays in Polanyi (1969).
7. There is no mention of Polanyi's work in Merleau-Ponty's writing. The first reference to Merleau-Ponty by Polanyi does not appear until 1964 (Polanyi 1969, 1964), most likely corresponding to the fact that the first English translation of Merleau-Ponty's *Phenomenology of Perception* did not appear until 1962.
8. Polanyi's life story is such that he experienced in turn the emergence of Communism in Russia, fascism in Hungary, and National Socialism in Germany. For biographical information, see Allen (1990), Ignotus (1961), Nagy (1994), Wigner and Hodgkin (1977).

References

Allen, R. (1990) *Polanyi*, London: Claridge Press.

Barnes, B. (1974) *Scientific Knowledge and Sociological Theory*, London: Routledge and Kegan Paul.

Bloor, D. (1976) *Knowledge and Social Imagery*, London: Routledge and Kegan Paul.

Campbell, D.T. (1989) 'Fragments of the Fragile History of Psychological Epistemology and Theory of Science', in B. Gholson, W.R. Shadish Jr, R.A. Neimeyer, and A.C. Houts (eds), *Psychology of Science: Contributions to Metascience: 21-46*, Cambridge: Cambridge University Press.

Danziger, K. (1990) *Constructing the Subject: Historical Origins of Psychological Research*, Cambridge: Cambridge University Press.

Danziger, K. (1997) *Naming the Mind: How Psychology Found its Language*, London and Thousand Oaks, CA: Sage.

Fleck, L. (1979) *Genesis and Development of a Scientific Fact*, F. Bradley and T.J. Trem (trans), Chicago & London: University of Chicago Press, (Originally published in 1935).

Gholson, B., W.R. Shadish Jr, R.A. Neimeyer and A.C. Houts (eds), (1989) *Psychology of Science: Contributions to Metascience*, Cambridge: Cambridge University Press.

Grover, S. (1981) *Toward a Psychology of The Scientist: Implications of Psychological Research for Contemporary Philosophy of Science*, Washington,

DC: University Press of America.
Haraway, D. (1991) *Simians, Cyborgs and Women: the Reinvention of Nature*, New York: Routledge.
Harding, S. (1986) *The Science Question in Feminism*, Ithaca & London: Cornell University Press.
Ignotus, P. (1961) 'The Hungary of Michael Polanyi', in P. Ignotus (ed), *The Logic of Personal Knowledge: Essays Presented to Michael Polanyi on his Seventieth Birthday: 3-12*. London: Routledge and Kegan Paul.
Keller, E. (1985) *Reflections on Gender and Science*, New Haven: Yale University Press.
Knorr-Cetina, K. and M. Mulkay (eds) (1983) *Science Observed: Perspectives on the Social Study of Science*, Beverly Hills: Sage.
Koch, S. (1976) 'Language Communities, Search Cells, and the Psychological Studies', in W. Arnold (ed), *Nebraska Symposium on Motivation, 1975: Conceptual Foundations of Psychology*: 477-559, Lincoln and London: University of Nebraska.
Koch, S. (1999) *Psychology in Human Context: Essays in Dissidence and Reconstruction*, D. Finkelman and F. Kessel (eds), Chicago & London: University of Chicago.
Kuhn, T. (1961) 'The Function of Dogma in Scientific Research', in A.C. Crombie (ed), *Scientific Change*, London: Heinemann, pp347-398.
Kuhn, T. (1970) *The Structure of Scientific Revolutions*, Chicago: University of Chicago Press (Originally published in 1962).
Kuhn, T. (1977) *The Essential Tension: Selected Studies in Scientific Tradition and Change*, Chicago and London: University of Chicago.
Lakatos, I. and A. Musgrave (eds) (1970), *Criticism and the Growth of Knowledge*, Cambridge: Cambridge University Press.
Latour, B. (1993) *We Have Never Been Modern*, Catherine Porter (trans), Cambridge: Harvard University Press.
Latour, B. and S. Woolgar (1979) *Laboratory Life: the Social Construction of Scientific Facts*, Beverly Hills: Sage.
Mannheim, K. (1936) *Ideology and Utopia*, L. Wirth and E. Shils (trans), New York: Harvest, Brace, and World (Originally published in 1929).
Masterman, M. (1970) 'The Nature of a Paradigm', in I. Lakatos and A. Musgrave (eds), *Criticism and the Growth of Knowledge*, Cambridge: Cambridge University Press, pp59-90.
Merleau-Ponty, M. (1962) *Phenomenology of Perception*, Colin Smith (trans), London: Routledge (Originally published in 1945).
Merleau-Ponty, M. (1964) *Le Visible et l'Invisible: Suivi de Notes de Travail*, Paris: Gallimard.
Nagy, E. (1994) 'After Brotherhood's Golden Age: Karl and Michael Polanyi', in K. McRobbie (ed), *Humanity, Society, and Commitment*, Montreal, New York and London: Black Rose, pp81-112.
Polanyi, M. (1940) *The Contempt of Freedom*, London: Watts and Co.
Polanyi, M. (1941) 'The Growth of Thought in Society', *Economica* 8: 428-456.
Polanyi, M. (1946) *Science, Faith and Society*, London: Oxford University Press.

Polanyi, M. (1951) *The Logic of Liberty: Reflections and Rejoinders*, London: Routledge and Kegan Paul.

Polanyi, M. (1958) *Personal Knowledge: Towards a Post-critical Philosophy*, Chicago: University of Chicago.

Polanyi, M. (1959) *The Study of Man*, Phoenix: University of Chicago.

Polanyi, M. (1961) 'Commentary on "The function of dogma in scientific research"', in A. C. Crombie (ed), *Scientific Change*, London: Heinemann, pp375-380.

Polanyi, M. (1964) 'The Logic of Tacit Inference', in Polanyi (1969), M. Grene (ed), London: Routledge and Kegan Paul, pp138-158, (Originally published in 1964).

Polanyi, M. (1966) *The Tacit Dimension*, New York: Doubleday.

Polanyi, M. (1969) *Knowing and Being: Essays by Michael Polanyi*, M. Grene (ed) London: Routledge and Kegan Paul.

Popper, K. (1958) *The Logic of Scientific Discovery*, New York: Harper & Row (Originally published in 1933).

Popper, K. (1967) 'Epistemology Without a Knowing Subject', in B. van Rootselaar and J.F. Staal (eds), *Logic, methodology and philosophy of science III*, Amsterdam: North Holland Publishing Company, pp333-373.

Shapin, S. and S. Schaffer (1985) *Leviathan and the Air-pump: Hobbes, Boyle, and the Experimental Life*, Princeton: Princeton University Press.

Taylor, C. (1989) *Sources of the Self: the Making of the Modern Identity*, Cambridge: Harvard University Press.

Wigner, E. and R. Hodgkin (1977) 'Michael Polanyi', in *Biographical Memoirs of Fellows of the Royal Society*, 23: 413-448.

Woolgar, S. (1988) *Science, the Very Idea!*, London: Tavistock.

The history and memory of childhood sexual abuse: true and false

Robert S. Steele

Freud's often repeated historical claim that in his first years of practising psychoanalysis he was taken in by his women patients' stories of having been sexually abused as girls is supported by Daniel Schacter in his recent positivist history of research on memory distortion. Schacter uses Freud's renunciation of his 'seduction theory' as an instructive warning about the power of false memories and abuse-survivor testimony. However, neither Freud nor Schacter accurately recounts the history of this work: Freud's original 1896 seduction theory papers show that Freud explicitly states that his patients never told him they were sexually abused as children. He claims that he constructed these accounts using his psychoanalytic method. The distortions in Freud's and Schacter's historical accounts of these earlier scientific findings are used to examine and illustrate how history, as well as memory, can be distorted by cultural biases surrounding male authority and female victimisation. Additionally, a detailed critical reading of Schacter's model of memory reveals not only the cultural narratives undergirding that scientific project, but also the omissions, attributions and denials necessary to sustain such an endeavour. This critical appraisal reminds us of the dynamic, interdependent boundaries of culture/science, truth/falsity, and personal/collective, helping to revitalise our sense of history and memory as lived-experiences always open to reinterpretation, re-plotting, and new understandings.

> How did we get here, to a land where forgetting becomes so central an issue for competing ideologies? (Hacking 1995: 126)

Memory is a major discipline within psychology and memory's absence, forgetting, is a topic that has been intensively studied for over a century. Within the psychological sciences, laboratory conceptualisations of memory flourish generating 'objective scientific knowledge', but not without contenders. Complex phenomenological perspectives on the narrative qualities of experiences are being developed as corrective supplements to scientific judgements about memories, or histories, being either true or false, or definitively knowable. These newer views foster more deeply textured understandings of remembrances of things past, understandings that try to accommodate the immense complexity and uncertainty of knowing our histories. These hermeneutic-phenomenological, and often feminist, readings seek to replace simple representational approaches, which assume a singular, veridical, non-perspectival historical viewpoint supported by an objectivist epistemology, with a multi-dimensional, intersecting dialectics of truth/falsity, imagined/real, and personal/collective.

Our detailed reading of a prototypically positivist and presentist work on the history of memory research, Daniel Schacter's *Memory Distortion: History and Current Practice* (1995), explicates the major impossibilities and biases that are engendered by the currently dominant scientific approach to explaining both the history of research on memories of childhood sexual abuse and the construct of 'false memories'. False memories have been the focus for much of the mnemic research over the last two decades. One of the forces driving these investigations has been the widespread reporting of recovered memories of childhood sexual abuse. This reading begins with a critical deconstruction of Schacter's historical account of Freud's 'seduction theory', and then moves to a broader consideration of the vested interests that scientists have displayed in their recounting of women's histories. Our analysis concludes with a consideration of Janet Haaken's creatively synthetic post-structuralist views of memory and history in her *Pillar of Salt: Gender, Memory, and the Perils of Looking Back* (1998). Haaken's work builds on the feminist demonstration that women's claims about their sexual abuse as children and adults be taken seriously and be seen as a particularly brutal manifestation of patriarchy's subjugation of women. Moving beyond this foundational empiricism, Haaken calls into question the positivism of such accounts about the past, asking us to consider how histories, both individual and collective, are a fusion of experience and imagination shaped by cultural narratives about what can, and cannot, be told, as well as who is to be doubted and believed.[1]

Textual comparison indicates that although Schacter's and Haaken's works have a common concern – the history of the psychological investigation of recovered memories of sexual abuse and the psycho-social significance of such memories – the laboratory science of memory and feminist-phenomenological perspectives on remembering are markedly different in their methodologies, ontologies, and perspectives on the relations of memory and history. They differ as well in their understandings of the dynamic influences of the social relations of power on collective as well as personal remembering. Direct comparison also makes it apparent that the different methodological and theoretical practices of the two perspectives produce widely divergent histories of both science and personal life.

False memories and tendentious histories

Experimental psychology, psychoanalysis, history and feminism have all addressed the vexing issues generated by the vicissitudes of both personal and social reconstructions of the past. Whether framed as a matter of knowledge of a collective past or an individual's remembrances of her or his life, questions arise about the veracity of memory. As memory becomes increasingly social and shared, it becomes – at some indefinable point on a cultural-temporal continuum – history. Schacter's (1995) text simultaneously serves as an overview for a collection of state-of-the-science essays on memory and a review of the history of psychological investigations of memory distortion. In this history, two accounts central to the narrative, and also paradigmatic for an investigation of history and memory, are of interest: Freud's 'seduction theory' and Schacter's recording of certain selected cases of alleged childhood sexual abuse. Both of these passages provide the opportunity to examine the ways history and memory intertwine. So too do they afford us with the chance to assess how a collective history, in this case a history of the scientific study of the relation of sexual abuse and false memories, is an interested history that evidences the asymmetrical, gendered power relations undergirding twentieth-century experimental science.

The control of history

In his review of late nineteenth and early twentieth-century work on memory distortion, Schacter highlights and praises the experimental breakthrough of Ebbinghaus who 'gained control over the input to the system'. He concludes that:

> The importance of exerting experimental control over the input to memory is so widely accepted in most modern research that one easily forgets what a giant step Ebbinghaus took when he invented the procedure. Indeed, it is precisely the absence of control over, or knowledge of, the inputs to memory that has made the current debate over recovered/repressed memories so vexing. When patients claim to remember an episode from their distant past, it is often difficult to obtain unambiguous external corroboration that the alleged event actually occurred (1995: 5).

Schacter here introduces two problems that beset history. First, in the passage 'one easily forgets ... Ebbinghaus', he notes that the sources of conventionally accepted ideas are often forgotten. Second, Schacter acknowledges that it is difficult to verify the historical accuracy of contemporary accounts of past events that were at the time of their occurrence not made public. The first problem seems relatively trivial: all that is needed to rectify it is a historical reminder – and, in the case of Ebbinghaus, Schacter provides it. However, this apparently straightforward problem becomes much more difficult if the historical refresher, while being part of received history or conventional wisdom, is in fact false and does not accurately represent what occurred in the past. This more complicated problem emerges when Schacter addresses Freud's work.

In reading Schacter's historical account of Freud's 'seduction theory' we see how difficult it is to uncover the truth when it is buried by conventional history. We see too in this account the difficulties that beset those people whose pasts are ignored, denied and replaced by more powerful individuals. Following Freud's own lead, and thereby simultaneously preserving the orthodox or 'received' scientific history and discounting the reported memories of psychoanalytic patients, Schacter incorrectly recounts the history of Freud's early researches on memories of childhood sexual abuse. Schacter writes, 'As is now well known ... Freud soon abandoned this "seduction theory" of early trauma in favour of the view that the "memories" that his patients retrieved were in fact fantasies or confabulations' (1995: 6). While appealing to conventional historical knowledge – 'As is now well known' – about Freud's renunciation of the theory, Schacter is neutral on the matter of whether Freud did this in order to save his career, as the revisionist Masson (1984) argues, or because he later realised that the memories were implausible and he had generalised from too small a sample of cases (Erdelyi 1985). Ignoring this crucial historical point not only covers over the problem of disputes about historical fact, but also enables Schacter to make a smooth passage to his account of false memory research.

Closer analysis of Schacter's historical method provides important information about this omission. In the human sciences, like historical scholarship, primary sources or original texts take precedence over convention in providing a grounding for interpretation (Gadamer 1975). In uncovering the history of Freud's theory of the relation of childhood sexual abuse to neurosis, it is important not to promulgate received history, but to use an historical method that directs examination to the original documents in which Freud set forth that theory and evidence for it. Although Schacter cites Freud's most often referenced paper on the seduction theory, *The Aetiology of Hysteria*, he does not cite Freud's two other 1896 texts in which the theory is presented. In each of those three original texts, Freud never once states, as Schacter maintains, that his patients 'retrieved' memories of having been sexually assaulted during their childhood. Freud never introduces any questions about the veracity of his patients' accounts; he, in fact, adamantly repeats three times over that they never told him directly that they were abused (1962 [1896a]: 153; [1896b]: 165-6; [1896c]: 204). For example, in *The Aetiology of Hysteria*, he summarises his views. He rhetorically asks if it is not possible that docile patients are telling the physician what he wants to hear and are simply making up stories of childhood abuse. He dismisses any doubts about the reality of these abuse scenes by arguing that before entering psychoanalysis patients know nothing about these incidents and that they are indignant when he suggests that such things might emerge in treatment. Freud says, 'Only the strongest compulsion of the treatment can induce them to embark on a reproduction of them' (1962 [1896c]: 204). He continues, saying that when recalling the sexual abuse, patients suffer violent emotions of which they are ashamed and which they try to conceal. Even when they have relived the incidents more than once, Freud emphasises, 'they still attempt to withhold belief from them, by emphasising the fact that, unlike what happens in the case of other forgotten material, they have no feeling of remembering the scenes'. He concludes, 'This latter piece of behaviour seems to provide conclusive proof' (p204). Here, then, proof that his patients are not making-up the scenes is that they deny any sense of remembering them.

Far, then, from having 'retrieved' memories of abuse in Freud's presence, his patients apparently refused to tell him they remembered such events. Indeed at the time Freud thought the importance of his new psychoanalytic technique was that it helped him piece together from his patients' stories, symptoms and associations, coherent accounts of childhood seduction. Accounts from which, according to Freud in all three 1896 papers, his patients 'withhold belief'. Freud's later historical recountings and the conventional psychoanalytic histories which follow his lead, for example Jones (1953), all deny what Freud so clearly wrote in the original 1896 texts. For example, eighteen years later Freud claims he had been far too ' ... readily inclined to accept as true and aetiologically significant the statements made by patients in which they ascribed their symptoms to passive sexual experiences in the first years of childhood – to put it bluntly, to seduction' (1957 [1914]: 17). In complete contradiction to his originally published findings, Freud states here in 1914 and again in a 1925 (1959) essay that he believed the stories his patients were telling him. He caps-off his denial of any responsibility for having been the creative force behind the construction of these memories of abuse in 1933 when he writes 'Almost all my women patients told me that they had been seduced by their fathers' (1964: 120).

Freud here has created the historical equivalent of a 'screen memory' (a fabrication that displaces traumatic memories of past events), retold three times and by this redundancy given credibility, that pulls a veil of plausibility over an unpleasant truth. The truth is that Freud constructed seduction scenarios from the fragments of memories, dreams, recollections and symptomatic expressions of his patients; however, it is unclear if even one of them ever told him that she/he had been sexually abused as a child. The historical 'smoke screen' which Freud creates positions him as dupe or innocent victim because he was too trusting.

Uncovering historical evidence of Freud's manoeuvring is doubly troubling for psychoanalysis and problematic for science in general. Not only does Freud abuse his power and the trust of his patients by ultimately blaming them for a mistake entirely of his own creation, but in trying to exonerate himself, he exposes psychoanalysis to a devastating criticism: its founder cannot accurately recount his own published findings and produces historical accounts of his work which are fictitious.

Without attending to these complexities of Freud's writings, Schacter concludes his review of this work saying, 'Unlike Ebbinghaus, Freud had no independent means of checking the accuracy of reported recollections, and therefore could never provide an entirely satisfying account of memory distortion' (1995: 7). Here Schacter employs an objectivist epistemological presupposition: if there were an 'independent means of checking the accuracy of reports' as there is in experiments, then the truth could be established. However, as we have just shown, even when independent sources from the past exist, as they do with Freud's three 1896 papers, subsequent historical gerrymandering can go not only unchecked, but actually be reproduced as truth, as is demonstrated by Schacter's own account of Freud's seduction theory.

By examining Schacter's text, especially the references he cites, it becomes clear that he did not compose an entirely accurate history even when reliable historical documentation was readily available to him. It becomes clear, too, that the history he composes is determined not so much by the past, but by the necessity of demonstrating that Freud was initially taken-in by the 'false memories' of his patients. As we demonstrated above, Schacter ignored Freud's direct statement in 1896 that his patients did not tell him they were sexually abused and it was he, Freud, who constructed accounts of abuse from their fragmented recollections. Further, although Schacter cites Masson (1984), he ignores Masson's central thesis that Freud's patients really had been assaulted as children, and that, 'Faced with his colleagues' hostility to his discoveries, Freud sacrificed his major insight' (p191). Given the evidence in both Freud's letters and publications, Masson is overly certain about the reality of childhood sexual assault in the lives of Freud's patients, but Schimek (1987), also cited by Schacter, is meticulous in documenting the textual evidence of Freud's creative interpretations. She writes, 'Freud's conclusion that hysteria always requires the occurrence of sexual abuse in early childhood was not based directly on the patients' reports and conscious memories, but involved a great deal of selective interpretation and reconstruction' (p938).[2]

Even though Schacter cites Masson only to dismiss his arguments, and Schimek as support for the idea that Freud was troubled by the suggestibility of his patients and the possibilities of 'obtaining false recollections' with his early procedures (1995: 6), both of these works radically disagree with Schacter's conclusion. He ignores this in favour of the account of Erdelyi (1985) who simply recasts Freud's (1953 [1906]) own self-serving exculpation that his 'material was scanty' and contained a 'disproportionately' large number of sexual abuse cases (p274). If taken seriously, the first part of the criticism that concerns inadequate sample size is troublesome for almost all Freud's work. The seduction theory actually was based on more cases than were most of Freud's findings. The second part of the argument concerning the representativeness of his cases is misguided because focusing on the disproportion or overrepresentation of sexual abuse cases misses the point: the fault did not lie in the patients not being representative of a wider population, because – as we have seen from Freud's own reports – his patients did not actually admit to being abused, therefore they could hardly represent an over-sampling of abused people. The fault lay with Freud's technique which he never significantly altered (Steele 1982; Schimek 1987).

Schacter's shaping of his history of Freud's researches is significant in two ways. Freud's renunciation of the seduction theory fits nicely with the accepted scientific view of science's past and the role of great men in science: in such valoristic accounts even when the scientist, in this case Freud, commits an error (believing his patients' seduction stories), he can learn from experience and correct the mistake (Freud realised the stories were fantasies). Additionally, Freud's work provides an historical cornerstone for Schacter's own thesis. Freud's dismissal of the reality of childhood sexual abuse is presented as reasonable scientific evidence against the notion that people can forget and then reliably recover memories of such traumas.

The culture of science

Scientific institutions and practice are shaped by broader, inclusive cultural dynamics. One such force that has received the attention of science studies is gender. As a category of persons that has structured asymmetrical social relations, gender has shaped the identity of scientists, the attitude of scientific practice, and the content of scientific theories and findings (Harding 1986; Schiebinger 1993). Resonating with the wider cultural views, normal scientific practices – whether in biology, medicine or psychology – repeatedly reinscribe master scientific narratives that explain the female as inferior, do not heed women's own accounts of their bodies and minds, and, ultimately, support the prevailing inequalities of gender (Fausto-Sterling 2000; Haraway 1989).

Schacter's recounting of Freud's work, coupled with his own observations about alleged childhood sexual abuse, contains several features of this dominant gender narrative. First, Freud's disingenuousness in telling the history of his own work on the role of childhood sexual abuse in the etiology of neurosis is a recounting that serves three obfuscating functions. It saves him from admitting that he was in error, casts doubt on the veracity of his women patients' testimony, and ultimately it confuses our understanding of how women's lives have been defined by our culture's practices surrounding rape and other forms of sexual abuse.

Many pages after presenting his history of Freud's work, Schacter himself employs an explanatory strategy very similar to the one Freud used. He discounts the veracity of people, who are overwhelmingly women, telling about having been raped as children: he calls evidence that childhood sexual abuse can be repressed and later recalled 'informal anecdotes' (1995: 28). Further doubt is cast on the veracity of abuse survivor testimony by Schacter when he gives considerable space to speculation, for which he admits there is 'no scientific evidence' (p29), that the 'recent explosion of recovered memories of sexual abuse involves a widespread "culture of victimisation"'. He adds that, 'such sociocultural influences could facilitate the production of false memories by suggestible individuals' (p30). In recognising cultural forces that might bias people's accounts, while not acknowledging the possibility that he (or Freud) might himself be influenced by other cultural beliefs, notably gender-related ones, Schacter reproduces an asymmetrical model of belief itself, choosing traditional hierarchical authority over an insurgent victims' movement.

Finally, in intensively focusing on and criticising the beliefs and claims of victims, Schacter gives no attention to perpetrators. This avoidance of even naming actors who are predominantly male, while intensively analysing female victims is, of course, another common expression of a gendered narrative (Lamb 1996). Nowhere in his text does Schacter consider or even note the longstanding gender hierarchy of abuse wherein women overwhelmingly are the objects of sexual acts of violence. Nor does he attempt to explain why both rape and childhood sexual abuse are so greatly under-reported (Armstrong 1994) – a fact that would seem to argue against the notion of a social order that was overly attentive to victims' voices. Even though, as Armstrong points out, victims' voices fill the media, the credibility of their stories is still in grave doubt because those voices have been pathologised, privatised and de-politicised by a profit-conscious therapeutic industry whose goals of recruiting new consumers and treating victims do not in anyway come into conflict with the acts of perpetrators and the androcentric legal-political system that sustains their privilege. Armstrong asserts that,

> The focus of incest-as-illness has served as a form of pacification of an otherwise potentially contentious population. [She concludes] Perhaps it is time to reclaim that contentiousness, and to set for ourselves the terms of the debate – not on the grounds of 'sick' or 'well', but on the grounds of a far-too-rampant sexual assault [by men] on children that continues to be quasi-legal (1994: 274).

The complexities of memory and history

History is not an experimental science. No one, Ebbinghaus-like, controls inputs while records of the outputs are inconsistent. Although laboratory memory research can, through the rigours of experimental science, so strip experience of its constituents of time and context that control of the inputs and outputs may be delimited to independent and dependent variables, experiential memory and history rarely unfold within the confines of the lab or the parameters of an experiment. In order to write histories that reproduce some of the complexities of experience, we benefit from more complex guides, like Haaken's *Pillar of Salt* (1998), to understand the intricate intertwinings of personal and collective remembrances. Writing about memory and the relations between images derived from external and internal sources, Haaken says, 'Fact and fiction, like history and mythology, infuse one another, making the boundaries between them imprecise' (1998: 255). While fact constituted scientifically requires confirmation, fiction needs affirmation. Schacter's account affirms Freud's historical narrative about seduction, although neither man's history is confirmed by Freud's own extant writings from 1896.

In the first part of this essay, our critique of Schacter's and Freud's accounts of Freud's work on childhood sexual abuse was driven dialectically by the necessity of uncovering biases in texts which purported to be objective by pointing out systematic inaccuracies and inconsistencies in them. We now return to psychoanalysis to construct a deeper understanding of Freud's abandonment of the seduction theory, an understanding which is based, in part, on psychoanalytic conceptions and which reconstructs Freud's history as a betrayal, in the name of the father, of his women patients' confidence. Following this critical reconstruction of Freud's work, we will then return to Schacter's 'Memory Distortion ...' (1995) and provide a more critically nuanced reading of the cultural myths inscribed in his text.

In the name of the father

Nearly thirty years after supposedly abandoning the seduction theory, Freud wrote that, 'The correct reconstruction ... of ... forgotten experiences of childhood has a great therapeutic effect, whether they permit of objective confirmation or not' (1959 [1926]: 216). This position is remarkably similar to the one he took in his seduction theory papers in which he first named his psychoanalytic method. In fact, Freud's methods remained consistent, and he never wavered in his belief about the importance of analytic interpretations in helping clients construct from dreams, memories, fantasies, symptoms and free associations more coherent and liveable lives. He also continued to maintain that childhood sexual abuse was a contributing factor in adult suffering. What Freud forfeited, when he abandoned the seduction theory, was a belief that never appeared in print in any of his three 1896 works on that theory, the belief that fathers raped their daughters.

In print, Freud refused to name fathers as sexual abusers. In the three 1896 seduction theory papers and in two cases presented in *Studies on Hysteria* (1950 [1895]), Freud named brothers, governesses, servants, nursemaids, teachers, tutors and close relatives, but never fathers. Freud also protected his own father. In referring to findings from his own self-analysis, he wrote to a friend, in 1897, about why he was abandoning his seduction theory. He said that, 'in every case the father, not excluding my own, had to be blamed as a pervert' (1966: 259). The lengths to which Freud went to protect fathers from accusations of abuse is illustrated by a passage in which he discusses the relative contributions of fantasy and reality to memories of sexual abuse. Many years after supposedly abandoning the seduction theory, he writes, 'Phantasies of being seduced are of particular interest, because so often they are not phantasies but real memories' (1963 [1917]: 370). He then claims that such real memories do not happen as frequently as he once thought, and concludes:

> Seduction by an older child or by one of the same age is even more frequent than by an adult; and if in the case of girls who produce such an event in the story of their childhood their father figures fairly regularly as the seducer, there can be no doubt either of the imaginary nature of the accusation ... (p370).

Although Freud almost never sought confirmation outside of analytic sessions for what patients said in session, he clearly and unambiguously states here that older children are often guilty of sexually abusing younger ones, and that he is equally certain that if a woman patient claims her father abused her when she was a girl, she is making it up. Freud's text provides no rationale for making such a marked distinction and no reason why a woman's account of paternal abuse would more likely be a fantasy than would her accounts of abuse by older children. However, Lerman's extensive analysis of Freud's views on women provides a clue to this bias: 'When the total body of his [Freud's] work is examined, the absence of psychological mechanisms dealing with paternal sexual impulses is noteworthy, particularly in view of the fact that the bulk of known criminal cases of incest are between father and daughter' (1986: 59).

In understanding the vicissitudes of memory, Haaken (1998) endorses the psychoanalytic view that what is remembered often has a defensive purpose and what is forgotten returns in disguised form. Using this principal as a guide, we might speculate that Freud at some level knew that fathers raped their daughters, but he could not say so. Therefore, initially in the 1896 seduction theory papers his defence against this knowledge took the form of the complete censorship provided by omission – the name of the father was simply left out of published accounts. However, as Freud became more certain of his theories, more adept at interpretation, and as decades of distance separated him from his seduction theory, his defence became more sophisticated. As was demonstrated in the above quote from 1917, fathers were named as sexual abusers only if such accusations could be discounted as the fantasies of Freud's women patients (Steele 1982; Westerlund 1986).

Returning to Haaken for guidance in trying to comprehend Freud's actions, we are directed by her observations that 'remembering is itself a gendered activity' and that, 'As receptacles and bearers of emotionally laden cultural knowledge, women have historically been both valorised and villainised' (1998: 12). Psychoanalysis and psychiatry share with other patriarchal systems a long tradition of blaming women for personal and social ills (Daly 1978; Lerman 1986). We have seen how Freud's attempts to protect 'the father' from accusations of sexual perversity, and himself from admitting to having played a significant role in constructing the seduction stories of his patients, lead him to assert that it was his women patients who made up such stories and especially when the father was named as the rapist, to declare that such tales were obviously fantasies. Freud's account – that he and fathers are blameless and that women patients are the ones who carry the onus of abuse – is encapsulated in a single passage in his essay on 'Femininity'. He says,

> In the period in which the main interest was directed to discovering infantile sexual traumas, almost all my women patients told me that they had been seduced by their fathers. I was driven to recognise in the end that these reports were untrue … (1964 [1933]: 120).

In this passage, Freud, once again, absolves himself of responsibility by saying, 'my women patients told me'. There is no trace of the fact that in his three 1896 papers he says it was he, himself, who constructed these scenes and that his patients resisted acknowledging his sexual interpretations. However, it should be noted, that unlike the 1896 papers where fathers were never mentioned as perpetrators, they are clearly named here. This may well be because by this time Freud was so certain that women patients were making-up these stories, that he could now openly admit that the most frequently named 'seducers' were the women's fathers.

Having thus cleared himself and fathers of involvement, Freud continues:

> And now we find the phantasy of seduction once more in the pre-Oedipus prehistory of girls; but the seducer is regularly the mother. Here, however, the phantasy touches the ground of reality, for it was really the mother who by her activities over the child's bodily hygiene inevitably stimulated, and perhaps even aroused for the first time, pleasurable sensations in her genitals (1964 [1933]: 20).

If we tie this quote to what immediately precedes it, we see that in this final attempt by Freud to work through the seduction theory, he has succeeded (after almost forty years) in fully absolving fathers of seducing their daughters, by asserting that the real origins of these women's fantasies about their fathers' actions were the unremembered, but sexually stimulating, ministrations of their mothers (Westerlund 1986).

In achieving this resolution in his own history of his work, Freud achieved conformity between his narrative and a common prejudice of his culture: men in authority are protected from the accusations of women by discounting the women's charges as fantasies and in turn blaming women for their own troubles. Even in the face of compelling evidence to the contrary and after publication of numerous books and articles criticising Freud's misogyny, an eminent psychologist and scholar like Schacter, can, with almost no reservations, repeat Freud's account. Only the operation of strong and persistent social forces shaping how we compose our histories could insure such uniformity in the face of overwhelming contravening evidence.

In the name of science

Freud's views on women have been widely criticised, yet his are not an unusual aberration of some pre-feminist misogynist. The same biases permeating Freud's accounts of women's memories of sexual abuse also pervade Schacter's very contemporary work, although they are expressed in different ways. Let us return to Schacter's text to explore how his degendering of the problem of abuse, questioning of women's reliability as witnesses and blaming of victims all combine to serve masculinist interests.

Schacter's account of sexual abuse is notable for its apparently comprehensive degendering of the phenomenon. Not once does Schacter (1995) mention that it is women who Freud blames for having deceived him, that women are far more likely to be victims of childhood sexual abuse than men, and that women's testimonies about all forms of sexual abuse have been discounted both historically and in contemporary society (Armstrong 1994). Schacter consistently and carefully uses the non-gendered terms 'person', 'people' and 'patient(s)' when writing about sexually abused individuals, and even when referring to Freud's clients (whom Freud identified as women) Schacter identifies them simply as 'patients'. Degendering abuse can be seen as a recognition that men too are sexually abused, but in his text it operates to depoliticise a long standing feminist issue by making it gender unspecified or neutral. Gender, for Schacter, is not an operative factor in the phenomenon.

This degendering of abuse would not be as problematic if Schacter did not then couple it with a denigration of women's testimony, a coupling that is, itself, clearly gendered. The three places in his 1995 text where the gender of abuse survivors is identifiable provide compelling evidence for Haaken's (1998) thesis that women's memories are distrusted and their testimony discounted. First, he mentions the George Franklin case in which recovered memories produced by his 'daughter Eileen' (1995: 20) were used to convict him of murder. The credibility of Eileen's testimony was seriously questioned by Loftus and Ketchum (1994), whom Schacter cites. They say that her testimony was 'so skillfully woven within the tapestry of a once-upon-a-time story that no one not even Eileen Franklin can say for sure what really happened' (p40). They conclude that 'Eileen's story is *her* truth, but it is a truth that never happened' (p65).

Schacter's next gendered reference is to the daughter of Gary Romana. Mr Romana won a large jury award when he 'sued his daughter's therapist for implanting false memories of sexual abuse' (1995: 200). The third case and the one male victim Schacter mentions is Ross Cheit, a 'Brown University ethics professor'. Cheit's work is given as an example of one of ' ... several credible reports of individuals who have forgotten and later recovered specific incidents of sexual trauma ... ' (1995: 28). Although there may be gender differences in how abuse is interpreted – men's sexual abuse is sometimes treated less seriously than women's because of conventional views about male invulnerability and female 'passivity and fragility' – there is no reason based on gender why the memories of male and female abuse survivors should not be equally creditable. While both King (1993) and Mendel (1995) say that male victims are reluctant to report abuse and that such accounts are often trivialised and doubted, in this paragraph of Schacter's essay which contains the only three accounts of recovered memories to which he amends a gender reference, it is the testimony of a male academic that Schacter endorses, while the women's accounts are either denied or thrown into doubt.

History and memory, as Haaken contends, are gendered. As shown in Schacter's review of Freud's work and in his own less purposeful accreditation of a male abuse victim's testimony, it is male authorities

– Freud and a Brown professor – who are to be believed and women – Freud's patients and female victims – who are too often doubted. This systematic marginalisation of women's experience and testimony is what Haaken has in mind when she asserts that because of their sense that 'many of the dominant legends and cultural scripts falsify women's experience' many women have rejected such 'conventional accounts' (1998: 57). In decontextualising incest survivor stories by making them real world instances of the more legitimate and controllable laboratory problem of false memory research, Schacter (1995) also engages in another typically gendered practice: he employs the power of the scientific objectivist approach – a perspective often associated with masculinity – to appropriate, relocate and redefine issues that are central to women's lives.

The gender politics of true and false

At the crux of the question of false memories and scientific veracity is *who* has the power to tell socially accepted stories. Within Schacter's text, victims of childhood sexual abuse do not have such power, either because of their female gender or because a small number who claim to have been abused, have lied. Although a small number of scientists, including Freud, have misrepresented their findings or misremembered their own published research, Schacter does not raise a single cautionary note about the prejudices and lies that haunt the history of science.

Near the end of his essay on memory distortion, Schacter writes, '... cultural myths typically become so embedded in the cognitive fabric of a society that it becomes virtually impossible to discern their origin' (1995: 30). Such discernment is one of the tasks of critical histories, and we have used textual analyses to both identify and trace some of the cultural myths, centred around gender, that have shaped Schacter's historical narrative and moulded his presentation of contemporary scientific evidence. We have traced the narrative of Freud's being taken-in, or perhaps seduced, by the sexual stories of his women patients to its source. We have tried to show how that narrative has been sustained because it conforms closely to a deeply embedded, well-rehearsed cultural-sensemaking pattern that is fascinated by, and yet simultaneously doubts and denigrates, the testimony of sexually abused women. This social schema rationalises the power of certain authorities, who have traditionally been men, to adjudicate the veracity of these women's experiences, memories and histories, by declaring them either true or false.

Looking back

Haaken's *Pillar of Salt* has guided our identification of a masculinist, objectivist worldview that dominates Freud's and Schacter's works and has aided us in reflecting on how they, and we, are situated within it. As expressed most earnestly through modern science and technology, this dominant practice has produced – by supplying well-rehearsed facts, scripts, histories and myths – the way in which many of us make sense of ourselves in the world. Haaken's feminist phenomenology also has informed our critical hermeneutic reading of these men's texts by clarifying some narrative devices, common social defences and cultural traditions that sustain and limit the objectivist ideology. Finally, she provides a significantly different perspective from that of Freud or Schacter on incest, memories of it, and its recent historical significance because she tries to understand it from the points-of-view of those who have most often been abused: women. Haaken says, 'Incest acquired a powerful social symbolic function within feminism ... ' both as a means of talking openly about the suffocating constraints of the family and also as a 'potent signifier of seductive, patriarchal authority' (1998: 126). She concludes,

> The incest survivor stands for every woman's seductions under patriarchy, for the myriad daily violations of her sense of self, and for the estrangement so many women experience from their own bodies ... In an era when child sexual abuse has come to represent the violation of the self at the deepest level, this same imagery may be employed to objectify a pervasive sense of anguish (pp180-181).

This is an 'anguish' that can only be exacerbated by approaches investigating childhood sexual abuse which marginalise women's voices by privileging as authoritative those methods professionally controlled by men and the histories of these endeavours authored by men.

Conclusion

Depending as it does on manipulation, observation and control a positivist-experimentalist epistemology will necessarily have difficulties when such discipline cannot be achieved. Extra-laboratorial memory, which is, of course, the way all people experience remembering as personal history, necessarily falls outside the paradigm preferred by experimentally oriented psychologists. We have seen the inaccuracies produced by one experimentalist's positivist methods as he applied them in recounting Freud's seduction theory. These are biases which repeated, and thereby reinforced, Freud's own self-interested accounts of this history. The collusion in these two scientists' accounts tends, as do all fictives, toward a well-rehearsed cultural narrative: blaming women, not men, for women's troubles.

Haaken's thematic construction of this patriarchal historical bias, beginning with the Biblical story of Lot's wife and ending with an analysis of today's recovered/false memory debate, guided an uncovering of common patterns in Schacter's and Freud's work on the recovery of memories of sexual abuse. Because collective memory moves toward a certain limited set of scenarios, critical histories are essential because they call into account such well-worn templates and ask for evidence of their fit with the past. The insight produced by a feminist-phenomenological reading has helped us to identify and question a typical masculinist narrative reproduced in both Freud's and Schacter's positivist accounts of the past. In addition, such critical appraisal reminds us of the dynamic, interdependent boundaries of culture/science, truth/falsity, and personal/collective, helping to revitalise our sense of history and memory as lived-experience always open to reinterpretation, re-plotting, and new understandings.

Notes

1. Haaken's criticism of Bass and Davis' (1992) unbridled certainty in the reality of the recovered memories of sexual abuse is based on her reading of the 'texts' of memory. Whereas Bass and Davis assert that survivors necessarily must believe in the reality of abuse – 'To heal from child sexual abuse you must believe that you were a victim, that the abuse really did take place' (1992: 86) and '... you have to come to terms with the fact that someone did those things to you' (p87) – Haaken says, 'Phenomenologically, however, sexual abuse assumes priority as a causal factor in female disturbances because it symbolises dilemmas common to women – specifically, vulnerability to masculine invasions and subjugation to male assertions of sexual entitlement' (1998: 181). After a re-interpretation of Gizelle's story, one of the accounts in Bass and Davis, Haaken writes, 'There may be, however, a complex interplay of fact and fiction, truth telling and deception, embedded in this narrative of memory retrieval' (1998: 182). For scientific positivists

like Schacter (1995) recovered memories of childhood sexual abuse are troublesome because they might be false, and for feminist positivists like Bass and Davis (1992) recovered memories are almost always certainly true, while for Haaken it is the fantasy of the reality of the abuse that can be established with some certainty. For a recent review of the tensions between feminist positivism and post-structuralism see Enns and Sinacore (2001).

Haaken attempts a synthesis of the 'dialectics of fantasy and reality' (1998: 104) and realises a practical, post-structuralist feminism using hermeneutical-phenomenological methods. While she repeatedly demonstrates that cultural/individual historical narratives are often fractured fabrications – symbolic mixtures of reality and fantasy constructed from diverse phenomena including the often inharmonious needs of the present and artifacts (memories, mementos, dreams and recalled realities) from the past, she is cautious about the 'hysterical poetics' (p106) of the more radical French feminists (see, for example, Marks and de Courtivron 1981). Her clinical goals are more modest than the subversion of phallologocentrism. She has chosen a more practical path of helping women to create progressively more inclusive and generative stories of their personal/collective pasts as they come to understand and free themselves from the repressions/oppressions inscribed by the disciplines of patriarchy on all its mothers-daughters and fathers-sons.

2. In making this argument Schimek does not cite the earlier works of Steele (1982; 1985). We can therefore assume her reading was done without prejudice and can be counted as an independent, unbiased confirmation of Steele's reading. See Westerlund (1986) for a similar interpretation.

References

Armstrong, L. (1994) *Rocking the Cradle of Sexual Politics: What Happened When Women said Incest*, Reading, MA: Addison-Wesley.

Bass, E. and L. Davis (1992) *The Courage to Heal: A Guide for Women Survivors of Child Sexual Abuse*, New York: Harper and Row.

Daly, M. (1978) *Gyn/Ecology: The Metaethics of Radical Feminism*, Boston: Beacon.

Enns, C.Z. and A. Sinacore (2001) 'Feminist Theories', in J. Worell (ed), *The Encyclopedia of Women and Gender* 1, New York: Academic, pp469-480.

Erdelyi, M.H. (1970) *Psychoanalysis: Freud's Cognitive Psychology*, New York: W.H. Freeman and Company.

Fausto-Sterling, A. (2000) *Sexing the Body: Gender Politics and the Construction of Sexuality*, New York: Basic Books.

Freud, S. (1953) 'My Views on the Part Played by Sexuality in the Aetiology of the Neuroses' (1906), in J. Strachey (ed), *The Standard Edition of the Complete Psychological Works of Sigmund Freud*,Vol. 7, London: Hogarth Press, pp271-279.

Freud, S. (1957) 'On the History of the Psycho-analytic Movement' (1914), in J. Strachey (ed), op. cit., Vol. 14, London: Hogarth Press, pp7-66.

Freud, S. (1959) 'An Autobiographical Study' (1925), in J. Strachey (ed), op. cit., Vol. 20, London: Hogarth Press, pp7-70.
Freud, S. (1959) 'The Question of Lay Analysis' (1926), in J. Strachey (ed), op. cit., Vol. 20, London: Hogarth Press, pp183-250.
Freud, S. (1962) 'Heredity and the Aetiology of the Neuroses' (1896a), in J. Strachey (ed), op.cit., Vol. 3,. London: Hogarth Press, pp141-156.
Freud, S. (1962) 'Further Remarks on the Neuropsychoses of Defence' (1896b), in J. Strachey (ed), op.cit., Vol. 3, London: Hogarth Press, pp157-185.
Freud, S. (1962) 'The Aetiology of Hysteria' (1896c), in J. Strachey (ed), op. cit., Vol. 3, London: Hogarth Press, pp187-221.
Freud, S. (1962) 'Screen memories' (1899), in J. Strachey (ed), op. cit.,Vol. 3, London: Hogarth Press, pp299-322.
Freud, S. (1963) 'Introductory Lectures on Psycho-analysis' (1917), in J. Strachey (ed), op. cit., Vol. 16, London: Hogarth Press, pp7-66.
Freud, S. (1964) 'New Introductory Lectures on Psycho-analysis' (1933), in J. Strachey (ed), op.cit., Vol. 22, London: Hogarth Press, pp5-182.
Freud, S. (1966) 'Extracts From the Fliess Papers', in J. Strachey (ed), op. cit., Vol. 1. London: Hogarth Press, pp177-280.
Gadamer, H. G. (1975) *Truth and Method*, New York: Seabury.
Haaken, J. (1998) *Pillar of Salt: Gender, Memory, and the Perils of Looking Back*, New Jersey: Rutgers University Press.
Hacking, I. (1995) *Rewriting the Soul: Multiple Personality and the Science of Memory*, Princeton: Princeton University Press.
Haraway, D. (1989) *Primate Visions: Gender, Race, and Nature in the World of Modern Science*, New York: Routledge.
Harding, S. (1986), *The Science Question in Feminism*, Ithaca: Cornell University Press.
Jones, E. (1953) *The Life and Work of Sigmund Freud*, Vol. 1, New York: Basic.
King, M.B. (1993) 'Male Sexual Assault in Community', in G. Mezey and M. King (eds), *Male Victims of Sexual Assault*, Oxford: Oxford University Press, pp1-12.
Lamb, S. (1996) *The Trouble with Blame: Victims, Perpetrators, and Responsibility*, Cambridge: Harvard University Press.
Lerman, H. (1986) *A Mote in Freud's Eye: From Psychoanalysis to the Psychology of Women*, New York: Springer Publishing Company.
Loftus, E. and K. Ketcham (1994) *The Myth of Repressed Memory*, New York: St. Martin's Press.
Marks, E. and I. de Courtivron, (eds) (1981) *New French Feminism: An anthology*, New York: Schocken.
Masson, J.M. (1984) *The Assault on Truth*, Toronto: Collins Publishers.
Mendel, M.P. (1995) *The Male Survivor: the Impact of Sexual Abuse*, Thousand Oaks, CA: Sage.
Schacter, D.L. (1995) 'Memory Distortions: History and Current Status', in D.L. Schacter (ed), *Memory Distortion: How Minds, Brains, and Societies Reconstruct the Past*, Cambridge: Harvard University Press, pp1-43.
Schiebinger, L. (1993) *Nature's Body: Gender in the Making of Modern Science*, Boston: Beacon.

Schimek, J.G. (1987) 'Fact and Fantasy in the Seduction Theory: Historical Review', *Journal of the American Psychoanalytic Association*, 35: 937-965.

Steele, R.S. (1982) *Freud and Jung: Conflicts of Interpretation*, with consulting editor S.V. Swinney, London: Routledge and Kegan Paul.

Steele, R.S. (1985) 'Paradigm Found: A Deconstruction of the History of the psycho-analytic movement', in C. Buxton (ed), *A History Of Modern Psychology: Concepts, Methods, Viewpoints*, New York: Academic, pp197-220.

Westerlund, E. (1986) 'Freud on Sexual Trauma: An Historical Review of Seduction and Betrayal', *Psychology of Women Quarterly*, 10: 297-310.

Knowing and feeling: new subjectivities and aesthetic experience

Estelle Barrett

An understanding of the relationship between images, words and the body as elaborated by Jeanne Achterberg (1985) underpins the arguments presented in this essay. I will also draw on the work of practitioners and theorists including Gerda Alexander, Sharon M. Hymer, Julia Kristeva, Shaun McNiff, Michael and Nancy Samuels and Gilbert Rose, who suggest that the use of expressive arts in therapy is a means of overcoming a negation of the role of the body and an over-reliance on verbal language in therapeutic practices. Visualisation and imagery are integrated, embodied processes involved in both verbal and non-verbal expressive arts. There is growing evidence that bodily processes activated through artistic and creative practices are intrinsic to reparation and healing. In aesthetic experience, physiological interactions involved in perception, feeling and affect are integrated in complex processes of meaning-making which provide forms for feelings to take. By objectifying the nature and pattern of bodily and emotional responses, the use of expressive arts in therapy promotes mind-body integration crucial to healing, psychic well being and the constitution of an alternative sense of self or subjectivity.

The tendency in traditional psychology to deny the body's role in mediating meaning is based on a general suspicion of the body as irrational matter, and negates a fundamental dimension of thought which is dependent on bodily processes. A number of practitioners and theorists suggest that incorporating expressive arts in therapy is a means of overcoming the negation of the role of the body and an over-reliance on verbal language in psychotherapeutic practices. Visualisation and imagery, which are integrated, embodied processes, are related to both verbal and non-verbal expressive arts. Vital bodily processes engendered through artistic and creative practices are intrinsic to reparation and well being.

With reference to Gilbert J. Rose, Shaun McNiff, Jeanne Achterberg, Julia Kristeva and others, I will consider how a physiognomic response to language and visual images is related to embodied processes. I will argue that physiological interactions involved in perception, feeling and affect are part of the continuum of meaning-making processes which allow feelings to be realised and given external expression. By objectifying the nature and pattern of somatic and emotional responses, the use of expressive arts in therapy promotes mind-body integration crucial to healing, psychic well being and the constitution of new or enhanced subjectivities.

The role of the body and primary processes involved in practices which are broadly defined as 'art' can be understood through an investigation of various medical and psychotherapeutic practices. These approaches incorporate theories of how the human organism processes information produced through its interactions with the physical and social environment. Carl Roger's client-centred approach with its emphasis on process rather than product is an example (Rogers 1961). This approach is concerned with reconnecting modes of producing meaning to the subject's vital biology and unconscious processes. Also pertinent are therapies which incorporate music, dance, the visual and verbal arts, and others, such as Gerda Alexander's method which focuses on bodily and sensory awareness as integral mechanisms of reparation (Alexander 1995).

I suggest that specific practices in the creative and expressive arts are a more deliberate and active intensification of other everyday practices in which these processes occur. Subjectivity, thought, language and the spectrum of 'knowledges' from which cultural experience is realised can be said to be the residues of such practices. Although they are harnessed and incorporated into discourses of social production, these practices do not belong exclusively to that domain but also serve a more immediate function of enablement for individuals that engage in them. They constitute what has been described as the human 'striving to affirm, to maximise its potentialities, its powers, its possibilities, in terms of the concrete options its situation affords it' (Grosz 1994: 13).

I am suggesting that creativity has survival value. This implies a striving for technical mastery not for its own sake, or for mastery over others, but as a function which extends the individual's capacity for change and growth. Michael and Nancy Samuels assert that what has been designated as 'art' is a manifestation of a more inherent and profound tendency of living processes, an intensification of what cybernetic science describes as processes which, at a primary level, operate as an 'automatic creative mechanism' (Samuels and Samuels 1990: 146).

An understanding of the body's intrinsic involvement in creativity is supported by Elizabeth Grosz' view that the body is the centre of perspective, reflection, desire and agency, 'the very stuff of subjectivity' (Grosz 1994: 13). Subjectivity may be posited not as fixity, but as perpetual interaction between the chaos and flux of internal and external environments and the dynamic integration required for the effective functioning of the organism. The processes involved are not exclusively biological. Grosz points out that 'biology must be understood as psychologically pliable' (Grosz 1994: 28), and I have, elsewhere, illustrated through the work of Julia Kristeva and others that somatic processes are always socially mediated. What I am proposing is that the subject be viewed as a process of body/mind and internal/external interplay involving multiple levels of fragmentation and integration required for effective functioning. The notion of interplay moves us away from cultural and social determinism permitting a conception of subjectivity as a fluid, open and unpredictable process of becoming. This perspective reinserts human agency and creative practices into accounts of social change.

Gerda Alexander explains the relationship between bodily or muscular activity, emotions and creativity through notions of tonus and eutony (Alexander 1995: 259). Tonus is the system by which one feels and reacts. It is the capacity for fibre muscles to change in response to effort required for various levels of action. Tonus changes not only with physical effort but also with every emotional change, and is also the basis for all artistic creation and experience (Alexander 1995: 260). Einstein and Nietzsche (amongst others) have been explicit in describing muscular and visual elements as essential to their creative thought processes. Einstein claimed that only when these had reached an adequate level of 'combinatory play' was he able to search for the words to describe the discursive or conceptual content of the process (Rose 1991: 133). Nietzsche commented, 'My most creative moments were always accompanied by unusual muscular activity ... I might often have been seen dancing in those days' (Nietzsche, cited by McNiff 1981: 110).

Alexander extends his explanation of the importance of tonus in creative practices through the notion of eutony (Alexander, 1995: 261). Eutony involves a level of awareness of the body's reactions and responses in relation to the environment. It requires a sense of 'presence' or neutral attitude that permits observations to occur which are not affected by mediated or prior expectations of results. Eutony produces a state of unity and integrity that liberates creative forces. This condition, accompanying creative practice, has been elaborated by Norman Bryson (1983) through his explication of art as interactive labour, Michael Polanyi (1969) through the notion of tacit knowledge and Julia Kristeva (1984) through her elaboration of the influence of bodily drives in creative textual production, a process which she terms *signifiance*. Artist Barbara Bolt has illustrated how this condition is realised in her own practice as a painter through the state of 'working hot'. In this situation sensory and other bodily responses are fully focussed on the demands of the unpredictable and uncontrollable materiality of paint interacting with the environment. Stimuli arise in the heat of the moment to which the painter's creative gesture becomes a reaction that is released from conceptual ways of thinking: 'The process of painting is a response to what happens in the interaction between paint, oil, turps, canvas, gravity, sun, heat, the occasional live beast and my body ... It is working in the heat of the moment' (Bolt 1998: 6).

The operation of 'body knowledge', as it pertains to art and craft, is advanced by Don Ihde's description of artistic practices as 'technics'. Drawing on philosopher Martin Heiddeger's theory of 'praxical knowledge', which asserts the material basis of all knowledge, Ihde describes the process of craft making as embodied practices which mediate and produce meanings and knowledges (Ihde 1990: 3). This view implies that, ultimately, ideas and theory are the result of practice rather than vice versa. It is a perspective that problematises the idea of the mind/body split which underpins overly cognitive and logocentric approaches in psychotherapy.

Gilbert J. Rose supports approaches in therapy that place less emphasis on verbal and cognitive processes and claims that where psychotherapy is most successful it operates as art (Rose 1991: 111). The development of art therapy as a discipline has emerged from the recognition of the expressive arts as therapeutic processes that operate independently and beyond the narrow diagnostic and interpretive limits of traditional psychoanalysis. Sharon M. Hymer has pointed out the therapeutic nature of art and its potential for self-reparation and non-compliance. She notes that the restoration of a person 'includes not only the integration and regulation of self, but also the transformation of self' (Hymer 1983: 61). Hymer suggests that the ambiguous nature of art allows for the individual shaping of feelings and experiences.

Shaun McNiff extends this in his view that the incorporation of expressive arts in psychotherapy is a way of overcoming the denial of the body in conventional psychotherapeutic practices, a denial which has been intensified in society by fixed expectations of action in daily life. Pragmatic and normative demands of everyday interactions limit possibilities for expressive play and communication. This constraint negates a fundamental dimension of thought which is dependent on the body's movement. In therapy people are often treated with programmes that 'manage their behaviour and provide emotional outlets only within the restrictions of controlled discursive speech' (McNiff 1981: 111). This denial of the body in traditional psychoanalysis is derived from a general suspicion of the body as the source of irrational and undesirable behaviour, a view that has been carried over from Victorian society and Freudian notions of subjectivity as repression and antagonism.

Central to the process of reparation is mind/body integration. McNiff suggests that the Descartian splitting of body and mind and subsequent fragmentation and specialisation of disciplines in the humanities and social sciences have produced approaches to health care quite different from earlier holistic practices (McNiff 1981: 111). He adds that the term 'psychotherapy' itself may prove inadequate because it perpetuates the mind/body split. The inclusion of the arts in therapy is believed to be a means of overcoming the effects of this split: 'The arts offer a valuable operational polarity to the use of discursive language in psychotherapy, and allow us to communicate with the emotions in their own language. Their multisensory rhythms must be kept intact rather than be absorbed within the more conventional verbal exchange of psychotherapy' (McNiff 1981: xii).

The incorporation of expressive arts in psychotherapy is associated with an understanding of the crucial role that action, and more specifically interaction with the external environment, plays in the development of body image required for physical and emotional balance. The lived body can be explored through creative practices which allow stored sensory information to interact with immediate experience. This process is central to the development and constant renewal of body image: 'The biological body, if it exists at all, exists for the subject only through the mediation of an image or series of (social/cultural) images of the body and its capacity for movement and action' (Grosz 1994: 141).

The development of body image commences in what Jacques Lacan has described as the mirror phase where the child sees a totalised image of itself as a Gestalt. This sense of wholeness or imaginary anatomy, and the ability to locate oneself in space, is in constant need of renewal. The process can be enhanced through expressive movement as well as other art forms in which visual elements of body schema are integrated into synergetically organised sensations, described by Oliver Sacks as the 'inner music' required for effective functioning of the organism (Sacks 1984). Sacks' metaphor promotes an understanding of imagery as an aspect of complex sensory processes that go beyond notions of static visualisation.

The recognition of play and art as psychotherapeutic processes in their own right has brought into question Freudian psychopathological interpretations of the content of art practice. The psychosexual orientation of Freudian theory posits all art as emanating from unconscious childhood experiences and as a projection of sexual conflicts, leaving little room for alternative explanations. McNiff claims that sexual conflict and childhood trauma are not the only motivations for art. Furthermore, 'The assertive action of art offers an alternative to passive resignation to psychopathology and personal dysfunction ... Art's value lies in its ability to transform psychopathology and emotional conflict into meaningful action' (McNiff 1981: 30).

Because of excessive emphasis on hidden motives, interpreters of art have given insufficient attention to explanations provided by artists themselves. Freudian interpretations of art have been developed by non-artists who have adapted visual artworks to psycho-diagnostic testing for the purpose of supporting their psychological theories (McNiff 1981: 153).

The move away from the therapist's interpretation initiated by Margaret Naumburg in the 1940s has revealed that personal symbols, emerging from the subject's creative practices and experimentation, followed by self-reflection and interpretation, provide a lasting manifestation of balance and order which has a parallel effect on consciousness. Emotional crises and other conflicts disrupt and fragment the perceptual process, and one of the goals of introducing the arts to therapy is to restore a sense of order within the sensory modalities. All of the arts, including visual arts and poetry, are a means of extending kinesis and inner movement. McNiff suggests that the term 'visual art' is misleading, since the graphic and plastic arts are both tactile and visual. The same may be said of poetry and its relation to body kinesis via synaesthetic responses. Hence, 'All of the arts in therapy must repossess the body if they are to actualise their healing powers fully. The denial of body ... is but symptomatic of the lack of mind body integration within society at large' (McNiff 1981: 111).

Inspiration comprises one element of the creative process. However it is one that may be readily dissipated without structure and integration. The ego must relax control so that inspiration can come from primary process sensations, and, as has already been mentioned, artists put themselves in situations where creative action involves letting go of conscious control and becoming immersed in sensory activities. Elsewhere I have elaborated, through various psychological theories of art including Gestalt theory, the way in which colour line and form induce processes of tension and relief that involve the integration of physiological, emotional and cognitive integration (Barrett 1996).

Jeanne Achterberg suggests that imagery produced in creative practices integrates mind/body processes promoting both mental and physical well being. Achterberg describes imagery, or the stuff of the imagination, as the 'communication mechanism' between perception, emotion and bodily change (Achterberg 1985). Again, this view of imagery is not confined to notions of visualisation, but implies particular phases of sensory activity. Imagery has profound and multiple effects on the body. For example memories of a lover's scent may simultaneously cause the release of hormones and other chemicals associated with emotions. Visualisations of presenting a speech or of competing in a physical event are accompanied by muscular change, activation of sweat glands, increased blood pressure and alteration of brain waves.

It can be said that the image represents a phase of intensity that occurs in processes that mediate between verbal or conceptual thought and physiological change. The process of image production may be viewed as an intermediary phase of complex processes influenced by various parts of the brain. Whilst such processes are not fully understood, the advent of electrode technology and chemical trace techniques have provided a theoretical framework by which these processes may, at least provisionally, be explained (Achterberg 1985: 116).

Achterberg's framework is one which demonstrates how images are inextricably woven into the fabric of the brain and the body. Her model presents an outline of the transformations that occur between mind and matter. It enables a view of imagination as a construct, 'a non-thing which is measured only through the observable behaviours of persons and their societies' (Achterberg 1985: 115). This view avoids casting the imagination in mystical terms or positing its operation in a purely biological framework. An understanding of imagination in this context has been applied in well-documented forms of medical treatment and therapy. Achterberg's successes with bio-feedback and visualisation techniques in the treatment of cancer and other patients are evidence of the complex role of imagery in therapeutic practices. These applications provide a basis for understanding the flow between physiological processes, visual imagery, emotion, thought and language. In simple terms, one can conceive of a multi-dimensional flow between physiological processes, images and words or conceptual thought: (body<—->image<—->word).

Suzanne Langer adds to Achterberg's explanation in her analogy of steam, water and ice, used to explain the relationship between physiological and psychological states. Langer puts forward a view of the relationship as one involving quality and quantity rather than difference and opposition. Affect, imagery and thought are not added factors, nor are they separate from physiological processes, but are complex, vital interactions, phases or modes of experience registering divergent stimuli through various levels of activity in the cortex (Langer 1967: 9).

The primacy attributed to imagery as a 'bridging' mechanism operating between bodily processes and thought is tied to its relation to language which is believed to have initially been based on images. 'Words functioned to evoke images' (Samuels and Samuels 1990: 13).

Words have come to serve the additional function of distancing the self from experience. Naming and categorising interfere with a fuller perception of objects or 'seeing with the mind's eye' – characterised by an 'inexhaustible and ineffable quality, by the profoundest interest in the object' (Samuels and Samuels 1990: 19). Because words as instruments of informational exchange have become more removed from experience, they no longer readily trigger the sensations of objects to which they may refer. The use and development of visualisation has largely been superseded by the development of language as a naming device. Central to the practices of healing and therapy that incorporate imagery is the development of techniques for improving the capacity for embodied visualisation in clients and patients.

It can thus be claimed that words or language do not belong exclusively to the domain of the cognitive or conceptual. Gestalt drive and its relation to tension and the release of tension have been shown to operate in response to language. Words affect the body not only as ideas or concepts, but also as 'objects'.

It has also been suggested that the physiognomic perception of words is a means by which semantic innovation is achieved: 'A physiognomic perception of words represents an extreme expansion of semantic space. It involves a rich unfolding of meanings over those twilight regions of meaning which mostly remain suppressed' (Kreitler and Kreitler 1979: 227).

Physiognomic response to language involves responding to the word or words with an integrated body/mind. J.E. Downey as well as Hans and Shulamith Kreitler have shown that this occurs more readily when one is 'conversing to oneself and in poetic language' (Kreitler and Kreitler 1979: 228). This notion of communicating with the self, and its association with semantic innovation, has been theorised by Yuri Lotman (1990) as the 'I-I' code of autocommunication, which I have already discussed in some detail in relation to Julia Kristeva's theory of the interrelationship between symbolic and semiotic dimensions of language (Barrett 1996). Purely formal qualities of language, such as rhythm, rhyme, varying combinations of particular vowel and consonant sounds, patterns of repetition, juxtaposition and other stylistic devices of languages that operate primarily through the perception of sound have been shown to evoke similar states of arousal to those produced in confrontation with visual forms.

Gilbert Rose has suggested that in certain therapeutic practices this alternative mode of language comes into play through what he terms the 'plasticity of words' (Rose 1991). By the time most thought reaches the point of ordinary discourse much of its raw physicality has been bleached out and the process of naming further obscures the perceptual impact of words. The plasticity of words is derived from the combination of physical sounds, affective weight and intellectual content. The aesthetic plasticity of words makes it possible to combine and correlate these seemingly disparate aspects of information-processing and links various dichotomies making them available for conscious reflection. In this process familiar objects and words can assume different features and take on unusual characteristics. This use of language operates as 'art' and accomplishes what the information exchange function of language cannot readily do. 'It provides forms for feelings to take, it objectifies and presents the nature and patterns of sensitive emotional life' (Rose 1991: 32).

The recognition that creativity and preverbal bodily processes are inextricably entwined in the creative process has been the impetus for a move towards more client-centred forms of therapy, or those therapeutic practices which permit, 'a free experiencing of the actual sensory and visceral reactions of the organism' (Rogers 1961: 80). Rogers suggests this experiencing may be viewed as a growth tendency or an urge which is evident in organic and human life to enhance, expand and extend the organism or the self. It is a mode of experiencing that is an alternative to construing experience in rigid ways (which are perceived as external facts) and it places personal power under personal control. It encompasses the constant movement of change and adaptation and activates preverbal, unconscious processes of desire linked to bodily drives.

I have attempted to show that creative practice involves an integration and an interplay between mind and body, language and materiality. The movement towards client-centred forms of therapy and the incorporation of the creative arts in therapy indicates a recognition of this integration as vital to the reparative process. Such processes in therapy facilitate the production of embodied or situated knowledges in which alternative subjectivities are articulated. This is realised through an interplay between given constructions of the self through social discourses and a perpetual striving in the human organism to maximise its potential despite limits placed on it by social mechanisms. Accordingly, these processes may be viewed as praxis which results from the intrinsic creativity and tacit knowledge of the body.

References

Alexander, G. (1995), 'The Holistic Discovery Of Total Person' in Don Hanlon Johnson (ed), *Bone Breath And Gesture*, 6, Berkeley, California: North Atlantic Books, pp273- 293.

Achterberg, J. (1985) *Imagery And Healing: Shamanism And Modern Medicine*, London: New Science Library.

Barrett, E. (1996) *Subjectivity and art* (unpublished Ph.D. thesis), Western Australia: Murdoch University.

Bolt, B. (1998) *Technics* (exhibition catalogue), Western Australia: Craftwest Centre for Contemporary Art.

Bryson, N. (1983) *Vision And Painting: The Logic Of The Gaze*, London: Macmillan Press.

Grosz, E. (1994) *Volatile Bodies: Towards A Corporeal Feminism*, Sydney: Allen & Unwin.

Hymer, S.M. (1983) 'The therapeutic nature of art in self-reparation', in *Psychoanalytical Review*, Spring, Vol. 70, 1: 57-68.

Ihde, D. (1990) *Technology And The Live World: From Garden To Earth*, Indiana: Indiana University Press.

Kreitler, H. and S. Kreitler (1979) *Psychology Of The Arts*, Durham: Duke University Press.

Kristeva, J. (1984) *Revolution In Poetic Language*, Margaret Waller (trans), New York: Columbia University Press.

Langer, S. (1967) *Mind: An Essay On Human Feeling*, Volume 1, Baltimore: John Hopkins Press.

Lotman, Y. (1990) *The Universe Of The Mind*, A. Shukman (trans) Bloomington: Indiana University Press.

McNiff, S. (1981) *The Arts And Psychotherapy*, Illinois: Charles C. Thomas Publisher.

Polanyi, M. (1969) *Knowing And Being*, Chicago: University of Chicago Press.

Rogers, C. (1961) *On Becoming A Person: A Therapist's View Of Psychotherapy*, Boston: Houghton Mifflin.

Rose, G. (1991) 'Abstract Art And Emotion: Expressive Form And The Sense Of Wholeness', in *Journal of the American Psychoanalytical Association* Volume 39 (1): 131-156.

Sacks, O. (1984) *A Leg To Stand On*, London: Gerald Duckworth & Co. Ltd.

Samuels, M.D. and N. Samuels (1990) *Seeing With The Mind's Eye*, New York: Random House.

TREE: a short story

William E. Cross, Jr

The glare of the media's preoccupation with black male dysfunctionality blinds one to the discovery that the black community, as the late Edwin Barnes (1972) once wrote, is more typically the site of positive self-concept development for black people in general, and, in the context of the current work, black boys and men in particular. In a short story grounded in the everyday comings and goings of a mythical black barbershop on the South Side of Chicago, black men voice their heterosexual and homoerotic tendencies; celebrate the common man; tell each other lies – in the tradition of Zora Neale-Hurston; allow a newly minted PhD to re-enter his space and place in the shop; reflect on the cultural conflicts that accompany higher education; help a young pre-adolescent find relief from excruciating shyness; and meditate about the death of Black Mothers. The story is not so much an 'analysis' as it is a series of jazz riffs that are meant to 'happen' to the reader. It is a story of how blacks help each other discover and sustain their humanity, despite everyday racism.

He swung me around and pressed his chest and stomach close to my face. As he raised his arms, I could detect that intriguing fusion of cheap but pleasant cologne and his base body odour that results in a very distinctive 'musk'. Sometimes he startled me, circling my body with great dexterity and athleticism, and other times he was clumsy, awkward, and lacking in grace. On occasion, he was quite simply too rough, and the sting of small cuts and nicks would generate a tear or two, though as a young boy, I had already learned to take stuff, without vocalising pain and discomfort. I never felt abused, in danger or mistrustful, but certainly the first few times, I simply did not understand his privilege, his right to shift me around, from one side to another, from one angle to another, his right to touch in a fashion that I thought was reserved for Mom or my Sisters. Here was this man, this barber, who could enter into my 'space' and for a half hour or so, and under the guise of cutting my hair, came as close as anything to giving me a bath without water.

Of course, the insinuated sensuality of my youthful haircuts gave way to a more welcomed treat, as an adult. Many black men will not admit it, but the entire process of the haircut culminates in a massage, which, if the truth be told, is scintillating. The barber splashes a distinctive tonic into the palm of one hand and then in a flash, he smacks his hands together, as if to further liquefy the tonic. Finally those strong hands attack the customer's head. He rubs and squeezes for only a few seconds, but the pressure of his hands and fingers and the slight burn and tingle of the tonic offers a special physical treat. If there is a time, during the process, when a man closes his eyes, it is then.

The taxi jolts to a stop, jarring me from my daydream about youthful experiences while seated in the barber's chair. The appearance of the taxi in front of the shop and its huge bay window visually announces my presence, my arrival at the *Johnson & Sons BarberShop*. No pretence, just a barbershop. The Johnson Brothers played with other names and '*Everyman's Shop*' almost won out. But, when their Father died, Mrs Johnson requested that they call it Johnson & Sons, for in her mind it stretched Roy's stay on earth. Most people knew that Sam and Kenny Johnson were the grown boys of Minnie and Roy Johnson. Roy cut hair at the *HairShack* for nearly thirty years, making and saving enough money to send both boys to college and purchase a small two-storey home near McCosh Elementary School. They lived just down the way from Auntie Kathleen, the most pretentious light skinned black woman in all of the South Side of Chicago. Roy was just the opposite and he wore his blackness like a suit of gold and silver and folks knew darn well that he caught hell, down in Philadelphia, Mississippi. White folks sweated in Roy's presence, so powerful was his display of self-pride and negritude.

Initially, Roy became depressed when the Sons dropped out of college to take over his modest four-chair shop on Cottage Grove. He could not imagine how they wanted to repeat his life, his drudgery, and the sense of being trapped by an inferior and limited education. Before he died, back in 1993, the whole picture changed, when Sam and Kenny opened their six-chair shop in the new three-storey building that anchored the new strip mall known as the J-Sons Shopping Mall. Roy cried at the opening ceremony.

The Johnson sons loved the art of black barbering and the atmosphere of the shop itself. As Shorties (little kids), Minnie would not allow them to stay long at the shop, for she feared the consequences of premature exposure to the raw side of male machinations. Minnie knew that the shop was a very special place wherein black men transacted not only their blackness and sense of community – values she could easily embrace – but their sexuality, self-esteem, and exaggerated Bravado. She recalled slipping into the shop unnoticed, during the climax of one of those black male bonding sessions, and though she kept her cool, she was nearly floored by the language, animation and unbridled crudeness.

But Roy persisted and soon his two young sons found themselves atop the shoeshine stand in the back of the shop, taking in just about everything. Eventually, as their arms grew stronger, they took over the shoeshine concession and thereafter had a constant jingle in their pockets. Of course, Roy and Minnie made them save most of their earnings.

Ken and Sam sat about three feet off the ground and looked around at the shop. To them, it was less a shop and more a stage, a place of performance, of high drama. Who needed BET, MTV, ESPN, or CNN, for that matter, when the kids had the shop. The late Harold Washington kicked off his campaign for mayor of Chicago in the shop, Jesse Jackson was and remains a steady customer, along with his son, who is now a Congressional representative from the South Side, and there was that amazing day when MLK stopped in for a shoeshine. Attorney Robert L. Tucker often explained the latest games white politicians were trying to run on the community. When Robert felt up to it, he would tell stories about the deep south that caused Ken and Sam to laugh till they cried. Oscar Peterson always made it a point to stop by, in between tickling the keys at the London House; Ray Brown once unpacked his bass and played for an hour; Jerry Butler often came in and just hung out for hours on end. A local favourite, Ramsey Lewis, charmed everyone with his cool self. Gerry Jackson, the self-made black historian, who claims to have known J.A. Rogers, often held the group in rapture, with tales of black accomplishments seldom referenced in textbooks.

Of course, what would a black barbershop be like without its visitors from the world of sports, both real and imagined? Real in the sense that, there before Ken and Sam might stand the likes of Floyd Patterson or Sugar Ray Robinson; and imagined to the extent that, constantly going in and out of the shop were janitors, bus drivers, mailmen and homeless folks, with the following label written across their foreheads: 'He was as good an athlete as so and so'. Ronald Green or the man they called 'Shoes' was such a figure. Shoes was said to be the best black basketball player never to play in the NBA. Sam and Ken saw him daily, at the back of the shop, when Shoes jumped off the sanitation truck to pick up garbage; the J-Sons once told their Dad they could never look directly at Shoes for too long, because he had the most vacant and lifeless eyes. More fun was old-man Josh Brown, whose memories of the black baseball league preoccupied the Shop regulars too many times to count. And then there were folks from the underside of black life: the likes of Rufus or Karl would describe the latest run-in with the police, or Joe-Silk, Smooth Lover Willy, or PaPa Goochee provided the spellbinding descriptions of the player's life.

But it was Leroy Short who owned the stage, insofar as male rawness was concerned. No one, I mean no one, could tell a story of love, lust and conquest as did Leroy. When others rapped, there was always some competing chatter in one or two corners of the shop, but when Papa Short started to get into the rhythm of his latest conquest, all mouths closed tight. Short could make you hear women's groans, his visualisation made pictures from *Jet* seem tame, and at certain turns in his monologue, one could literally smell the woman's sweat or perfume, and taste her love juices. And he loved every woman he made love to but showed never a grain of commitment to any one. At some point during his storytelling, smoke began to rise from the heads and out of the ears of every man in the shop. After a particularly good evening of love making, Minnie teased Roy by suggesting that he had learned some new stuff from one of Leroy's tales of conquest. At first Roy was annoyed but then he and Minnie laughed so hard, they fell off the bed and woke the boys. For some strange reason, the Sons had a sudden increase in their allowance for a week or two.

Most of Short's monologue went over the heads of Roy and Kenny. Their favourite was Yasser Williams. Yasser worked in the homes of really rich white folks and he spun stories of white stupidity, white ignorance, white vulnerability, white craziness and white defeat. He levelled white folks and made them less powerful and more human.

Jesus, he made people laugh and laugh to the point they almost lost sight of the fact that many of the whites about whom he was speaking were stone-cold racists.

After high school, Kenny and Sam headed for college and a 'brighter' future. Sam was one year short of graduating from Morehouse and Kenny, the younger sibling by two years, was a sophomore at Cornell University, majoring in business and accounting. They both found themselves talking on the phone about the impact of reading Carter G. Woodson's sometimes rambling and tautological treatise on the *Miseducation of the Negro.* They shared how much they loved their dad, and were intrigued by his advanced perspective on what makes for a successful business and a strong community. Their vision of the future involved taking up where Roy left off, and to move in an aggressive economic way to take ownership of the land and property that surrounded the original shop. Sam and Kenny's dream is to become millionaires by age forty, but their daily avocation, their respite, their site of personal meaning and playfulness is the barbershop.

And what a shop it is. Its twenty-five by seventy foot dimensions are huge, compared to most shops. To the left is a bank of six barber's chairs (it can accommodate far more). The first five are very modern, with every conceivable gizmo attached. The sixth chair is an antique. It is the centrepiece of what everyone calls Roy's corner. It replicates every aspect of the workspace Roy had in the original shop. For about a year or so following Roy's passing, each morning found Minnie dusting and checking all the cutting implements, in anticipation of a visit by his spirit. At first the customers did not know what to make of Minnie's actions and were awkward observers and reluctant participants. But Minnie encouraged them to engage Roy's memory, and that meant striking up a conversation with Roy's spirit. As Minnie walked in the door, invariably one of the old timers found a way to recall a memorable conversation he once held with Roy and before you knew it, he was acting out the exchange. James Cheeks had Roy's voice down to a 'T' and he could almost raise the hair on your back, so real was his imitation. The topics were wide ranging, from the silly to philosophical to joyful. It was a surreal way to start the day, but Minnie, who loved Roy to the depth of her soul, felt refreshed by the daily ritual. After a fashion, Minnie stopped this ritual; she came to terms with his death.

Toward the back of the shop, right next to Roy's corner, is a two-seat shoeshine stand with brass ornamentation, which Dewitt, a slow-minded middle-aged man from the neighbourhood, runs to perfection. Dewitt was once an egghead, but after a terrible car accident, his IQ dropped from 140 to below 85. He had the wrong name to befall such a disaster and in short order, a few of the neighbourhood kids were calling him Dewitt the Dimwit. At first his family coveted his every move but they finally relented and allowed him to 'work' at the barbershop. His injury took nothing away from his dexterity and in short order his reputation preceded him. He can rehabilitate any pair of shoes and his general shine leaves a sparkle that lasts for up to thirty days! On the days they are scheduled to get a cut, labourers remember to bring their 'Sunday-go-to-meetin' shoes and some, looking rather hilarious in make-shift day labour clothes and Stacy Adams pin-toes, wear their good shoes into the shop, having changed shoes in their trucks or cars. On rare occasions, a stone fox comes in for a shine. Dewitt can keep his focus, even when a black women's private essence is looking him dead in the eye. However, the generally raucous bystanders slip into a strange silence, when a Fox with a short skirt climbs up on one of Dewitt's chairs. As she exits the shop, her shoes all a twinkle from Dewitt's magic, the men seem to participate in symbolic masturbation, as each takes turn describing how much leg and thigh they think they saw. Of course, certain exhibitionists know full well what is happening, and one can imagine her lady friends waiting in a nearby coffee shop to compare notes on the collective insanity of the gawking dudes.

Day in and day out, Dewitt smiles and follows the flow of the group, so pleased with himself that he has two families: His Mom and Dad, who never abandoned him, and the brothers at the shop, who create a daily space for him that involves adult love, acceptance, affection and laughter. I'm not certain that some of the other customers, who are functioning with all their marbles, do not envy Dewitt's situation.

To the right of Dewitt's stall is an amazing, hand crafted display case containing hair products from firms that are black owned. Kenny and Sam make it a point to test every hair product imaginable, but most intriguing is the care with which they display the products. The case measures about five feet wide, four feet tall, and two feet deep. The wood is commonplace but treated with a rich mahogany stain. The glow of the wood, combined with indirect lighting inside the case, makes even the most inexpensive products seem, well, expensive. About 10 per cent of their yearly profits are derived from hair product sales. Women, especially, women, come from miles around not simply to buy certain items, but to pump Ken and Sam, for information about the special needs of their hair. Many a husband confesses to going out of his way to engage the shop's services, at the insistence of their wives, who demand that the J-Sons be supported. Of course, once they get a haircut by either Ken or Sam, their resistance fades.

There is considerable space between the barber's chairs and the row of chairs that face the barbers, where waiting customers sit. In the expansive space above the chairs and the twelve foot ceiling are displayed various paintings and works of art by black students from nearby Chicago State University and the Chicago School of Fine Art. The chairs are moveable and at the far end, where Dewitt operates and just before the hallway that leads to the bathrooms, chairs have been arranged to accommodate a checkers game and a chess set. The little game tables have well-worn mechanical timers, which, after making his move, a player presses, starting the thirty or sixty second time-window, for his opponent's move. In the summer, the games and tables are set-up just outside the shop's bay window. Between getting a haircut and watching the games, many a customer has turned a thirty-minute haircut into an unplanned four-hour visit. It's not always clear what is the main attraction: The competence of certain players, or the signifying skills of others. In any case, for every game completed, at least ten rounds of the dozens also unfold.

The J-Sons selected bold black and white tiles to decorate the floor. In the middle of the shop are four purple coloured tiles, and flowing from the entranceway is a three-by-six foot strip of bright red carpeting, set into the floor itself, so as to minimise the chance of a person's tripping. The carpeting signals the welcoming of every man who enters the shop, regardless of his status in the community. On the other hand, the purple tiles mark the spot where each customer must stand immediately after his cut. He stands on the purple tiles and waits for the approval of everyone in the shop. If something is off centre, neither Ken nor Sam take offence and a touch-up or refinement follows. The customer again hits the spot, and approval is now forthcoming. For the most part, Sam and Ken get it right the first time. Then, someone, often Sam or Kenny, occasionally Dewitt and frequently one of the old timers who sits in the shop all day long, makes this comment: 'You are looking rather special, (name of customer), and if you take care of yourself, your wife, your children and your community, then maybe we will welcome you back the next time!' Each observer finds a way to play the statement like a jazz artist, so there are a thousand versions of the script.

One can only imagine how a customer feels being greeted by the red carpet, saluted by a chorus of hellos and friendly significations, flooded with images of black art, a shoe shine that overpowers one's field of vision, a bathroom cleaner than the ones at home, conversation unique to any other setting, a haircut that transforms even the most homely dude into a prince, and a parting salutation that lifts the spirit.

I could see Ken Johnson leaning awkwardly around his customer's shoulders to get a glance at me stepping from the cab. Few customers arrive by taxi and Kenny surmises that this is someone going out of his way. The J-Sons appreciate such efforts. They want to provide a class act that will draw customers back to the community. This is surely my case, for it would be much more convenient to be serviced by a shop near my suburban home. Like others, I am not shy about 'experimenting' with barbers closer to where I live. Kenny always knows when I have gone astray, so to speak. I will be absent for twice the amount of time between cuts. The experiment always fails, and there is nothing more destabilising to one's sense of well being than a bad haircut. I am coming off such an experiment, but my hair is now long enough to be rehabilitated by Kenny's magical hands and clippers.

Ken stoops over and twists his body so that his eyes can better see around the posters and signs that dot nearly a third of the shop's bay window – people refer to the shop window as the community bulletin board announcing everything from concerts by Puff Daddy or Little Kim or lectures by Na'im Akbar or Badi Foster. At that special moment of recognition, he stands straight up and turns to the row of men on the opposite side of the barbers' chairs. I can see his lips form the words: 'Hey, it's the professor', as folks in the shop are fond of calling me.

Social mobility is hard on the soul; it fractionates one's allegiances. Born and raised in the ghetto, my Princeton doctorate has taken me far beyond the boundaries of the community that received me from my Mom's bosom; nurtured me in segregated schools that were pregnant with acceptance, love and motivation; shaped and rocked my soul, during Sunday morning church services; taught me how to protect my self-esteem when confronted with racist ideas; and, ironically, pushed me toward the white world, in anticipation that once successful, I would never forget my roots and find a way to pay back the community a thousand times over. What the black community has never learned to accept, is that social mobility changes a person in a fundamental way. I speak not of deracination, but of outgrowing the provinciality of one's ethnicity, as the lenses of multiculturalism, biraciality, and gender and class sensitivity reconfigure one's worldview. You see and feel things differently. It is not that one becomes 'better' – just 'different'. I still laugh at Mr Short's stories but I see and feel his sexism; Papa Goochee's gay jokes remain imaginative but no less homophobic; Gerry Jackson's home-grown black history is as truthful as it is too linear and too one-sided; and my cluster of white, Asian, Jewish and Native American friends and lovers position me beyond the pale of Afrocentricity, even when that is not my conscious intent. The fact of the matter is I no longer prefer and can no longer function, twenty-four hours a day, in a totally black environment. Having lived the ghetto and experienced the world, I like elements of both.

Yet I return, time and again. First, because, for all the progress that has been made, not only are white men unable to jump very high, they still cannot cut black hair! But beyond the practicality of it all, I cannot possibly explain to others or to myself, for that matter, just how exhilarating and comforting it is to enter a black barbershop and feel the warmth and acceptance of a large group of black men. In the United States and the Western world in general, much is made of self-acceptance, self-accomplishment and self-esteem. However, for such a universally despised group, as we black men are, self-acceptance is only part of the solution. It is not enough for me to accept myself in the privacy of my inner psyche, I need public spaces where I am publicly recognised, and publicly roasted or played with, in a loving and accepting way. Going to a black barbershop does not satiate my needs, but it goes a long way. I go back because I must and when I leave, I feel better, less fractionated, more whole and at peace with myself, as an individual and as an icon of black success. And when I enter our space – their space – I experience no difficulty in accepting Short, Papa Goochee or whoever, on their own terms. I can no longer speak their voice without experiencing some philosophical perturbation, but I have not lost the ability to 'hear' them.

After I received my doctorate, I had to re-negotiate my 'place' in the shop and my re-acceptance came in the aftermath of a personal tragedy. When Mom died, my sisters said that as the oldest son, I had to speak for the family. Two weeks after the funeral, I was climbing out of

Kenny's chair, and I gave him a copy of the eulogy I had written. I told him that I tried to capture the passing of everyone's Mom, to pay homage to all overlooked black washerwomen, maids and factory workers. Someone else's servants were our Mothers! I found out later that he read, aloud, the entire statement to the whole group and had copies made and set next to the door, in the bay window. Word got back to me that one particular passage struck a chord with everyone in the shop. In the passage, God explains to the Angels why Margaret, a washerwoman, is accorded a Royal reception, at the Gates of Heaven:

> 'My children, this is not a commoner. When she was born, I gave her a thousand talents and a million charms and in the history of earthly affairs, she surely would have gone far had it not been for the colour of her skin and her African heritage. But look children, she did not despair and sink into nihilism. Can you not see the magnificence of her earthly efforts in the distinctive features of her children? She used a painter's brush to colour their emotions, the poet's ways to sculpture their character and the scholar's insight to fill the depth of their intellect and intuition. And what manner of art or fame could match the love and devotion she gave to each? Like so many Afro-American mothers, Margaret took all those charms and talents and poured them into her family life, and I dare say I have grown tired of their lack of recognition. And so I mark her passing and stir my memories of the many beautiful Black Mothers who have gone before her'. Pausing for a moment he continued (instructs the Angels), 'Take this crown and place it upon her head'.
>
> The Angels took the crown of African Violets and slowly put it on Margaret's halo of white and gray hair. As they did, they could see that each of the small vague figures in the foreground of Margaret's image, those spirits from God's memory (images of other Black women), also appeared to adorn crowns. At that instance, God spoke again and his voice thundered a joyous affirmation: 'Hark, I bring (to Heaven) not a commoner, but an African Queen!'

Entering the shop today, I feel as welcomed as anyone. I linger, while standing on the red carpet, and am greeted with catcalls and a chorus of voices saying, 'What's Happening'. By the time I reach Dewitt's stand for my shoeshine, I exchange high-fives with everyone in the shop. My comfort level makes me all the less prepared for what will transpire over the next sixty minutes.

Mostly regulars are present: PaPa Goochee, a local pimp, decked out in a garish purple and white suit, with white fake fur on the rim of his matching purple hat; Gerry Jackson, the resident black historian, who, while never attending college, has read more books on black history than most accomplished scholars; John Sinclair, whose background is a mystery to everyone – when he's not around we call him the Creeper; a real surprise is Mr Short's presence, as he is seldom around on weekdays; he just turned seventy-five and recently had a hip replacement but all indications are that he's still going strong to the basket; of course Dewitt is there, along with several youthful customers, each of whom is currently being given a haircut by Ken and Sam, respectively.

Lester, a bright eyed youth on the cusp of that hormonal explosion called adolescence, is seated in Ken's chair. After my welcoming fades and blends into the greeting for the next customer, I become aware that something is amiss; the atmosphere is simply off centre but the reason is unclear. Then I notice that Mr Short and Papa Goochee are trying to hear what Ken is whispering to Lester, and Lester looks like he is about to break into tears. Ken takes hold of the situation and says: 'Lester, I think I may have nicked you, just behind your (left) ear – why don't you go to the bathroom and put some water on it'. Now Ken has all that is needed to treat cuts and nicks, right there at his fingertips, so his directive simply confirms to all that Lester is going through some changes. When Lester moves out of ear-shot and disappears into the bathroom, Ken says: 'You know Lester is an orphan and he's being raised by Mama Tuere, who is a Pentecostal, and never permits open discussions about sex. The boy's juices are starting to flow and he's feeling like a complete idiot around girls. He thinks he's the most shy and sexually naive person alive'. 'Jesus', Ken continues in exasperation, 'what do I tell him? He says he recently tried to kiss a girl and missed her lips and practically bit off her nose, instead' (groans are expressed by some of the regulars).

Mr Short leans forward on his chair but before he can get a word in edge wise, the entire room is filled with waving arms, as a gesture to Mr Short to remain silent (to shut the fuck up). But Short persists and says: 'Look, give me a break; I am well aware that this kid is not ready for my advice and counsel' (everyone breaks into laughter).

'Well then,' asks Papa Goochee, 'are you seeking the spotlight or what?'

'No, No, No, I'm not focusing on me, I was going to recommend that the Professor get involved', says Short. I respond: 'Jesus, Short, Why me?'

Mr Short replies 'Look, up until this Lester character came along, you have got to be the most shy and socially backward person we know (laughter from group) and surely you must know some story that will provide this boy with some insight and relief' (laughter, again).

Ken chimes in, 'Short's right. This kid sees you as someone special; when his Mom died six months ago, I gave him a copy of the eulogy you wrote and he carries it around with him all the time. Lester needs to know that there's nothing wrong with being shy. Chris (my name is Christopher but Ken calls me Chris), remember that story you told me in confidence last year, about the tree?' (a moan of curiosity rolls across the room).

I respond: 'Oh no you don't, you're not going to get me to tell that story in front of this group!'

'The boy needs to know that even someone of your stature can be shy and that the world does not come to an end, when one makes a social mistake, like kissing a girl's nose, instead of her lips' (broad laughter).

Short asks: 'You been holding out on us, Professor?' (laughter and one senses a growing level of curiosity, among the group).

Before I could answer, Lester turns the corner and is back in the room. Ken signals for me to start my rap. Mr Short is sitting three chairs down from me and without warning he looks over and says: 'Professor, what is this tree story I have been hearing about, fill me in on the details. Is it a true story or what?' I pause and find the strength to sink deep into my actor role, my performance persona that generally only makes its appearance when I am giving a lecture or talk. Papa Goochee is mildly startled with the role-shift. I start walking up and down the centre of the shop, crossing over the purple squares, and moving my body with considerable expressiveness, in order to give each utterance maximal meaning and impact. I look deep into each person's eyes and a silence takes hold of the shop. I launch into a story telling mode, using call-and-response.

'I'm at a multicultural conference and for five straight days, I hold fort in a dynamic black identity seminar' (Audience: 'Chris is doing his thing').

'I'm consumed by my work and am totally unprepared for her appearance' (Audience: 'Look out, here she comes').

'It's early in the morning and I have just completed a three-mile jog. I'm bent over, catching my breath and I hear a soft voice inquire: "Did you overdo it'. Before coming upright, I see these incredible legs that never seem to end'. (Audience: 'Fine legs will do it every time').

'She is no less than six feet tall but her proportions are so perfect that her height seems ordinary' (Audience: 'What he means is she's a stone-fox').

'I manage the small talk for the moment but as I walk away, I feel my knees buckle' (Audience: 'Someone call 911').

'Aretha is singing a love song deep inside my eardrums' (Papa Goochee sings a few lines from one of Aretha's songs).

'This running into each other continues for several days but one afternoon, we take off for a walk around the campus. What was to be a fleeting conversation turns into a two hour exchange, which we cannot bring to an end' (Audience: 'Both their noses are wide open').

'Within no time we are sharing stuff that suggests instant and complete trust. An hour into the conversation, she is in tears, as she shares a particularly painful event in her recent history' (Audience: 'Goodness, things are getting serious').

'We have circled the campus three times (it's a fairly small campus) and I hint at still a fourth walk-around to which she agrees. I want to kiss her' (Mr Short: 'Finally, he's takin' care of business').

'There is a tree halfway round the campus and it provides a certain degree of privacy and closeness' (I say the words 'privacy and closeness' slowly and playfully and the audience responds by imitating me).

'As we get closer and closer to the tree, I use my imagination to rehearse my moves, and it reaches a point that I am not listening to what she is saying' (Audience: 'Lookout, he's uptight – he's losing his cool').

'We come to the tree and I position myself close to her face' (Audience: A sudden hush grips the room – everyone knows the punchline is near).

'At what seems like the right moment, I make my move but at the last second, my coordination disappears and instead of kissing her lips, I nearly kiss the tree, instead!'

For a split second, everything moves in slow motion; I'm scanning the room to see if the story and punchline have had the intended effect. In this twilight zone between the room's hush and the impending roar,

I see men start to open their mouths and widen their eyelids. Several are starting to form the words 'shit' or 'mother-fuck' in tones that reflect acceptance and a story well told. Others turn to the person sitting next to them, in anticipation of a high-five exchange, where both persons simultaneously leap to their feet, jump about three inches off the ground, and at the apex, slap each others hands. Some of the older guys, whose legs cannot sustain any kind of flipping around, can be seen raising their legs a few inches off the ground, as a prelude to stomping the floor. In that split-second of observation, I go from anxiousness to relaxation – the story has worked. As the sense of accomplishment starts to feed my self-esteem, the action shifts back to real-time.

The shop falls apart and I cannot help but laugh myself. I make it a point to peek at Lester's face to see how he is responding. I wink at him and give him the thumbs up and he quickly and playfully returns the favour. He says not a word but the sense of relief on his face is palpable. His chest expands a little and the slouch in his shoulders is replaced by sharp contours.

Before I know what is happening, Papa Goochee and Mr Short are acting out the story, with Short playing me, and Papa Goochee the woman. Someone directs Dewitt to stand on the purple squares and a barber's cloth is thrown over his head. His arms are lifted away from his body, making him the tree. With utter delight, Dewitt softly says: 'I'm the tree, I'm the tree'. Short walks Papa Goochee around the tree four times, counting as he goes. By the second pass, everyone in the shop joins in unison with Mr Short's counting. At the end of the third time around, he mimes his intention to steal a kiss, and the crowd is wound-tight with anticipation. At just the right moment, Papa Goochee shifts his body and Short's full lips miss their mark and end up on Dewitt's forehead, which protrudes in relief beneath the barber's cloth. The room is in a total uproar and Dewitt is going nuts saying, at the top of his voice, 'Tree! Tree! Tree! – The professor kissed the Tree!'

It is a year later. Now, when I enter the shop, Ken greets me as the professor and Mr Short simply says: 'What's happening, Chris.' But most regulars call me Tree. This often confuses many of the young customers, because they cannot figure out for which pro-basketball team did I once play. I'm not that anxious to retell the story so I generally simply say: 'It's just a nickname I picked up along the way.'

Eulogy for Mom

> ... when an evil one dies, the day
> simply passes but when a person of
> much good dies, God cries and his
> tears fall to the earth as rain.
>
> An old African proverb

Margaret L. Cross, 1911-1983

A Tribute from Her Family

We come tonight to give witness to a washerwoman, a labourer, a mother of many children, a commoner. And in that faithful moment on May 1st, 1983, when God saw fit to finally end her protracted and difficult struggle against the ravages of cancer, God mercifully sent his secret messengers, who quietly marked her last breath and escorted Margaret's spirit to the Promised Land. Since she was a commoner, the Angels presumed their flight would be problematic and unpredictable, for the forces from below would at some point make their bid for Margaret's soul. But no sooner had the Angels cradled Margaret's inner being and begun their ascent, when quickly they sought the safety of a tranquil cloud, under which to hide. Much to their disbelief, God was actually interceding. He waved his arms wildly to stir the most violent wind and thus clear the air of any competing forces. No, the Devil would not have his due, in fact he dared not make an appearance, for God was taking extraordinary efforts to make certain that Margaret, the commoner, would be transported by the peaceful breeze that follows a tumultuous storm. Thus, on May 1st at 10:05 a.m., the wind blew in a furious way and shortly thereafter, the earth seemed to stand still, except for a gentle breeze, the kind on which Angels glide.

No history book will bear her name, no monuments with her deeds etched on metal will sparkle in the noonday sun, and no poets or writers will weave tales or mysteries that are transparent interpretations of her life. Margaret was a commoner. Such people pass and typically there is only dreadful silence. For them there is even the failure of an outline to appear in the mirrors that line the entranceway to Heaven – mirrors set to only reflect the images of 'important' people.

Still surprised by their uneventful and smooth ascent, the Angels took a still sleeping washerwoman before the golden gates. With the sprinkle of a little stardust they awakened Margaret; she immediately sensed her surroundings and softly she could be heard to say, "Oh my, I'm here before the house of the Lord." She had suffered from cancer for three years and the final months were beyond human endurance. Margaret had come to doubt whether her destiny would extend toward the sky, for surely her illness was some sort of punishment that only the Devil could inflict. But all seemed well, now, since the shape and colour of those gates just ahead were unmistakable.

The Angels could not find the time to query God about the storm, for no sooner had they entered His domain, when He requested that they cry for a day. The next day, He, himself, was indisposed, and the gentle rain on Monday became a downpour on Tuesday, as God cried with the passing of the washerwoman. By now the Angels were thoroughly beside themselves, for even they recognised that all the events of the past three days marked the death of anyone but a commoner; hence, with some urgency, they pressed God to please clarify Margaret's status.

Still God said nothing, instead, He commanded that the gates be opened so that Margaret could enter. The Angels did not move or speak, as Margaret walked pass the entrance and approached the mirrors. When she stopped at the mirrors, the Angels let out a gentle gasp, for not only did Margaret's image appear, but also the vague outline of a thousand common women garlanded her more distinct image. As Margaret paused, God summoned the Angels, for He was finally ready to speak. Almost in unison the Angels asked God, 'How could a commoner be accorded such a greeting?' He answered:

> My children, this is not a commoner. When she was born, I gave her a thousand talents and a million charms and in the history of earthly affairs, she surely would have gone far had it not been for the colour of her skin and her African heritage. But look children, she did not despair and sink into nihilism. Can you not see the magnificence of her earthly efforts in the distinctive features of her children? She used a painter's brush to colour their emotions, the poet's ways to sculpture their character, and the scholar's insight to fill the depth of their intellect and intuition. And what manner of art or fame could match the love and devotion she gave to each? Like so many Afro-American mothers, Margaret took all those charms and talents and poured them into her family life, and I dare say I have grown tired of their lack of recognition. And so I mark her passing and stir my memories of the many beautiful

> Black Mothers who have gone before her'. Pausing for a moment he continued, 'Take this crown and place it upon her head'.

The Angels took the crown of African Violets and slowly put it on Margaret's halo of white and gray hair. As they did, they could see that each of the small vague figures in the foreground of Margaret's image, those spirits from God's memory, also appeared to adorn crowns. At that instance, God spoke again and his voice thundered a joyous affirmation:

> 'Hark, I bring you not a commoner, but an African Queen!'

He moved forward to greet her. They slowly began to walk toward the Spirit Hall and as they did, God instantly took notice of Margaret's strength, her vision, her caring, her delicacy, and her penetrating warmth and humility. Strange, he thought to himself, I came here to welcome and comfort her but perhaps it is I who will find much comfort in her presence.

The Family.

References

Barnes, E. J. (1972) 'The Black Community As A Source Of Positive Black Self-Concept For Black Children: A Theoretical Perspective', in R.L. Jones (ed), *Black Psychology*, first-edition, New York: Harper & Row, pp166-192.

Labouring in the counter story factory: experiential teaching about authority

Linda C. Powell

Through a case study on a graduate class on leadership, the question of what happens when counter stories are publicly named and spoken is analysed. Lifting counter stories from the shadows where they typically reside sets into motion psycho-dynamics that reveal essential information about leadership, authority and power that are rarely addressed – and even more rarely 'taught' – in the classroom. The analysis focuses particularly on faculty and students' differentially positioned refusal to analyse pedagogically the very paradoxical relations of authority that interrupt, and define, organisational life.

Authority, anxiety and innovation

The 'Emperor's New Clothes' is a perfect example of the Master Narrative, the power of the Counter Story, and the dilemma of what comes next. In the classic version of the tale, the entire kingdom colludes in the belief that the Emperor's new garb is the best and the most beautiful ever. Actually, the Emperor is conned by a succession of people who fear (or refuse) to tell him anything other than what he desires to hear. Finally, a young person speaks a counter story by telling the truth as (s)he sees it: the emperor has no clothes! This story spotlights the vanity and foolishness of those in formal authority, the anxiety evoked in various court members when confronted with his power, and the impact of expressing an alternative version of reality than the dominant view.

And yet, few of us contemplate the meaning of the end of the myth: in one version, the people cast the Emperor into exile. Without him (or without what he represents), the previously prosperous and peaceful kingdom flies apart and falls into unrest and disruption. This suggests that naming the fact that the emperor had no clothes was an important revelation, but it was insufficient. The people in the kingdom needed to imagine something new, to tell a different story about who they were and who they wanted to be. Someone or something needed to emerge to fill the void left by the expulsion of the Emperor. In addition to their actions, they needed clearer and deeper analyses: Why was the Emperor so vulnerable to flattery? Why was everyone incapable of telling him the truth? Why did so many collude for so long with such foolishness?

As a clinical psychologist involved in urban school change, I am convinced that naming, speaking counter stories, and asking these 'why' questions are critical to creating lasting improvement. Those who hold formal organisational authority must be prepared to understand and deal with the irrationality they will inevitably meet in their roles. Leaders who would be change agents must have the internal capacity and external skills to both learn from anxiety as well as use their authority to manage genuine innovation. Individuals who would improve educational systems must be able to diagnose and intervene in these processes, not be held captive by the dominant discourses that comfort and sustain them. My challenge has been to develop a pedagogy for change agents and leaders who are capable and confident when confronted with counter stories about covert organisational processes.

While this pedagogy uses a complex mix of psychoanalysis, social psychology and systems theory, three simple notions form its framework. And each of these core notions is, itself, a counter story. First, groups take on personalities of their own that can have powerful covert undertows and dynamics (Wells 1985). They can have an entire 'life' that is hidden, affecting individuals in unexpected ways. This is a counter story to the master narrative about the stability and centrality of the individual personality. Second, individuals and groups can take on symbolic meaning as ideas, thoughts and values are 'projected' into them: some are made smart, right and trustworthy while others are made incompetent, wrong and unreliable. This creates the 'scapegoat' dynamic that is so familiar and relentless in groups, organisations and society (Smith and Berg 1987). This idea is a counter story to the master narrative about individual merit and power; it suggests that those dimensions are contextual and co-created. Finally, new knowledge about these dynamics and projections can be discovered and created by sticking with the immediate experiences of group life, paying exquisite attention to the 'here-and-now' details of what actually happens (Palmer 1979). This is a counter story to the master narrative that tells many of us that 'truly important' events are in the past or the future, or in the experiences of unnamed 'others'.

I had no clue what this pedagogy would liberate in and among students; I was unprepared for the de-centring impact of these three simple ideas put to work in a graduate school classroom. Teaching from this perspective is, literally, a factory for counter stories. This essay will describe the essential elements of the course and explore four specific counter stories that emerge. The essay will close with my reflections on the pitfalls and delights of it all.

Generating counter stories: designing a course

Forty students enter a conventional classroom, expecting the first meeting of a course about leadership and authority. In place of the predictable tables-in-rows arrangement, they find chairs in a double horseshoe. As they struggle to select seats in this unfamiliar arrangement, someone walks to the solitary chair in front of the room and announces, 'this is the opening session of "Understanding Authority and Exercising Leadership". Where would you like to begin?' A stunned silence follows.

Since 1993, I have been experimenting with methods of teaching that would prepare urban educators to deal constructively with the irrationality in the systems they confront everyday. As it has emerged, the course is an example of the four-stage professional development for change model developed with colleagues in the Philadelphia School District (Powell, Barry and Smith 1997).[1] The primary theoretical frame for the course is drawn from the fifty-year tradition of the study of leadership and authority at the Tavistock Institute for Human Relations in Great Britain (Rice 1975; Rioch 1975; Powell 1997).[2] And of course, the design of this course has been enriched by similar courses and preparation programmes in schools of management, government, theology and public service.

The initial event described above signals students that this will be very different from other graduate school courses about leadership.

Following the stunned silence, students employ a staggering variety of behaviours, including 'respectful' questions, whiny requests and infantile confusion aimed toward a single end: to persuade me to relieve their anxiety by telling them what to do. Their relentlessness and creativity, are, in themselves an important lesson: mid-career professionals running huge organisations are suddenly undone by the simple absence of the expected authority dynamic that constitutes the dominant narrative.

Despite substantial innovations such as the opening, the course retains several familiar academic elements; these form the 'ego' of the course where we can all return to anchor our thinking in the midst of strong feelings. A traditional syllabus with readings from social psychology, systems theory, and adult development is distributed, although the staff freely admit that it is part roadmap, part framework and part fiction. As the semester proceeds, changes are made to the syllabus and new resources substituted if they seem useful to the learning. Students write weekly memos about their experiences as well as two major papers; they prepare a final portfolio to demonstrate their learning. The written elements of the course are a primary basis for grades with class participation as another factor.

The major innovation is the inclusion of four interrelated experiential elements that distinguish this from philosophical or prescriptive courses 'about' leadership or authority. Experiential work provides the opportunity to excavate, explore and legitimate various voices and support the collaborative development of knowledge about leadership and authority.

Completing the learning contract secures admission into the course. Students are asked to respond in writing to four key ideas: 1) the importance of intellectual work as the basis for grading in the course, 2) the necessity of regular attendance in a group-based course, 3) the issue of confidentiality for all members and 4) the fluid complex boundary between psychotherapy and a learning experience. Completing this contract initiates the entry process to the course; it begins the work of making the professor's authority – and how I intend to use it – available for their inspection.[3] Not surprisingly, most students assume that the contract is an exercise in compliance: the way to assure acceptance to the class is to 'say whatever' they imagine the professor wants. They 'promise' to accept the professor's judgement of their writing, to never miss a class, to share openly and to keep every secret they hear in the class, and to never cross the line to therapeutic experience. These contracts are usually both short and insubstantial.

These students are generally shocked during the semester when they discover that I 'actually meant something' by the contract. For example, when they stop by to 'get my permission' to miss class for something completely reasonable (the father's surgery, the friend's wedding, the paper due in another course) I am not 'understanding'. I do not threaten to lower their grade or lecture them about their responsibility to the course. I simply ask whether their request is consistent with what they said on their learning contract. I do not 'grant' or 'withhold' permission; I ask, instead, what the request reveals about their attitudes toward their own authority and mine.

Other students invest differently before even submitting the contract. They use it to inquire into their own values. Will they miss class for a serious snowstorm or a sick child? Is their thinking and writing good enough to sustain their grade? How do they really feel about grades? How do they imagine the boundary around their private life and what they would choose to share in class? Are they at a stage in their life for a cognitively and emotionally demanding learning experience? These students state their values more candidly and relinquish their imagined control over 'getting in'. They also initiate a very different relationship with the professor – one based on the aims of the course in learning about leadership and authority. These students launch themselves on a far different trajectory of 'authorising' their learning and the meaning of the class.

Students rarely inquire about my review process, but the projections into me are telling: I have a preference for African American students; I choose for race and gender diversity and white male students are at a disadvantage; I only take the students I think are 'psychologically healthy'. Yet, because students don't ask, they don't learn until later in the semester that everyone who completes a contract is admitted.[4] The resource (of the course) is assumed to be limited and selective solely because the contract makes the boundary of in/out of the class explicit.

The second experiential component is the work of the entire class as a group. All enrolled members meet for one hour to explore their experience in the here-and-now. The primary task of these meetings is learning about leadership and authority as they emerge within the group. Without the professor's specific direction to orient their contributions, these sessions are initially disorienting and upsetting to students who are accustomed to the professor controlling or at least facilitating (covertly or directly) most of the course agenda. Cast onto their own resources, many students are confused (what are we supposed to talk about?), often angry (I'm *paying* for this?) and only later, empowered to direct their own inquiry (I observe that this is happening and I think it means ...). Learning to think collaboratively to build knowledge rather than passively absorb it from me is a developmental hurdle for the class. First they must understand and internalise the novel notion that they are actively co-creating the learning experience with the teaching staff and with each other. Unlike other kinds of learning, students must engage or there is no 'course'. It is difficult to sit this class out. Students often report that this pressure and visibility alone gives them tremendous insight into themselves as those who act or refrain from acting, into the unexplored dynamics of other classes and into the real-world organisations with which they are connected.

Second, students must cope with a variety of choices revealed by experiential methods and the implications of their participation: what does it mean to speak vs remain silent? Who gets listened to and who is ignored – for the same idea? What does competition look like in an intellectual environment, and how does it influence 'achievement'? A primary cycle throughout the class is the desire to please formal authority, then reacting to the desire to please me and then resenting the desire to please me! We attempt to examine and excavate this cycle, looking beneath it for the authentic dreams and hopes of rebellion, yearning and interdependence. Students and teaching staff discover, develop and test new ideas in real-time with others, framing multiple hypotheses about what happens rather than adopting 'pathological certainty' (Shapiro and Carr 1991) about complex issues. Shapiro and Carr describe this approach of bringing all of the information we have about ourselves, our relationships and our context to a given moment as 'the interpretive stance'. Throughout the course, students and teaching staff adopt this stance, 'moving from heuristic to heuristic' rather than toward a false certainty which is insured by dominant discourses and practices.

The third experiential element of the course is a weekly consultation group. Students are informed about the critical role of these groups, and are asked to self-manage a process to divide themselves in whatever way will 'maximise their learning'. While this is the only official directive given about the groups' composition, the process inevitably raises questions about the meaning and value of group composition. Students routinely struggle with the racial and gender balances in their group for reasons that remain unclear to me. Often they seem to do this as a 'politically correct' tic. Or perhaps they seek unconsciously to please the (African American woman) professor who must (in their projection) think those issues critical. Or perhaps they sense that heterogeneity strengthens the group's ability to consult on complex problems. In any event, reviewing the precise way in which the large group went about the task of dividing itself teaches us all about the nature of leading and authorising, about the complexity of learning from our own experience, and about who we unconsciously believe is 'in charge'.

The sole task of these consultation groups is to learn about leadership and authority. This task is pursued by providing each student with the opportunity to present an experience of 'leadership failure'. A leadership failure is an unresolved experience about which they still feel strongly; they are encouraged to tell it as a story, filled with the nuance and murkiness with which they experienced it. They then receive consultation from their group members on what happened, why and what can be learned from it. Teaching staff are not present for the consultation group meetings; another member of the group serves as the 'Designated Authority'. This role goes far beyond the typical facilitator role. While it is every member's responsibility to move the learning work of the group, the DA bears a special responsibility to use their formal authority to help the group learn from the case presented. For example, the DA might raise issues that the group seems to be avoiding, might support a minority opinion that is not being heard, or might risk an inquiry that goes beyond the defensive limits on 'professional discourse' (especially around race, power and sexuality). In a real sense, their job is to help generate counter stories, or at the very least, seed alternative narratives to explain complex events. In a recent case, there was clearly a 'secret' that the presenter circled but could not quite reveal. Without this information, his story was flat and the group disengaged. Finally, the DA said with some exasperation, 'it's either that someone is gay or someone has been having an affair with a student'. This comment galvanised the group and was discovered to be partially accurate. This both forced and freed the presenter to tell a more complex story filled with real people, real bodies and real consequences.

The fourth experiential component is a weekend-long group relations conference. Derived from the work of the Tavistock Institute for Human Relations in Great Britain and the A.K. Rice Institute in the United States, this is an intensive opportunity for students to study group dynamics, authority and leadership in real time. This is an immersion experience which uses external staff to explore questions of leadership and authority. During this intensive experience, participants in the conference (which can include students from other courses throughout the College and members of the community) create a temporary institution and study its dynamics. Working in groups of varying sizes and compositions, students have an intensive opportunity to study intra- and interpersonal, group and intergroup dynamics. Students do not 'enjoy' these weekends, due in part to the shock of having material that is generally repressed or 'politely' withheld made so available for examination. However, without fail, students routinely report that this weekend provokes a paradigmatic shift in learning about themselves and social and organisational change.

The fundamental assumption of this course is that learning about authority requires that authority be exercised transparently and made available for inquiry and interpretation. As staff, we do not 'share authority' with students but we are open to their exploration and critique about the choices we make in the exercise of our authority. We do not pretend to create perfect authority dynamics; we simply stay committed to studying the ones we create. We refuse the comfort and trouble the control seductively offered through the dominant discourse of our authority in the room. We make the course 'rules' as clear as possible; we invite inquiry when *our* inevitable covert rules come to the fore. While more overtly confrontational, challenging and difficult, this stance actually leads to the more important learning. By allowing ourselves to be hated, we give students the opportunity to experience the full range of reaction to authority that is usually forbidden. Without fail, this generates new information and broader options for action. It is, in psychoanalytic terms, a 'working through' of previously repressed material. Most students will return to organisations where they need to inhabit hierarchy and bureaucracy. They probably will not have sufficient informal or formal authority to recreate their organisations overnight. Or they may work in circumstances where hierarchy suits the task of the organisation. For these reasons, the course is designed to prevent individuals from being blindsided by unconscious issues about their own authority or the authority of others. We hope that students will have a clearer grasp of their own story and on the mechanisms by which they can see and generate authentic counter stories.

To encourage this kind of learning, the teaching staff is an explicit hierarchy constituted by the professor and two to three teaching assistants. As a sub-group within the class, we play a critical role in two specific ways. First, teaching assistants – who are often doctoral students themselves – are fully authorised to work in the class sessions and to forward student learning whenever and however they judge possible. They interpret, prod or contradict the professor if this is useful. They provide extensive and at times controversial comments on the weekly class memos. They are 'middle management' providing additional opportunities for students to think and feel about how authority is exercised in the class. Their authority goes far beyond the traditional 'grade papers' and 'keep office hours' paradigm with which most students are familiar.[5]

Second, the hierarchical relationship between the teaching assistants and the professor is available for inspection and interpretation by members of the class. They can generate counter stories about us. There are also more opportunities for students to question the professor, the teaching assistants and each other about their experiences and decisions. Taking these opportunities often crosses unexamined and unspoken boundaries that students have about 'appropriate' behaviour in the classroom.

For example, as DA in the first leadership failure case of the semester, I challenged the presenter directly on his 'confusion' about the case. He was avoiding pointed questions from his classmates about the issue of race and his leadership behaviour in the case. He believed that his problems stemmed from the fact that there were 'so few teachers of colour that he could persuade to come to his school'. Finally, using my own anger and disconnection in that moment, I stated that I could understand that because, as an African American, I would never work for him. I yelled, was not polite and was clearly not detached or 'neutral'.[6] There was, again, that stunned silence. My comment did shift the presenter's aloofness and helped him get in deeper touch with his concerns about whether he was perceived as genuine by his staff and the community. The climate in the room also shifted: discussion became freer. I modelled the full range of behaviour available to the DA role: passion, clarity, forcefulness. But some students felt that I had gone way too far. Many believed that I had misused my authority by being so pointed with him; not only had I been impolite, I had crossed some line of what is 'simply not done'. Although they felt it strongly, putting words to their analysis was difficult, and these students spent the rest of the semester exploring, challenging and testing my decision to go after him so intently. Each question about my use of authority was met with an invitation to learn from their experience: what was my responsibility in the DA role? To the presenter and to the rest of the class? How did I choose to intervene in the way that I did? This was just one example of the strong feelings that emerged in class throughout the semester. What is it like to be angry at the professor or competitive with other students or victimised in class – and be not only free but at some level *expected* to explore it in order to learn?

The simplest elements of the course lead to the most critical lessons. For example, the workload of the course makes unreasonable time and emotional demands compared to more traditional courses. Many students who have never 'broken a sweat' academically discover that they cannot easily excel; for some, it is the first time they have ever received a note to 'see the professor' about the marginal quality of a paper. For the first time in their academic lives, they have a sense of what it is like to not be the best, the smartest and the most-beloved. These students discover that 'their' experience of class and school is not 'the' experience. Theirs is only a single narrative among many, shattering a sense of centrality and security. This realisation alone can provoke tremendous feeling and thinking about the covert psychological nature of organisational life. One student wrote his weekly memo about his decision to set limits on his own participation in the course. When he considered his multiple roles as student, husband, father and job-seeker, he decided not to invest the eight to ten hours per week that his early memos demanded. He was willing to take the lower grade that (he assumed) would be forthcoming. The teaching staff found his revelation very helpful, and understood this as his taking up his authority to determine his own investment. When we raised this during the weekly course meeting, other students admitted to similar struggles about depth of involvement and time commitment to the course. However, they could not believe that *he told us*! They assumed that 'we were doing it on purpose', 'that we wouldn't care', in short that we were taking some masochistic pleasure out of their feeling overburdened. (This is a common projection taken by people in authority: it relieves a responsibility to share experience with those in formal authority). Without this memo, the teaching staff would not know how seriously the workload affected them, nor could we make clear that these decisions were the heart and soul of the course: how do you authorise what will be important in your life?

The construction of multiple counter stories

Teaching this course has become a routine process of discovery. Once real experiences are 'authorised', for example once students discover that the structure of the course actually has authenticity and integrity, then the entire semester becomes about creating new and multiple versions of what is real. The joint experience of teaching staff and students lays naked the master narrative about formal authority and leadership: that it is heroic and individual behaviour; that we can probably identify the leader by what he (sic) looks like or the organisational role he holds; that leadership is based on an unshakeable personal vision that never wavers; that the leader must have more answers/wisdom/patience than others.

This narrative carries two protective fantasies that explode under scrutiny in class. The first is the notion that the leader is immune from uncertainty and protected from the rigours and pains of change (which is one reason we may unconsciously wish to be the leader!). Week after week, students watch the teaching staff and each other grapple with complex phenomena and 'not know' in public. We are all less and less protected by expert status, or a claim to 'higher' or better knowledge. The staff works to model this questioning, not-knowing with genuine humility. An additional defensive aspect of this master narrative is that the leader is solely accountable and 'followers' are relieved from any responsibility (along with any real power). I often comment early in the semester that the aims of the course can be easily defeated if students do not participate. We demonstrate the immense power of groups and individuals to 'not authorise' an idea or an exploration simply by not 'getting with it' – enhancing, exploring or refining it; the idea will then wither for lack of attention. Conversely, the student who risks sharing a dream that galvanises the group's sense of itself, or the young Latina who says quietly that she'd rather not dilute the people of colour 'among' the consultation groups or the subgroup of students who come to me with an alternative proposal for the final paper, are instances of the power of self-authorisation and participation.

The course is truly a factory for counter stories about many topics, including all of the elements of what the authors of the AAUW report, *How Schools Shortchange Girls* (1992) called 'the evaded curriculum', issues of power which so rarely get an open hearing and are generally avoided in teaching and learning. However, given the topic of the course, four distinct and yet interrelated counter stories emerge.

Leadership is a function, not a role: As the actual work of the course reveals, mobilising groups to tackle tough problems can be done by anyone with the informal authority to move minds and hearts. This is not always the person we might predict (like the professor!), but the person who has the clarity and courage to say the hard thing that inspires or provokes a shift. 'I think we're angry at the professor and afraid of what that means'. 'I wonder if we're avoiding the issue of gender and maybe we should return to the earlier discussion'. 'I think the problem in this case is like the issue in this room now'. An old Tavistock definition of leader was 'the person who is best at the task'. This functionally oriented definition shifts the focus from the individual or their formal role to the behaviour.

Leadership and authority are relational – group, not simply individual – variables: Leadership and authority cannot be studied apart from the group context in which they exist. Authorising is a dynamic, requiring the yielding or joining of an individual, group or subgroup to the values or aims of another individual, group or subgroup. Given the nature of our current social and organisational challenges, we can no longer afford a 'leadership class'. There is work for all of us. No one can 'lead' without followers. A group can defeat any individual in authority by simply refusing to work. This is routinely evident in the class, although the impact of becoming conscious of this simple fact often surprises students. Their power comes as a revelation. Members who do not participate can defeat the efforts of others, simply by withholding themselves, their experience and their contribution.

Authentic transformation is messy: This course does not fit in a traditional time slot. The tables must be moved out of the room in the ten minute break between classes. This course appears expensive compared to more typical teaching pedagogies. This course leaks emotionally into other courses, as students take up their authority to learn differently with other professors who may not be interested in this innovation. This is a metaphor for genuine change: by its very definition, innovation does not fit neatly into the current structure.

Given the power and novelty of the experiential work, many students make new connections about their internal lives and their external circumstances (Kahn and Kramm 1994). These are often not connections they would have expected to make at graduate school. For example, students routinely reconsider childhood incidents of abuse as well as sexual harassment in organisations in a new light. They now see these incidents as profound abuses of authority. They can make the connection between these incidents – and their resolution of them – to the construction of their inner world and their own leadership behaviours as adults in organisations. Many students discover how little they really know about themselves and about how they are seen by others. It is as if the course awakens them, and the degree to which they have been sleepwalking through their organisational lives is initially unsettling. Students routinely report that this course 'changed their lives', but not without nightmares about the class, creating stress in their marriages, causing them to neglect other responsibilities, inspiring them to try risky behaviours at work. One student recently contrasted it to low-cost learning: this course was demanding and costly in terms of what he gave of and learned about himself compared to his seventeen years of more traditional learning.

Social identity matters: The variations on this counter story emerge loudly and clearly throughout the course. When most of my students begin their exploration of their varying feelings (surprise, shame or excitement) about having a black woman professor, they are beginning a critical exploration about the ways in which social identity influences unconscious aspects of leadership and authority. Who is authorised, who leads and with what impact are deeply influenced by the social identity variables of the individual and group. This idea comes as no surprise to women students, men of colour or younger students: their organisational experiences have led them to suspect that their value and contribution have been distorted by issues related to stereotypes and prejudice about social identity.

However, few of us are prepared for the intensity and relentlessness of the master narratives regarding race, gender, age and authority. And the extent to which, under stress, we all revert to the master narratives for relief from our anxiety. When there are genuinely scarce resources demanding hard choices, let the professor decide. When there is frightening new learning about race or gender or class in the room, let the older white male students talk about the readings. When the women are afraid of their power, provoke the men to fight. We are willing to authorise the most unlikely people or behaviours if they will protect us from our own anxiety about change. And it is a genuine act of leadership to struggle against that anxiety toward some more authentic and complex 'truth' than to passively cling to the avoidant, defensive posture.

Second and third thoughts

Why is this teaching so fraught with emotion? Why do staff and students dream about this course? Because we ask students to take significant risks in this course. Most students have real reason to distrust authority, to believe that we will 'screw them on their grade' if they say what they really believe. Trusting the course structure and the staff enough to test us is, in itself, a risk within an academic setting.

Students are hungry for what they find in this course. Not just for the group relations interpretations of unconscious group process, although they are importantly provocative. Not even for the intense opportunities to tell their truths about their experiences in the moment. Students and staff are hungry to be in the present and to pay close attention to what they see, feel and taste. And the present, collaborating with others, is incredibly fertile ground for the 'seeing' and 'telling' of counter stories.

The course is harrowing for me because at every moment I can be tempted to re-take my expert status, to fall back on the unexamined (and far more comfortable) authority relations as they are known in the academy. I can use that master narrative of the 'all-knowing, all powerful professor' to beat innovative ideas into submission (especially if they are about my unconscious process). In fact, if I enter this honestly, any expert status I might have – even around the basics of this work – is put at risk every week by any student or teaching assistant. Although I have my formal authority as professor, I can only exercise leadership if I encourage, persuade, and influence students and staff to pursue the tougher tasks of the course. Each semester I learn more unwelcome things about myself, my fears, my greeds and ambitions. I do not necessarily welcome these insights at the moment, but I am always grateful for and inspired by the course's ability to generate them.

A commitment to social or organisational change requires an exploration of the least examined and most hallowed traditions of teaching and training. Can 'transformation' or 'improvement' or 'innovation' be simply added on to our current modes of instruction and assessment, or does preparing individuals to assume change roles demand a reassessment of basic assumptions about the psychological function of authority in teaching and learning?

The relational processes of teaching and learning evoke deep feelings in everyone involved. As in all human relationships, our earliest and most conflicted experiences of dependency are reawakened. When we enter the classroom without attention to the unacknowledged issues of student projections of our expert status, or to the hierarchies they have created and sustained through a lifetime career of being students, we inadvertently teach lessons about authority. If and when we can hold onto these experiences and explore them, they provide tremendous insight into our internal models of authority and the world around us.

In order to prepare leaders of change-oriented efforts, those who teach must make our authority available for exploration and inquiry; when we do not inquire or comment, we enact authority relations already at play in the dysfunctional systems which have been imported into the classroom by our students. We structure learning environments that package or manage rather than confront the anxiety of innovation (Schall 1995).

This is not simply about developing or preparing leaders: the true danger is that our over-reliance on traditional teaching methods prepares people for compliance and an unconsciously assigned niche in various hierarchies. We must aggressively pursue any pedagogy that creates artists and architects of counter stories. This is a key leadership skill enabling individuals who feel the desire and have the skills to make a difference, and to make meaning of their increasingly complicated worlds.

Notes

1. The design of this course is influenced by a number of other experiential courses, most notably those developed by Clayton Alderfer and David Berg at the Yale School of Management; Ken Smith at the University of Pennsylvania School of Social Work; Ron Heifetz, Marty Linsky, Ron David and Robin Ely at the Kennedy School of Government, Harvard University; Ellen Schall and Emily Style at the Wagner School of Public Service at New York University; Debra Noumair and Sarah Brazaitis at Teachers College; and Terri Monroe and Brian McDermott at the Weston School of Theology.

2. For the purposes of the course, we teach Heifetz's (1994) distinctions between leadership (mobilising people to tackle tough problems), formal authority (official roles within organisations) and informal authority (trust and willingness to follow bestowed by others).
3. In group relations work, this response is called 'teaching across the boundary' established in the entry process. I maintain my role as professor on one side of an imaginary zone established by the student's own response to the contract. I then try to work across this zone to make meaning of what is happening between us. Students rarely experience this kind of teaching as neutral; I am often perceived as hostile. Much of the 'as if' nature of the academy is revealed in conversations around the four points of the learning contract. Students patiently explain that we've all agreed to play a very specific game in graduate school; my actually holding them to the terms of their learning contract is a serious breach of the (unspoken) rules of that game and feels to students like an attack.
4. In seven years of teaching this course only three or four students have not been admitted. They were clearly seeking a 'psychotherapeutic' or 'self-help' experience that, in my judgement, would not accommodate a larger organisational focus.
5. Obviously, the course would not exist in its most complex form without the effort, investment and courage of teaching assistants. I specifically must thank the three who have worked with me most recently: Francois Guilleux, Ed.M., who has partnered with me in developing this course since 1994; John Barrengos, Ed.D., whose research and practice demonstrate his passion for and commitment to group relations; and Maggie Barber, a 1999 alumna of the course who leapt across the faculty-student boundary and co-taught with us three times in one year. Many thanks for the early review of this manuscript.
6. During that discussion, I countered with the argument that the unacknowledged white privilege in the case was, in its own invisible way, a form of force that I simply replied to 'in kind'. This argument, itself, is a counter story.

References

Heifetz, R.A. (1994) *Leadership Without Easy Answers*, Cambridge, MA: Harvard University Press.

Kahn, W.A., & Kram, K.E. (1994) 'Authority At Work: Internal Models And Their Organizational Consequences', *Academy of Management Review*, 19: 17-50.

Palmer, B. (1979) 'Learning And The Group Experience' in W.G. Lawrence (ed), *Exploring individual and organisational boundaries: A Tavistock open systems approach*, Chichester, England: Wiley, pp169-158:.

Powell, L.C. (1997) 'The Achievement (K)Not: Whiteness And Black Underachievement' in M. Fine, L.C. Powell, L. Weis, & L.M. Wong (eds), *Off White: Readings On Race, Power, And Society*, New York: Routledge, pp3-12.

Powell, L.C., Barry, M., & Davis, G. (1997) 'Facing Reality In Urban Schools: Using Racial Identity Theory In Family Group', in C.E. Thompson & R. Carter (eds), *Racial Identity Theory: Applications For Individual, Group, And Organizational Interventions*, Mahwah, NJ: Lawrence Erlbaum, pp147-158.

Rice, A.K. (1975) 'Systems Of Organization', in A.D. Colman & W.H. Bexton (eds), *Group Relations Reader* 1, Washington, DC: A.K. Rice Institute, pp71-158.

Rioch, M.J. (1975) 'All We Like Sheep – [Isaiah 53:6]: Followers And Leaders', in A.D. Colman & W.H. Bexton (eds), *Group Relations Reader*, 1, Washington, DC: A.K. Rice Institute, pp159-177.

Schall, E. (1995) 'Learning To Love The Swamp: Reshaping Education For Public Service', *Journal of Policy Analysis and Management*, 14: 202-220.

Shapiro, E.R., & Carr, A.W. (1991) *Lost In Familiar Places: Creating New Connections Between The Individual And Society*, New Haven, CT: Yale University Press.

Smith, K.K., & Berg, D.N. (1987) *Paradoxes Of Group Life: Understanding Conflict, Paralysis, And Movement In Group Dynamics*, San Francisco: Jossey-Bass.

Wellesley College Center for Research on Women (1992) *How Schools Shortchange Girls: The AAUW Report,* Washington, DC: American Association of University Women Educational Foundation.

Wells, L. (1985) 'The Group-As-A-Whole Perspective And Its Theoretical Roots', in A.D. Colman & M.H. Geller (eds), *Group Relations Reader* 2, Washington, DC: A.K. Rice Institute, pp109-126.

What's in a name? western terms and non-western experiences

Anne-Marie Tupuola

This essay explores the limitations of Americo-centric and Euro-centric concepts of human development when applied to differing Samoan contexts. The following discussion illustrates the restrictions of universal models of psychology and poses questions that need to be explored in future research with young Samoan women. Although the intention here is not to provide an alternative Samoan model, it does address the difficulties of adopting fixed models of development for both papalagi (European) and Samoan populations.

Diasporic populations of multiple identities and transient experiences are a useful starting point in illustrating the problematic nature of single labels and theories for populations shifting 'in-between' local and outside worlds. This 'in-betweenness' is further elaborated upon through the author's position in both western and Pacific academia. Some of her own challenges in promoting local and indigenous concepts in both western and Pacific academia are discussed as is her concern with the ongoing use of westernised terms and labels to describe all Pacific populations.

> it is not just important what we speak about, but how and why we speak (hooks 1990: 151).

My interest in the intra-cultural complexities of both westernised and traditional cultures stems from the writings about multiple subjectivities by third-world and black women of the diasporic condition

(Abu-Lughod 1991; Chen 1992; Lotfalian 1996; Mani 1992). In many instances these writings about their familiarity with western, non-western, traditional and global cultures seem to reflect my own multiple identities as a woman of Samoan descent born in New Zealand and currently residing in the United States of America. Can and should transient experiences be identified and made sense of by a single label and theory? Bhaskaran (1993) and Rasiah (1993: 267) argue that scholars need to accentuate the disparities within cultures rather than rely on essentialist labels that deny 'the diversity within group identity and contribute to the creation of false assumptions'. For example, Abu-Lughod (1991), Chen (1992) and Mani (1992) introduce the concepts of 'halfies' and 'in-betweens' to define researchers that are both inside and outside and 'in-between' their local and western worlds. The practice of such researchers is to unsettle the boundary between self and other and to 'reflect on how moving between different "configurations of meaning and power" can prompt different "modes of knowing"' (Mani 1992: 309).

My intention is to blur the polarised boundaries between Samoan and westernised world views by weaving in between western, cross-cultural and indigenous narratives of psychology through both overt and covert lenses. The use of terms such as 'western', 'non-western' and 'indigenous' in this text is to illustrate the language found in popular psychology texts (Adelson 1980; Berzonsky 1981; Lerner 1986; Santrock 1987; Sebald 1984) and is not meant to essentialise or homogenise these groups nor to ignore their own cultural disparities. In analysing western psychology narratives I do not wish to undermine the value of their contribution to the discipline or to suggest that all western theories of psychology are problematic in Samoan contexts. Making reference to fa'aSamoa (Samoan culture) here is not to speak on behalf of all Samoans nor to assume that the experiences of young women are the same but, rather, to shed light on some of the cultural disparities within fa'aSamoa and indigenous experiences. In taking an intra-cultural stance I want to make visible the continuum of western language and concepts in westernised, cross-cultural and indigenous human development and psychology studies and theories, irrespective of the diverse cultural backgrounds of researchers and authors. Do cross-cultural and indigenous studies contribute different modes of knowledge? Or are they extensions of westernised master narratives of psychology?

The Samoan component of this essay raises several issues. In the traditional Samoan context the privilege of voice is generally given to the elders or someone of chiefly status (see Hereniko 1995). My lack of status in fa'aSamoa coupled with the inclusion of voices of young Samoan women, who are generally voiceless in traditional Samoan societies, challenges the protocol and etiquette commonly associated with speaking out and about Samoan issues (see Freeman 1983; Tupuola 1996). My birthplace of New Zealand also poses a challenge as there have been numerous occasions when I have been publicly questioned by some Samoans on my authenticity as a Samoan and have been asked to cite my Samoan lineage and ancestry. Thus, by speaking out about delicate issues relating to my Pacific and Samoan peers, there is a risk of facing ostracism as well as tarnishing the honour of my family's name (see Tupuola 1996). While I am respectful of my Samoan culture and peers, it seems important that the voices of young people be considered and the perspectives of a new generation of Pacific scholars be recognised: 'The shaping of local peoples' cultural subjectivity can no longer go back and look for origin, purity and authenticity; it must be connected to the here and now of everyday life. If cultural formation is always open ended and interactional, then it is no bad thing to encounter outside forces' (Chen 1992: 482).

In consideration of these challenges, this essay's aim is to go beyond the common polarised discussion about western and non-western master narratives by paying attention to the disparities within them. What are the master narratives of psychology in the twenty-first century for differing cultural groups? What role, if any, do cross-cultural and indigenous models have in sustaining the status quo of westernised narratives of psychology in the twenty-first century?

Introduction

> ... no behaviour and no spoken word has an irreducible objective meaning. Members of different groups or nations place meanings on what goes on around them, and the nuances of these meanings often serve to define identity (Smith & Bond 1998: 9).

Non-western and third-world psychology studies have assisted in broadening the cultural base of psychological theories and in challenging the 'Americo-centrism' of most social sciences (Featherman 1993).

Some of these writings poignantly address the cultural bias of mainstream psychology theories and the limitations of universal eurocentrically defined terms and concepts (Garrod, Ward, Robinson & Kilkenny 1999).

This essay takes a similar stance to such third-world writings in that it analyses the limitations associated with the terms 'human development' and 'adolescence' in Samoan contexts. Reference is made to the findings of my Master of Arts (1993a) and Doctoral (1998) studies of young women of Samoan descent in New Zealand to address the following issues: How valid are these terms for Samoan communities where it is appropriate to speak of the person as the 'person-in-relationships, rather than as a discrete, well-bounded unit' (Hollan 1992: 284)? Why are both Samoan and non-Samoan researchers continuing to use western terms to describe the maturational processes of Samoan people? This is especially important at a time when non-western writers have started to 'formulate their own literary and critical methods, long giv[ing] up the attempt to use an alien literary language' (Watt 1985: 288). The closing sections discuss the complex assimilation process undergone by some of my Samoan and Pacific peers in western academia to reiterate the hardships of prioritising non-western scholarship and of validating local terms and concepts in western and Pacific academia.

Re-appropriating psychological terms

> ... the growth of an indigenous third-world psychology could potentially lead to fresh ideas that could only spring from the work of third-world psychologists, with beneficial results for all of psychology (Moghaddam 1987: 917).

Third-world and non-western psychology researchers are a diverse group with varied perspectives and research approaches to studying human development. A large proportion of non-western studies have relied on North American and Western European theories and on the English language rather than on locally generated measures, frameworks and terms (Ongel & Smith 1994; Smith & Bond 1998). The concerning tendency for some non-western psychologists to assimilate to westernised narratives of identity, autonomy and attachment and separation has urged other third-world researchers to instead promote local theories and scholarship in their studies (Garrod, Ward, Robinson & Kilkenny 1999; Wierzbicka 1993). Theorists such as Ardila (1996), Mpofu (1995) and Sinha (1997) emphasised locally generated data, concepts and theories in their studies while Bond (1996), Doi (1973) and Palsane and Lam (1996) used native language and native terms to replace western, universal concepts of development and to illustrate clear variations of maturational processes within non-western and third-world contexts.

Similar diversity can be seen in the works of researchers and psychologists of the South Pacific. Some have relied on North American and Western European concepts and theories to analyse Pacific experiences while others have used their own local language, concepts and world views to make sense of their own people's maturational process (Helu-Thaman 1992; Koloto 2000; Macfarlane 2000; Penetito 2000; Tupuola 1993a, 1998). My own research with young women of Samoan descent in New Zealand examined the terms 'human development' and 'adolescence' in differing Samoan contexts (Tupuola 1993a, 1998). The notion of 'human development', as defined by western psychologists in popular psychology texts (see Bird & Drewery 2000), proved challenging to explain. Many of these women seemed to associate their maturation process with cultural and familial expectations and had some difficulty identifying with a concept that seemed age-defined and progressive in nature: 'I still find it hard to understand ... I never thought about human development ... probably 'cause my aiga [family] and the culture have really determined the way I've turned out ... I wasn't even aware of my own development 'til now' (Born in Samoa, cited in Tupuola 1993a: 278).

This young woman's comment captures the strong influences of both the Samoan culture and the aiga in shaping and defining the maturational process of young Samoan women. In traditional Samoan societies the behaviour of the young Samoan woman is a reflection of her family's honour (see Huntsman 1995; Shankman 1984). Thus, her daily routine is defined by rigid cultural and familial codes of conduct such as obedience, deference, servitude and chastity, leaving little room for her to shape and determine her own process of growth: 'I'm constantly being protected by my brothers, my parents and my extended family and so there is never the opportunity for me to do things independently or to even make my own career choices ... that's all laid out for me' (Born in New Zealand, cited in Tupuola 1998: 131).

In recognising the strong influence of fa'aSamoa in the maturation process of these participants, my research used the Samoan term 'tuputupua'e' (growth) in place of 'human development' as it captured not only the holistic nature of maturation but also the interconnected relationship between the physical, emotional, psychological and spiritual. A term that instigated a lot of debate and that reflected the diversity amongst the participants was 'adolescence'. Definitions of adolescence in both traditional and cross-cultural texts of human development and psychology seem to identify it as a universal period of experimentation, individuation and sexual maturity (Blos 1967; Erikson 1968; Hall 1916; Hansburg 1980). My research found the concept of adolescence problematic and not as universally applicable as these theories seemed to suggest. When I asked the women 'Are any of you familiar with the term adolescence?' their responses varied, as did their experiences, despite them all being raised in New Zealand. The following comment alludes to the limitations of experimentation and individualism in Samoan contexts as well as to the influential role of the Samoan culture in the woman's maturation process: '[adolescence] sounds so limiting ... It has to do with the way my Samoan culture shapes me ... I am not expected to experiment nor allowed to make my own decisions. So, I don't relate to this label adolescence and I'd be shocked if it was encouraged in the Samoan culture' (Born in New Zealand, cited in Tupuola 1998: 121).

Another participant provides an interesting view. Although she was born in New Zealand, a predominantly westernised and developed country, she appears to have greater affiliation with her Samoan culture, suggesting that the processes of adolescence may not necessarily be an attainable reality for all young people born and raised in western societies:

> I think if I wanted to I could easily say, 'oh yeah, well I was born in New Zealand and I'm a typical ... adolescent' but I can't because there's always this influence from my Samoan side ... I don't really have the opportunities to experience all the things ... adolescents are supposed to. Um, I'd like to but it's like the Samoan culture protects us ... so we don't get to experience for ourselves (Born in New Zealand, cited in Tupuola 1998: 121).

These comments support literature that describes the Samoan community as a population less inclined to assimilate with New Zealand

and papalagi (European) lifestyles (see Pitt & Macpherson 1974) and the view that 'in some cultures there is no period of adolescence, as Westerners know it, and there are no words to describe it' (Côté 1994: 149).

Thus far I have provided a rather polarised analysis of adolescence whereby the comments of women have been used to support the seemingly westernised characteristics of adolescents and the limitations for traditional non-western societies such as fa'aSamoa. The following comments portray a more complex discussion of adolescents. They illustrate the changing and shifting population of young Samoan women and point out the need for researchers to examine the overt and covert characteristics and realities of youth of diasporic and mixed ethnic backgrounds to make sense of adolescence into the twenty first century:

> I think I am an adolescent but then ... um like you look at me and if you saw me from the outside you'd probably think, 'oh yeah, she's an adolescent 'cos her upbringing is pretty liberal', but underneath all this there is still a lot of cultural restrictions ... See, so adolescence ... maybe the term is wrong ... it doesn't describe us in-betweens properly (Born in New Zealand, cited in Tupuola 1998: 126).

This woman identified herself as 'in-between', as someone who is a product of a mixture of cultures that cannot be categorised as either Samoan or papalagi. The term 'adolescence' seemed limiting for reasons different from those of her traditional and predominantly westernised peers. While she appeared to have the opportunities to experience adolescence as her western peers seemed to, such opportunities were ambiguous and contradictory in nature. Thus, her overt experiences are not necessarily reflective of the contradictory role she lives on the covert level: 'It's so frustrating, one minute I'm given adolescent privileges, and, then suddenly out of nowhere, I have to obey Samoan ways and expectations ... So where does that leave me?' (Born in New Zealand, cited in Tupuola 1998: 127).

What are the boundaries between who is and who is not an adolescent for someone who is in-between? These women's comments point to a limited definition of adolescence for youth of westernised societies and perhaps suggest that an alternative label be created to interpret a maturation process that is reflective of their weaving in and out of different social and cultural conditions, blurring the binary between western and fa'aSamoa.

My search for a suitable Samoan word to replace 'adolescence' proved difficult. The three terms that were considered were 'tupulaga' (young generation), 'autalavou' (youth group) and 'tamaiti' (child) as they all had some reference to youth. However, in Samoan contexts the meanings of these terms are broad, can include age groups outside 'adolescence' and may be used varyingly at the discretion of the community and family. The use of a single Samoan term to define an 'adolescent' therefore seemed inappropriate and problematic as it would have overlooked the overlapping and less compartmentalised nature of growth, the intra-cultural disparities of fa'aSamoa as well as the complex and changing cultural conditions for young Samoans in New Zealand: 'I've not gone through life in a prescribed order ... from childhood to adolescence to adulthood ... I have an unpredictable role and my development is not as clear cut in fa'aSamoa' (Born in New Zealand, cited in Tupuola 1998: 121).

The way that westernised psychological terms are used in different cultural contexts deserves attention. That is, making reference to terms such as 'Samoan adolescence' or 'Samoan human development' without clarification and definition can be problematic, especially as the perception of adolescence and human development in Samoan contexts is complex and seemingly different from that of popular western psychological theories (Tupuola 1993a, 1998). Additionally, using these references loosely can dangerously simplify the heterogeneous backgrounds and maturational processes of Samoan youth:

> My western side allows me the independence ... to experiment, but it's like my Samoan side places some degree of limitation. ... I can go out with boys but only if I'm chaperoned ... I can go to 'varsity and choose my subjects but only if I join the Samoan choir. So I guess my maturational process is one of compromising, um part Samoan and part western – it's like a combination of the two – the boundaries are unclear (Born in New Zealand, cited in Tupuola 1998: 129).

Traditional psychology narratives

> The term human development refers to development [as] an evolution process based upon a universally experienced sequence of biological, psychological, and social events (Maier 1969: 29).

It is interesting to note how traditional popular psychology theories of the twentieth-century continue to be seen as master narratives, whether intentional or not, with reference to Samoan and cross-cultural research in human development (Tupuola 1998). Ongoing storm and stress and nature versus nurture debates seem to promote adolescence as a universal stage of growth and appear to simplify and essentialise non-western communities and realities (see Freeman 1983; Holmes 1987; Mead 1943). Similarly, the current discourse on personal and ethnic identity seems predominantly preoccupied with the ideas of Erikson (1950, 1968) and his fellow psycho-analysts (Blos 1967; Marcia 1966, 1967, 1976) who compartmentalise adolescence and human development into specific stages and statuses and emphasise an individualistic and universal developmental assumption: 'Development proceeds from dependence to autonomy. To grow is to separate' (Marcia, Waterman, Matteson, Archer & Orlofsky 1993: 94).

Some cross-cultural studies of psychology also seem filtered through western and mainstream psychological theories and ideas. Much of the research about Pacific youth, while useful, seems to reiterate western norms of development such as decision-making, experimentation and sexual maturation. It also refers to models of ethnic and personal identity that connote optimal levels of maturity and identity and generalisations about western and non-western youth (Bird & Drewery 2000). In some instances the studies about personal identity for non-western youth also seem to rely on models of development and methods of analysis specific to white, middle-class and/or modern conditions that emphasise western and androcentric characteristics such as autonomy and independence as essential developmental necessities (see Kroger 1989).

Inter and intracultural challenges

> The fact that most of us are blind to our own cultural heritage, except when we become aware of contrasting practises, makes the explicit study of culture an essential resource for studying the human condition (Rogoff & Morelli 1989: 341-342).

Has there been much change in the way human development and adolescence are theorised, measured and studied as we move into the twenty-first century? The growing amount of cross-cultural study and the participation of more third-world psychologists in the discipline of psychology is to be applauded. However, as this paper has shown, not all cross-cultural and third-world studies see it as necessary to promote local concepts or prioritise terms outside the English language. I have faced considerable challenges with my own work in re-addressing the use of western psychological terms in non-western studies and writings. It seems that, while there is some encouragement within western academia for non-western researchers to provide alternative perspectives, the support to do this is not always consistent. Although I have been encouraged by academics receptive to my work, there have been other times when I have faced both non-Samoan and Samoan academics alike who view the Samoan culture through a western lens, labelling my work as 'unscholarly' because it prioritises Samoan terms, research protocols and notions of knowledge (Tupuola 1993b). Despite a growing sympathy toward the 'insider's' perspective, western academic expectations and criteria often result in research that 'appeals to a small, educated élite ... firmly confined to the universities' (Watt 1985: 286). My own questioning of western theories and thought has received mixed reaction from my Pacific and Samoan peers. While limitations of western psychology theories are acknowledged by Pacific educators and academics, the reluctance to replace these with local concepts and terms is interesting. At public gatherings I am reminded of the effects of assimilation when some of my peers accentuate the value of western education and how inappropriate it is for me to question western thought and mainstream ideas (see Jones 1991). It is frustrating to hear both Pacific and non-Pacific researchers refer to 'adolescence' and 'human development' without clarification, and to be challenged by them for promoting terms that are of local relevance to the Pacific youth themselves. Why are some Pacific researchers more accepting of western world views than those of the Pacific? Is this form of assimilation by these researchers any different from the ethnocentrism found in some early twentieth-century psychology theories?

The assimilation of westernised terms by some of my Pacific peers is a complex issue that deserves some attention. My use of assimilation here refers to their academic adoption and duplication of papalagi academic terms and concepts while many of them continue to adhere to traditional customs, protocol and etiquette in their private lives outside the academic arena. This code switching and seeming reliance on western cultural capital reflects several factors. One is the predominantly westernised education system during the early 1970s and 1980s in Samoa and New Zealand where the expectations of Samoan parents for their children to excel in things western was high (Bray & Hill 1973; Jones 1991). Secondly, the concept of scholarship and knowledge in western academia calls for a mastering of westernised terms and concepts. This preferred cultural capital has become a problematic reality for Pacific academics as they strive for academic credibility and respect not only in mainstream academia but also within Pacific academia. In my own experience as a Master of Arts student I faced many challenges from both Samoan and non-Samoan peers when I wanted to use Samoan terms and a Samoan methodology for my research. Irrespective of the Samoan nature of my study, I was expected to meet particular criteria and adhere to specific papalagi scholarly guidelines. This illustrated to me the disparity between literature in both western and Pacific academia pushing for alternative cultural discourses and the difficult reality of putting these into practice (Hereniko 1995; Tupuola 1993b). Thus, while the institutional and social barriers to creating and prioritising Pacific codes of knowledge are great, it is still concerning that some Pacific researchers are unquestioningly recycling theories and maintaining the dominance of western terms and concepts that researchers like myself are trying to minimise.

Closing thoughts

How does one perceive master narratives in cross-cultural psychology? This essay has illustrated how westerners and non-westerners alike are relying on traditional western psychology theories to tell their stories. Despite the useful contribution made by many cross-cultural psychologists, the extent of assimilation cannot be ignored. As briefly mentioned here, some non-western and third-world researchers are adopting foreign terms to define and analyse their own populations. There are also cross-cultural studies that do not acknowledge the intra-cultural dynamics within cultural groups and thus rely on terms and concepts that are essentialist and reductionist such as 'Samoan adolescence' and 'Samoan human development'.

Indigenising western psychological terms is one approach suggested here for emphasising the local and creating alternative forms of knowledge. In this era of minorities, indigenous populations and third-world countries, it seems appropriate that both western and non-western psychologists take more caution in the terms and concepts that they use. It is also necessary that future studies of psychology focus less on the polarisation between western and non-western and more on the integrated relationship these cultures have in the maturational process of diasporic communities. My own research of young Samoan women is valuable in that it begins to explore alternative perspectives and interpretations of human development and adolescence. Furthermore, it illustrates the diverse backgrounds of these women and my own difficulty in finding a single term and concept to accurately describe and define their maturational process. Tuputupua'e seems to be a valid concept in Samoan contexts in that it projects a holistic process of growth and recognises the covert influences of fa'aSamoa for the young woman. However, despite its value, it needs to be used with caution as it was a concept that was adopted to interpret and define the cultural experiences of a specific group of Samoan women in my research. Thus, the use of indigenous terms and the context in which they are used in intra-cultural and cross-cultural studies deserves further attention. As shown in this paper, a name can have many connotations. It seems pivotal that current and future psychology researchers must clearly define, interpret and use the concepts of human development and adolescence in their appropriate cultural contexts:

> Interactants need to coordinate both the content and the process of what they are doing ... they cannot even begin to coordinate on content without assuming a vast amount of shared information or common ground – that is, mutual knowledge, mutual beliefs, and mutual assumptions ... And to coordinate on process, they need to update their common ground moment by moment (Clark & Brennan 1991: 127).

References

Abu-Lughod, L. (1991) 'Writing Against Culture', in R.G. Fox (ed), *Recapturing Anthropology: Looking In The Present*, Sante Fe, NM: School of American Research Press, pp137-162.

Adelson, J. (ed) (1980) *Handbook Of Adolescent Psychology*, New York: John Wiley.

Ardila, R. (1996) 'Ethnopsychology and social values in Colombia', *Interamerican Journal of Psychology* 30: 127-40.

Berzonsky, M.D. (1981) *Adolescent Development*, New York: MacMillan.

Bhaskaran, S. (1993) 'Physical Subjectivity And The Risk Of Essentialism', in Women of South Asian Descent Collective (eds), *Our Feet Walk The Sky: Women Of The South Asian Diaspora*, San Francisco: Aunt Lute Books, pp191-202.

Bird, L. & W. Drewery (2000) *Human Development In Aotearoa: A Journey Through Life*, Auckland, NZ: McGraw-Hill.

Blos, P. (1967) 'The Second Individuation Process Of Adolescence', *Psychoanalytic Study of the Child* 22: 162-186.
Bond, M.H. (1996) *The Handbook Of Chinese Psychology*, Hong Kong: Oxford University Press.
Bray, D., & C. Hill (eds) (1973) *Polynesia and Pakeha in New Zealand Education Vol 1: The sharing of cultures*, Auckland, NZ: Heinmann.
Chen, K-H. (1992) 'Voices From The Outside: Towards A New Internationalist Localism', *Cultural Studies* 6: 476-484.
Clark, H.H. & S.E. Brennan (1991) 'Grounding In Communication', in L.B Resnick, J.M. Levine & S.D. Teasley (eds), *Perspectives On Socially Shared Cognition*, Washington DC: American Psychological Association, pp127-149.
Côté, J. (1994) *Adolescent Storm And Stress: An Evaluation Of The Mead-Freeman Controversy*, NJ: Lawrence Erlbaum.
Doi, T. (1973) *The Anatomy Of Dependence*, New York: Harper Row.
Erikson, E.H. (1950) *Childhood And Society*, New York: Norton.
Erikson, E.H. (1968) *Identity: Youth And Crisis*, London: Faber and Faber.
Featherman, D.L. (1993) 'What does society need from higher education?', *Items* 47: 38-43.
Freeman, D. (1983) *Margaret Mead And Samoa: The Making And Unmaking Of An Anthropological Myth*, Canberra: Australian University Press.
Garrod, A., J.V Ward., T.L. Robinson, & R. Kilkenny (1999) *Souls Looking Back: Life Stories Of Growing Up Black*, New York: Routledge.
Hall, G.S. (1916) *Adolescence* 2 vols. New York: Appleton.
Hansburg, H.G. (1980) *Adolescent Separation Anxiety: A Method For The Study Of Adolescent Separation Problems*, New York: Robert E. Kreiger Publishing Company.
Helu-Thaman, K. (1992) 'The Kakala metaphor', *ACCESS* 11: 44-50.
Hereniko, V. (1995) 'Indigenous Knowledge And Academic Imperialism', paper presented at the *Contested Knowledge and Power in Pacific Studies* Conference, Hawaii.
Hollan, D. (1992) 'Cross-Cultural Differences In The Self', *Journal of Anthropological Research* 48: 283-300.
Holmes, L.D. (1987) *Quest For The Real Samoan: The Mead/Freeman Controversy And Beyond*, South Hadley, MA: Bergin and Garvey.
hooks, b. (1990) Yearning: Race, Gender And Cultural Politics, Boston: South End Press.
Huntsman, J. (ed) (1995) *Tonga And Samoa: Images Of Gender And Polity*, Christchurch, NZ: Macmillan Brown Centre for Pacific Studies.
Jones, A. (1991) *'At School I've Got A Chance': Culture/Privilege: Pacific Islands And Pakeha Girls At School*, Palmerston North: Dunmore Press.
Koloto, A. (2000) 'A Tongan Perspective On Development', in L. Bird & W. Drewery (eds), *Human Development In Aotearoa: A Journey Through Life*, Auckland, NZ: McGraw-Hill, pp34-39.
Kroger, J. (1989) *Identity In Adolescence: The Balance Between Self And Other*, New York: Routledge.
Lerner, R.M. (1986) *Concepts And Theories Of Human Development*, (2nd ed),

New York: Random House.
Lotfalian, M. (1996) 'Working Through Psychological Understandings Of The Diasporic Condition', *Ethos* 24: 36-70.
Macfarlane, A. (2000) 'The Value Of Maori Ecologies In The Study Of Human Development', in L. Bird & W. Drewery (eds), *Human Development In Aotearoa: A Journey Through Life*, Auckland, NZ: McGraw-Hill, pp46-51.
Maier, H.W. (1969) *Three Theories Of Child Development:The Contributions Of Erik H. Erikson, Jean Piaget And Robert Searls And Their Application*, New York: Harper Row.
Mani, L. (1992) 'Multiple Mediations: Feminist Scholarship In The Age Of Multinational Reception', in H. Crowley & S. Himmelwait (eds), *Knowing Women: Feminism And Knowledge*, Cambridge: Cambridge Polity Press, pp306-321.
Marcia, J. (1966) 'Development And Validation Ego-Identity Status', *Journal of Personality and Social Psychology* 5: 551-558.
Marcia, J. (1967) 'Ego Identity Status: Relationship To Change In Self-Esteem, "General Maladjustment" And Authoritarianism', *Journal of Personality* 35: 118-133.
Marcia, J. (1976) 'Identity Six Years After: A Follow Up Study', *Journal of Youth and Adolescent Psychology* 5: 145-160.
Marcia, J.E., A.S. Waterman, D.R Matteson, S.L Archer & J.L. Orlofsky (1993) *Ego Identity: A Handbook For Psychological Research*, New York: Springer-Verlag.
Mead, M. (1943) *Coming Of Age In Samoa: A Study Of Adolescence And Sex In Primitive Societies*, New York: Penguin.
Moghaddam, F.M. (1987) 'Psychology In The Three Worlds,' *American Psychologist* 42: 912-20.
Mpofu, E. (1995) 'Exploring The Self-Concept In An African Culture', *Journal of Genetic Psychology* 155: 341-54.
Ongel, U. & P.B. Smith (1994) 'Who Are We and Where are We Going? JCCP Approaches its 100th Issue', *Journal of Cross-Cultural Psychology* 25: 25-53.
Palsane, N.M. & D.J. Lam (1996) 'Stress And Coping From Traditional Indian And Chinese Perspectives', *Psychology and Developing Societies* 4: 89-104.
Penetito, W. (2000) 'The Social Construction Of Maori Identity: The Roles And Tastes And Preferences', in L. Bird & W. Drewery (eds), *Human development in Aotearoa: A journey through life*,. Auckland, NZ: McGraw-Hill, pp52-61
Pitt, D., & C. Macpherson (1974) *Emerging Pluralism: Samoan Community In New Zealand*, Auckland, NZ: Longman Paul.
Rasiah, D. (1993) 'Mississippi Masala And Khush: Redefining Community', in Women of South Asian Descent Collective (eds), *Our feet walk the sky: Women of the South Asian Diaspora*, San Francisco: Aunt Lute Books, pp267-273.
Rogoff, B. & G. Morelli (1989) 'Section Introduction', *American Psychologist* 44: 341-342.
Santrock, J.W. (1987) *Adolescence: An introduction*, Iowa: Wm. C. Brown Publishers.
Sebald, H. (1984) *Adolescence: A Social Psychological Analysis* (3rd edition),

Englewood Cliffs, NJ: Prentice-Hall.
Shankman, P. (1984) 'The Samoan Conundrum', *Canberra Anthropology* 6: 38-57.
Sinha, D. (1997) 'Indigenising Psychology', In J.W. Berry, Y. Poortinga & J. Pandey (eds), *Handbook Of Cross-Cultural Psychology: Theory And Method*, Boston: Allyn and Bacon, pp129-169.
Smith, P. & M.H. Bond (1998) *Social Psychology Across Cultures*, Hemel Hempstead, UK: Prentice Hall Europe.
Tupuola, A.M. (1993a) *Critical Analysis Of Adolescent Development: A Samoan Women's Perspective*, unpublished manuscript, Victoria University of Wellington, New Zealand.
Tupuola, A.M. (1993b) 'Raising Research Consciousness The Fa'asamoa Way', *New Zealand Annual Review* 3: 169-190.
Tupuola, A.M. (1996) 'Learning Sexuality: Young Samoan Women', *Women's Studies Journal* 12: 59-76.
Tupuola, A.M. (1998) 'Adolescence': Myth or Reality for Samoan Women? Beyond the Stage-like Toward Shifting Boundaries and Identities', unpublished manuscript, Victoria University of Wellington, New Zealand.
Watt, J. (1985) 'Literature And Liberation: Black Consciousness In Recent South African Writing', *Ethnic and Racial Studies* 8: 227-291.
Wierzbicka, A. (1993) 'A Conceptual Basis For Cultural Psychology', *Ethos* 21: 205-31.

Social constructionist psychology: almost critical?

John Cromby & David J. Nightingale

Introduction

Social constructionist psychology is not a unitary body of theory, method and practice, but a disparate collection of approaches which share a 'family resemblance' (Burr 1995). This critique is directed at that vociferous member of the constructionist family which proclaims a universal and totalising relativism as its philosophical ground (e.g. Edwards, Ashmore and Potter 1995; Gergen 1994). This variant, broadly consonant with the 'light' strand of constructionism described by Danziger (1997) and sometimes characterised as 'discursive psychology' (Edwards and Potter 1992; Parker 1997), has been much discussed by critical psychologists (for example, Gill 1995), notably in the 'realism-relativism debate (Parker 1998). Here, our focus is not on realism or relativism *per se*, but on the limitations of a wholly relativist social constructionist psychology (hereafter, SCP) for critical psychology.

To complicate matters further, critical psychology is itself a multiplicity of approaches and although definitions have been offered (Fox & Prilletensky 1995; *International Journal of Critical Psychology* 1,1 and 1,2) no consensus around any one of these has yet emerged. For our purposes, we define critical psychology as a heterogeneous matrix of interconnected activities directed at supporting or creating progressive social transformation, such activities necessarily entailing a fundamental interrogation and reconstruction of the basic categories and underlying binaries (individual/social, mind/body) which constitute culturally dominant, institutionalised psychological knowledge. Thus, we both emphasise the goal-directed nature of critical psychology and acknowledge its sometimes covert relationship with the mainstream, identifying critical psychology partly by contrast with what is not. Below, we will briefly describe some of the inconsistencies and problems of SCP, then discuss its value for critical psychology. We conclude by suggesting that a *critical realist* social constructionism ultimately has far greater potential for progressive social transformation, and hence for critical psychology.

Social constructionist psychology (SCP) and relativism

SCP's wholesale commitment to relativism produces inconsistencies and effects which we will now summarise (for a fuller account see Cromby and Nightingale 1999; Nightingale and Cromby 1999a). Relativists argue that relativism is 'the quintessentially academic position' (Edwards et al 1995: 37) and claim for it a meta-epistemological superiority since it 'can include both realism and relativism alike, viewed as rhetorical practices' (p41). Such arguments seem to confer upon relativism a degree of coherence and internal consistency, but on closer examination this apparent coherence disintegrates. As Eagleton (1996: 28) says: 'epistemological anti-realism [relativism] ... consistently denies the possibility of describing the way the world is, and just as consistently finds itself doing so'. Thus in SCP, ontological claims that persons and their psychological characteristics are socially constructed (not the outcome of biology, genes or internal essences) accompany an epistemological stance which simultaneously denies the possibility of making *any* ontological claims: 'because disquisitions on the nature of things are framed in language, there is no grounding of science or any other knowledge-generating enterprise in other than communities of interlocutors. There is no appeal to mind or matter – to reason or facts – that will lend transcendental validity to propositions' (Gergen 1994: ix).

The incoherence of a universal relativism is further demonstrated by the selectivity with which it is deployed. SCP is legitimated by historical, cross-cultural and anthropological evidence, which shows that notions of the person vary greatly across time and between cultures – yet the typically uncritical acceptance of this evidence constitutes a realist stance towards it. A similar implicit realism is visible in the treatment of 'transcripts', 'discourse' and 'talk' in SCP, which also commonly appear as unproblematically real. Consequently, despite its vocal commitment to relativism, SCP tends towards an unexamined naive realism with respect to some aspects of human life.

The commitment to relativism symbiotically sustains the close focus on language and discourse that characterises SCP, but simultaneously leaves it unable to address human embodiment and the materiality of our world as anything other than *talk* of bodies and the world. SCP implicitly adopts both a 'uniform plasticity of the body' (Nightingale 1999: 169) and an indifferent stance towards the material, ecological, environmental and physical aspects of human life. Murphy (1995) argues that such a stance, which is only sustained by avoiding comparative research that would highlight material influences, produces conceptual errors, reifies the 'social', and causes a substantial loss of ecological validity.

SCP as critical psychology

The simultaneous loss of both embodiment and materiality leaves SCP unable to adequately address the issue of *power*. For without some conception of embodied beings in a material world, beings facilitated and constrained by their physical features, spatio-temporal location and access to resources, there is nothing 'really' at stake any more. Bodies and power are intimately connected, as illustrated by both academic theory (see for example, Bourdieu 1977; Foucault 1977; Young 1990) and the lives of people whose bodies deviate from conventional norms. Materiality, too, both structures and is structured by power – from armies and weapons of mass destruction, to striking global inequalities and access to basic living resources. But SCP cannot incorporate embodiment and materiality (and hence power) as *influences partly beyond the text*:[1] consequently, enduring global or socio-political inequalities (around gender, ethnicity, sexuality) either dissolve into ways of talking, rhetorical practices, discursive strategies; or alternatively remain under-theorised and must appear as simply, naively real.

SCP rose to prominence concurrently with the cultural phenomenon of 'political correctness', and may gain political credibility from its correspondences with this strategy of monitoring and manipulation of everyday language – especially in academia, where we have a duty to use language responsibly. But in progressive social transformation much more is at stake than mere words. Despite political correctness, inequality and injustice continue to grow, both between nation states (Oxfam 1991; WHO 1995) and within them (see for example, Joseph Rowntree Foundation 1995; World Bank 1993). Some decades ago, Orwell's *Nineteen Eighty-Four* (1954) described how changing language in the context of oppressive structures simply concealed their existence; more recently, Ehrlich and King's (1992) empirical study pointed to similar conclusions. Earlier still, Marx brought his reading of Feuerbach to bear on Hegel's dialectic and argued that '... ideas sprang from conflict instead of causing it. In his own words, he found Hegelianism standing on its head and put it the right way up' (Taylor 1967: 9). Marx's point was that ideas are rooted in material forces, not independent of them. We (the authors) are not Marxists, and are aware of the unhelpful determinism it can introduce. But nor are we idealists, and we recognise in SCP a tendency towards idealism which we find equally problematic. SCP's rise to prominence was broadly contemporaneous with the collapse of the Eastern Bloc, proclamations of the 'end of history' (Fukayama 1993) and the triumph of capitalism, a historical context which made it difficult to criticise SCP from a materialist, dialectical perspective. Historically, though, not all opposition to capitalism has been Marxist (Hampton 1984; Marshall 1993). Whether recent anti-capitalist protests (in Seattle, Prague, London, Sydney and elsewhere) are the seeds of a new movement or the last gasp of an outmoded tradition remains to be seen, but in either case the idealist tendencies of SCP make it incompatible with them.

This leads to another problem of SCP, arising from its confused, ambiguous conception of subjectivity. That SCP lacks a coherent conception of the embodied subject has been acknowledged (Bayer and Shotter 1998; Cromby and Standen 1999), but in relation to critical psychology this lack becomes especially pertinent. Some notion of the desiring, agentic subject (however fragmented, split, multiple and irrational) has long been central to critical thought (Fay 1987). Lacking this, SCP is incapable of properly theorising alienation, oppression, submission, protest, resistance and the desire for progressive social transformation. These are fundamental issues for critical psychology: indeed, detailed examination of why and how people cope with, endure and adapt to inequitable social structures might constitute the greatest strategic contribution towards progressive social transformation that critical psychology can currently deliver. Moreover, because of this lack proponents of SCP 'who do suggest active subjects ... often have leaned on humanist notions of autonomous actors' (Morawski 1998: 222); just as inadequately theorising embodiment and materiality leads to naive realism, so not theorising the subject leads to naive humanism.

Despite these shortcomings SCP has nevertheless challenged mainstream psychology, questioning its core assumptions and typical practices. However, Burman (1990) observes that the totalising relativism of SCP is a dangerous tool which deconstructs solutions as readily as it deconstructs problems. This point is amplified by studies of critical thinking (see for example, Held 1980; Fay 1987) which demonstrate that realism and relativism are typically deployed strategically, not universally: writers ground their critique in aspects of the world they wish to make or remain real, and from this grounding relativise those aspects they wish to question or deny. So a further problem of SCP as critical psychology is that its wholesale commitment to relativism undermines its political ability and intent. Importantly, this problem is not confined to academia but also may impact upon social movements: for example, Segal (1987) describes the negative consequences for feminist 'consciousness raising' groups of relativist, poststructuralist theories.

Conclusion

SCP declares its commitment to a universal, totalising relativism, but simultaneously deploys a naive realism with respect to various features of psychology and human life. That is, SCP is already selectively relativist but fails either to acknowledge its selectivity or critically examine its selection criteria. By contrast, advocates of a critical realist social constructionist psychology (such as, Parker 1992; Willig 1999; Nightingale and Cromby 1999b) posit an intransitive realm to which we can never have direct access (Bhaskar 1978); hence we must maintain a vigilant, critical engagement with ontology which may help us avoid the naive realism that ensnares unwitting proponents of SCP.

In critical psychology, the critical realist approach is superior to SCP since it can comprehensively include embodiment, materiality and power: not as naively real 'things in themselves', nor as mere discursive traces, metaphors, tropes or texts. Materiality is mediated by language, artifacts, the body (including its sensory and perceptual apparatus, an apparatus which is itself modified by experience), and activity in a complex, multidimensional fashion. The nature of our world is not simply a matter of how we talk about it, but nor is it simply given, naively real. Critical realists are also able to theorise subjectivity without falling back on naive humanism, for example using a critical, reflexive humanism (Parker, 1999), psychoanalysis (for example, Henriques, Hollway, Urwin, Venn and Walkerdine 1984), or the concepts of subjective possibility spaces and action potence drawn from German Critical Psychology (Tolman 1994). Consequently, critical realists can contribute to the interrogation of capitalism's *emotional* economy.

The impossibility of unmediated access to the world means that ontological commitment (to whatever local, mediated version of reality) is not merely a matter of empiricism (naive realism) and argument (SCP). Shotter (1993) suggests that the question of 'who shall live in whose reality?' is inevitably a moral, ethical, political matter. However, SCP's rhetorical relativism problematises any moral-ontological commitment, allowing it to appear either radical or apolitical as suits the occasion. In these reactionary times such coyness is understandable, but inappropriate for critical psychology. SCP is almost critical; certainly sceptical; at worst, perhaps, cynical. A critical realist constructionism, by contrast, remains theoretically consistent, morally and politically engaged, and wholly sensitive to the disputed, constructed character of human life.

Notes

1. By this we do not mean that embodiment and materiality are not shot through with discourse, or that our experience is not mediated by language. Embodiment and materiality are indeed mediated, and not just by language (as we explain later). Our point is that embodiment and materiality are not *reducible to* language, that not all of their aspects and influences are matters of how they appear in discourse. We could not, for example, stop bodies from carrying out respiration by excising this term from our vocabularies, conversation and texts. More tellingly, perhaps, nor could we cure a tumour by renaming it as an abscess and then bursting it.

References

Bayer, B. and J. Shotter (eds) (1998) *Reconstructing The Psychological Subject: Bodies, Practices, Technologies*, London: Sage Publications.
Bhaskar, R. (1978) *A Realist Theory Of Science*, Brighton: Harvester Press.
Bourdieu, P. (1977) *Outline Of A Theory Of Practice*, R.Nice (trans), Cambridge: Cambridge University Press.
Burman, E. (1990) 'Differing With Deconstruction: A Feminist Critique', in I. Parker and J. Shotter, *Deconstructing Social Psychology*, London: Routledge.
Burr, V. (1995) *An Introduction to Social Constructionism*, London: Routledge.

Cromby, J. and D. Nightingale (1999) 'What's Wrong With Social Constructionism?', in D.J. Nightingale and J. Cromby, *Social Constructionist Psychology: A Critical Analysis Of Theory And Practice*, Buckingham: Open University Press.

Cromby, J. and P.J. Standen (1999) 'Taking Our Selves Seriously', in D.J. Nightingale and J. Cromby, *Social Constructionist Psychology: A Critical Analysis Of Theory And Practice*, Buckingham: Open University Press.

Danziger, K. (1997) 'The Varieties Of Social Construction', *Theory and Psychology*, 7,3: 399-16.

Eagleton, T. (1996) *The Illusions of Postmodernism*, Oxford: Blackwells.

Edwards, D., M. Ashmore and J. Potter (1995) 'Death And Furniture: The Rhetoric, Politics And Theology Of Bottom-Line Arguments Against Relativism', *History of the Human Sciences* 8,2: 25-49.

Edwards, D. and J. Potter (1992) *Discursive Psychology*, London: Sage Publications.

Ehrlich, S. and R. King (1992) 'Gender Based Language Reform And The Social Construction Of Meaning', *Discourse and Society* 3,2: 151-166.

Fay, B. (1987) *Critical Social Science*, Cambridge: Polity Press.

Foucault, M. (1977) *Discipline And Punish: The Birth Of The Prison*, Harmondsworth: Penguin.

Fox, D. and I. Prilletensky (1997) *Critical Psychology: An Introduction*, London: Sage Publications.

Fukayama, F. (1993) *The End of History and the Last Man*, Harmondsworth: Penguin.

Gergen, K. (1994) *Realities And Relationships: Soundings In Social Construction*, Cambridge, Mass: Harvard University Press.

Gill, R. (1995) 'Relativism, Reflexivity and Politics: Interrogating Discourse Analysis from a Feminist Perspective', in S. Wilkinson and C. Kitzinger, *Feminism and Discourse: Psychological Perspectives*, London: Sage Publications.

Hampton, C. (1984), *A Radical Reader: The Struggle For Change In England 1381-1914*, Harmondsworth: Penguin.

Held, D. (1980) *Introduction To Critical Theory: Horkheimer To Habermas*, Berkeley: University of California Press.

Henriques, J., W. Hollway, C. Urwin, C. Venn and V. Walkerdine, (1984/ reprinted 1998) *Changing The Subject: Psychology, Social Regulation And Subjectivity*, London: Routledge.

International Journal of Critical Psychology (2001) 1,1 and 1,2, London: Lawrence and Wishart.

Joseph Rowntree Foundation (1995) 'Income And Wealth: Report Of The JRF Inquiry Group', (Social Policy Foundation), York: Joseph Rowntree Foundation.

Marshall, P. (1993) *Demanding The Impossible: A History Of Anarchism*, London: Fontana.

Morawski, J. (1998) 'The Return Of Phantom Subjects', in B. Bayer and J. Shotter (eds), *Reconstructing The Psychological Subject: Bodies, Practices, Technologies*, London: Sage Publications.

Murphy, R.(1995) 'Sociology As If Nature Did Not Matter: An Ecological Critique', *British Journal of Sociology* 46,4: 688-707

Nightingale, D.J. (1999) 'Bodies: Reading the Body', in I. Parker and the Bolton Discourse Network (eds), *Critical Textwork: An Introduction to Varieties of Discourse and Analysis*, Buckingham: Open University Press.

Nightingale, D.J. and J. Cromby (1999a) 'Reconstructing Social Constructionism', in D.J. Nightingale and J. Cromby, *Social Constructionist Psychology: A Critical Analysis Of Theory And Practice*, Buckingham: Open University Press.

Nightingale, D.J. and J. Cromby (eds) (1999b) *Social Constructionist Psychology: a critical analysis of theory and practice*, Buckingham: Open University Press.

Orwell, G. (1954) *Nineteen Eighty-Four*, Harmondsworth: Penguin.

Oxfam (1991) *The World: A Third World Guide*, London: Oxfam.

Parker, I. (1992) *Discourse Dynamics: Critical Analysis For Social And Individual Psychology*, London: Routledge.

Parker, I. (1997) 'Discursive Psychology', in D. Fox and I. Prilletensky, *Critical psychology: an introduction*, London: Sage Publications.

Parker, I. (ed) (1998) *Social Constructionism, Discourse and Realism*, London: Sage Publications.

Parker, I. (1999) 'Critical Reflexive Humanism And Critical Constructionist Psychology', in D.J. Nightingale and J. Cromby, *Social Constructionist Psychology: A Critical Analysis Of Theory And Practice*, Buckingham: Open University Press.

Segal, L. (1987) *Is the Future Female? Troubled thoughts on contemporary feminism*, London: Virago Press.

Shotter, J. (1993) *Cultural Politics Of Everyday Life*, Buckingham: Open University Press.

Taylor, A.J.P. (1967) *Introduction to The Communist Manifesto* (Marx, K. and F. Engels), Harmondsworth: Penguin.

Tolman, C.W. (1994) *Psychology, Society And Subjectivity: An Introduction To German Critical Psychology*, London: Routledge.

WHO (1995) *World Health Report*, Geneva: World Health Organisation.

Willig, C. (ed) (1999) *Applied Discourse Analysis: Social And Psychological Interventions*, Buckingham: Open University Press.

World Bank (1993) *World Development Report 1993: Investing In Health*, New York: Oxford University Press.

Young, I.M. (1990) *Throwing Like A Girl And Other Essays In Feminist Philosophy And Social Theory*, Bloomington, Indiana: Indiana University Press.

Reviews

E.A. Wilson, *Neural Geographies: Feminism and the Microstructure of Cognition*

Routledge, New York and London 1998
(ISBN 0-415-91600-3)

Ian Hodges

Neural Geographies is a thoughtful and challenging work, aiming at a novel synthesis of an impressive range of topics – from feminist (and queer) criticism through to psychoanalysis, cognition and connectionism. It is the desire for a 'liaison' (p4) between critical and scientific systems that lies at the heart of Wilson's arguments, a plea for a place *in between* science and phenomenology, a deconstructed non-present space of indetermination which nonetheless engages with the *ontological* features of the realms of biology and neurology. However, this book suffers from a narrow formulation of critical practice and restricted initial definition of its key themes (for example, cognition). Overall, it fails to deliver a coherent way forward for feminist-critical psychology.

Chapters one and two explore two different and often opposed areas of psychology, feminism and science. Wilson begins by asking 'In what manner and how effectively does feminism inhabit psychology?' (p32). She highlights a number of concerns about the current state of feminist psychology, in particular its lack of attention to the those areas which ' ... appear to cover a more neutral or sexually indifferent terrain (perception, cognition, neurology)' (p32). Wilson concludes that feminist psychology fails to adequately challenge mainstream psychology because of its reliance on a narrow reading of the concerns of women and the concomitant neglect of the seemingly more gender-neutral areas described above. Alternatively, by engaging with these neglected arenas the very nature of feminist psychology might undergo a positive transformation.

Chapter two explores the notion that the problematic status of psychology as science might be considered a strength. In particular she concludes that the anti-empiricist tendencies of feminist critique may be remedied through the adoption of a deconstructionist critical practice which draws upon connectionist principles and which seeks to reformulate the project of scientific psychology as one in which the tensions between science and interpretation (for example biological and anti-biological positions) are exploited rather than erased.

Wilson goes on to examine the tensions between 'computational' and 'neurological' understandings of mind, lamenting the immobility of cognitive psychology's 'morphology of mind', and that ' ... the anatomical and topographical space that neurology exemplifies is confined with a logic of location and hierarchization' (p132). In chapter four Wilson explores the synergies between Freud's early attempts at a neurological theory of the psyche, connectionism and Derridean deconstruction. It is here that Wilson begins to work through the ideas outlined in earlier chapters, in particular the Derridean reading of Freud's term *bahnung* (literally 'path breaking') as *diférrance*, retranslated as 'breaching', which Wilson suggests offers a template for understanding science, cognition, neurology, psyche; ' ... by resolutely deflecting a conventional topographical location to the psyche, breaching provides the possibility of radically reformulating neurology and psychology.'

By chapter five Wilson has turned her attention to the differing nature of the psychical trace within cognitive psychology and deconstructionist practice (and how the cognitive and the neuropsychological traces are taken as *a priori* in their respective sub-disciplines). Reexamining the work of Bartlett, Neisser and others Wilson juxtaposes the 'self-present trace' of cognitive psychology with the connectionist trace which ' ... functions in a manner surprisingly faithful to certain Derridean considerations of inscription and mobility' (p189). Finally, this emphasis on the (deconstructed) trace posits cognition as non-present, mobile and unidentifiable and reflects Wilson's ultimate desires for critical practice within psychology, ' ... under the logic of breaching, our critical procedures may become more than contained and repetitive analyses of static objects and places' (p207).

The significant force of this text is its opposition to absolutist positions within debates about science, cognition, biology and feminism in psychology. In particular Wilson condemns feminist-critical approaches for their lack of attention to the properly biological aspects of Being, accusing them of focusing on embodiment (culture) as opposed to the body (biology). While critical psychologists in my view are much more aware of the problem of the body (not only embodiment) than Wilson suggests, the invitation to recognise danger in the seemingly 'neutral' zones of psychology is at minimum a useful call for debate.

There are however several problematic aspects of the book. One difficulty with this text is that the chapters read as stand-alone papers. Although there appears to be a broad overall thesis, it is difficult to identify accurately. For example, the issues raised in chapter one concerning the status of feminism in psychology are neglected towards the end of the book. This problem is further compounded by the fact that overall the material is primarily a critique of previous frameworks and models.

However my principal criticism is that Wilson's arguments do not seem to bear the weight of her stated objectives. Critical practice is represented only by deconstruction and, as Wilson reminds us, deconstruction cannot move beyond its object of analysis. Thus the well-rehearsed dispute with cognitive and neurological approaches remains; how is one to properly account for historical, moral, economic, political and cultural conditions of possibility. These are particularly marginalised in the final two chapters when cognition and PDP take centre-stage. It is one thing to point to the problem of cultural determinism as a mirror image of biological determinism but another to simply engulf history and culture within the processes of the 'text'.

Furthermore, the definitions given for key terms like cognition and cognitive psychology are too simplistic to form a substantial enough starting point for what becomes a complex theoretical journey. Likewise, because of the breadth of Wilson's thesis the various key frameworks, for example connectionism and feminism, do not receive the detailed consideration and discussion required for a representative picture of these areas to emerge. Also, I would have liked a greater acknowledgement of the differences between cognitive science and cognitive psychology. For many working on problems of cognition this distinction is an important one.

Wilson's major argument – that ultimately we must move towards a novel deconstructed scientific psychology – is thoughtfully presented; however it is not clear exactly how we would recognise such a psychological practice. Wilson several times reminds us that deconstruction does not offer alternative epistemologies (p163, p165); however it is not clear where these suggestions lead feminist-critical psychology. Put another way, the culmination of the logic of breaching remains enigmatic. Nowhere in the book are we offered a worked-up version of this new deconstructed critical-cognitive practice. Ultimately it is this lack of a coherent programme, whether theoretical, empirical, political or something in between, that will disappoint readers. Cognitive psychologists will be alarmed at the jettisoning of a recognisable empirical structure; critical psychologists will be frustrated by the lack of sustained attention to a feminist (and queer) agenda.

M. Wetherell, S. Taylor and S.J. Yates (eds), *Discourse Theory and Practice: A Reader*

London, Sage, 2001 (ISBN 0-7619-7156-4)

Patrick J. Leman

As a final year undergraduate (in the early 1990s) I stumbled into a first encounter with discursive psychology. I was finishing my studies at an institution that revelled in its title of the 'Department of *Experimental* Psychology'. With exams looming I felt that the discursive approach offered, at the very least, some relief from the endless box-diagrams I was committing to memory. But I had strayed off the reading list. In a subsequent tutorial I was left with the distinct impression that I was meddling with dangerous nonsense. Meekly, and in the interests of a decent final mark in those exams, I focused on committing still more box-diagrams to memory. It was a strategy that worked. After nearly a decade of decidedly experimental work of my own, I found that my own research, linking children's interaction with cognitive development, led me to return to this dangerous nonsense.

My interests in discourse theory and practice have emerged from my background in mainstream psychology. In this sense this review is informed by at least two perspectives. Firstly from that of an open-minded experimentalist: as a critical psychologist with a small 'c', if you like. And secondly, from a perspective of unabashed self-interest; I am not asking what I can do for discourse theory and practice but rather what discourse theory and practice can do for me?

Discourse Theory and Practice: A Reader goes a fair way towards answering that last question. It only goes a fair way because there is an accompanying volume, not reviewed here, that focuses more closely on methodological issues. The two volumes taken together would, I imagine, constitute a pretty comprehensive introduction to the area. That said, this reader also stands on its own as a book that succeeds in illustrating and introducing a broad range of research in discursive psychology. It is accessible to a relative novice in the field but is never patronising. It introduces key ideas and debates and leaves the reader wanting to pursue further readings in new directions. Most of all, it communicates and helps to shape for its reader a diverse and growing field that is rich in potential for future inquiry.

The book is intended for advanced (Masters) students in the social sciences. It is divided into four parts. The first part, 'Foundations and building blocks' consists of new writings introducing the range of approaches that fall under the umbrella of discourse theory. The remaining three sections, 'Social interaction', 'Minds, selves and sense making' and 'Culture and social relations', are made up of a selection of previously published writings by key figures in a field. Each of these three sections, the bulk of the book, is preceded by editorial introductions to the group of writings presented. These introductions serve a pivotal role in locating papers in both an historical and a theoretical context and ensure that the reader is guided though a disparate collection of papers. There is not space here to review nor even to list each chapter in any detail (there are twenty-seven). Instead I shall try to give a feel for the book as a whole whilst pointing only to parts if it.

The opening section consists of seven newly commissioned pieces that introduce a particular area of research and theory in studies of discourse processes. These include a clear and well-written introduction to some central themes in discourse research (Wetherell), and excellent introductory chapters on conversation analysis (Heritage), speech communities (Fitch), Bakhtin and Volosinov's writings (Maybin) and Foucault (Hall). Generally the introductory chapters that work best are those which illustrate theoretical points with examples of discourse and its analysis. In fact, as a route into understanding discourse theory I can think of no better means than to be led through the steps involved in analysis to see how theory and method are fused. All these introductory writings are good. But two (notably those by Kress and Potter) are short on such examples and, as a result, are perhaps a little drier than the others.

Another good feature of this reader, and not just the introductory sections, is the brevity of the chapters. All too often one comes across reports and discussions of qualitative research that are long and densely packed tracts which would surely be alienating for any novice. Yet here the student can take time to pay attention to the details of the text, the analysis and the points being made. It is clear that the editors are sensitive to what will work best for their audience and are enthusiastic about the material. It is evident that careful thought has also been given to the sort of empirical work and discourses reported. Perhaps it should not be so, but the one thing that was guaranteed to capture *my* interest was an intrinsically interesting topic or subject matter. And there are plenty of these: calls to a hospital emergency line and the talk and events in the delivery room of a hospital to name just two.

Part II, 'Social interaction' comprises key readings from, amongst others, Goffman, Gumperz and Tannen. The focus here is very much upon conversation. Part III, 'Minds, selves and sense making' takes a rather more 'psychological' stance with an excellent collection of important papers. There is a strong emphasis on discourse analytic approaches here although work from within this tradition (for example, Billig, Edwards, Potter and Wetherell) is complemented by work from outside it (see Gergen and Wertsch).

The final section, Part III, 'Culture and social relations' develops the post-structuralist turn in discourse research. Again readings are located within a theoretical and historical context but Hall's chapter seeks to extend techniques for analysing discourse to other forms of data, thus giving the reader a linkage to broader and more Foucauldian notions of 'discourse' and to wider research in the social sciences. Finally, in a concluding chapter Wetherell ties together the range of ideas in the book.

This reader works very well as a teaching text. It works because it allows the student a direct connection with the work of researchers in the field and combines this with a sense of where their work fits into discourse theory and practice. It is, though, a text for advanced students. It assumes some familiarity with approaches to and the rationales behind the analysis of talk and text. All in all this is an excellent book that students can dip into and gradually become more familiar with this growing research area. And I am happy to report that, after an extensive inspection, I could find no box-diagrams!

Couze Venn, *Occidentalism: Modernity and Subjectivity*

Sage Publications in association with *Theory, Culture and Society*, London 2000
ISBN 0761954112, 0761954120 (paperback)

Martha Michailidou

How can we think about the forms of subjectivity appropriate to the challenges of the post-modern era? This is the ethical and political question at the heart of Couze Venn's *Occidentalism*.

The book's definition of occidentalism is framed by two thematic preoccupations, clearly stated in the introduction: first, the New World as a condition of possibility for the emergence of modernity, and second, the particular conception of the subject, of a particular form of and reflection on Being, for what we now recognise as the developed western world. The book 'tries to dislodge from post-Enlightenment philosophical discourse a number of critical elements that enable one to indicate a discourse of being which opens towards a different postmodernity, a transmodernity, one which is the correlate of a postcoloniality to come' (p2). In order to achieve this the author draws, in the first three chapters of the book, a broad genealogy of the philosophical foundations of subjectivity crucial for the institution of western modernity, and then, in the last two chapters engages with alternative traditions of conceptualising the subject, drawing mainly from hermeneutics, phenomenology and deconstruction.

Chapter one 'Remembering Modernity' argues that the fundamental moment of modernity is signalled with the passage to a type of consciousness defined not through reference to Christian narratives of moral completion in the afterlife, but through reference to a historical project of realisation of Autonomy and Reason. Venn counterposes to this a different conception of the subject, one that defines the self as a heteronomous being, drawing from Derrida and Lyotard's work on the gift, debt, sacrifice and responsibility. He then argues that conceptualising the postmodern through the postcolonial entails an engagement with this alternative conception of the subject, a conception which would posit ethical responsibility to the Other as the centre of subjectivity and sociality.

The next two chapters expand on these arguments. 'Historicity,

Responsibility, Subjectivity' breaks down the process of subjectification into processes of: *folding* (drawing from the recent work of Nikolas Rose); *bonding* (drawing from Levinas' and Kristeva's postulations on the essentially grounded character of being); and *desiring* (which breaks away from the economy of trauma and lack of Lacanian psychoanalysis, emphasising the materiality and sociality of embodied subjectivity drawing from Grosz, Gatens, Braidotti and Butler). These are supplemented with Ricoeur's formulation of the narrative character of identity, in an attempt to theorise the radical temporality of processes of subject formation. This, Venn argues, allows us to view the refiguration of particular selves as a process akin to 'working through' in psychoanalysis or to processes of rememoration, an argument to which he returns later on in the book.

'On the Emergence of Modernity', on the other hand, takes a more historical route to the same issues. The chapter outlines the emergence of modern subjectivity through a discussion of the ontological consequences of the epistemological events of Descartes' Cogito, of the post-Enlightenment project of the domination of nature through science and the emergence of instrumental rationality, and of the 'discovery' of the New World. Venn's argument, meticulously well documented through reference to counter-histories of colonisation as well as readings of Montaigne and Bacon, is that 'epistemology came to be privileged in the founding discourses of modernity as a result of the disruptions which the discovery of America provoked for the conceptual structure that had framed explanation and meaning from Judeo-Christian times to the dawn of the Renaissance' (p146).

'Enlightenment and After' puts forward the author's arguments about the possibilities of rethinking and reconstituting subjectivity in a way that will be adequate to the postcolonial moment. Starting from a Foucauldian interpretation of the legacy of the Enlightenment as a 'critical ontology' of the self, Venn first turns to a discussion of aesthetics and poiesis shaped by the work of Benjamin, Lyotard, and Derrida in order to propose a conception of ethics which will no longer rely on the epistemological strictures of the Enlightenment. The aim here, following Levinas' writings on the face relation, is to think through the ethical relation between Self and Other in a way that does justice to the complexity of the irreducible difference of the Other. The process of rememoration, put forward by Toni Morrison in her discussion of her novel *Beloved* as a reworking of memory and history in a way that refigures the self and identity, is then discussed extensively by Venn as an illustration of the ethical function of the aesthetic.

The focus on Levinas' work on ethics continues in 'Heteronomy, Alterity, Embodiment: on becoming otherwise', the last chapter of the book. The basic principles of a Levinasian ethics – unconditional responsibility to the other, passivity, irreducability of the other – are supplemented in this chapter by a discussion of Merleau-Ponty's phenomenology. The argument here is that Merleau-Ponty's postulation of the subject as always already embodied in a grounded relation to concrete others, together with Levinas' aforementioned ethical imperative, can provide the basis for conceptualising 'a way of being that recognizes, at one level, the common humanity of all on the basis of the experience of suffering and fragility, the within-timeness of being and the responsibility – of hospitality, care – triggered in the face relation, and at the other level, in spite of the radical alterity of the other, a way of being which acknowledges the impossibility of an I by itself existing' (p234).

This is a complex and ambitious book, with a project that is both timely and necessary. It is also a very scholarly work, engaging with important strands in the ontological and epistemological traditions which have defined self and Other from the Enlightenment onwards. The book's main project of thinking the future through the reconstitution of the self, however, remains firmly within philosophical discourses of the ontological and ethical constitution of the subject, and while ethics is clearly related to politics, as the author and many before him have convincingly argued, it does not necessarily translate into specific politics. Following this, the reader is left wondering whether this persistence in the grand philosophical narratives of the ethical composition of the self inadvertedly privileges the separation of ontology and politics, and the primacy of the former over the latter, which the author goes to such lengths to deconstruct. A firmer engagement with more materialist approaches to the constitution of the subject, such as Donna Haraway's work on cyborg subjectivity and the global informatics of domination, Elizabeth Grosz's and Moira Gatens' Deleuzian and Spinozist analyses of bodies and selves, and Gayatri Chakravorty Spivak's work on postcoloniality and the New World Order could have greatly enhanced the phenomenological insights into the relational nature of subjectivity, substantiating the claim that subjectivity is always already socially situated, historically embodied and politically efficacious.

Notes on contributors

Estelle Barrett completed her Ph.D. in 1997 and currently teaches Visual Theory in the School of Contemporary Arts at Deakin University, Australia.

John Cromby is Lecturer in Psychology at Loughborough University, UK.

William Cross is Chair of the Sub-program in Social/Personality Psychology at the Graduate Center, City University of New York, USA.

Ian Hodges is Senior Lecturer in Psychology at the University of Westminster, UK.

Lawrence Johnson completed his Ph.D. in English at The University of Queensland, Australia in 1999. His first book *The Wolf Man's Burden* is available through Cornell University Press.

Patrick Leman studied psychology and philosophy at Oxford University, UK before moving to the University of Cambridge to pursue a Ph.D.

Martha Michailidou completed her Ph.D. thesis at Goldsmiths College, University of London, UK in 2000. She has taught in the Department of Media and Communications, Goldsmiths College and is currently teaching in Greece.

David Nightingale teaches critical psychology in the Psychology Department at Bolton Institute, UK.

Christopher Peet is a Ph.D. candidate in Theoretical Psychology at the Department of Psychology, University of Alberta, Edmonton, Canada.

Linda Powell is a clinical and organisational psychologist at Teachers College, Columbia University, USA.

Robert Steele is Professor of Psychology and Chair of the Psychology Department at Wesleyan University in Connecticut, USA.

Nikki Sullivan lectures in Critical and Cultural Studies at Macquarie University, Sydney, Australia.

Anne-Marie Tupuola is a Fulbright Senior Scholar, affiliated with the Asian/Pacific/American Institute at New York University, the Department of Arts and Humanities, Teachers College, Columbia University and the W.E.B. Du Bois Institute for African American Research, Harvard University, USA.

Nicole Vitellone is currently a post-doctoral fellow in the Sociology Department, Manchester University, UK.